Behavior therapy

Behavior therapy

Scientific, philosophical, and moral foundations

EDWARD ERWIN

Professor of Philosophy
University of Miami

CAMBRIDGE UNIVERSITY PRESS

Cambridge
London   New York   Melbourne

Published by the Syndics of the Cambridge University Press
The Pitt Building, Trumpington Street, Cambridge CB2 1RP
Bentley House, 200 Euston Road, London NW1 2DB
32 East 57th Street, New York, NY 10022, USA
296 Beaconsfield Parade, Middle Park, Melbourne 3206, Australia

© Cambridge University Press 1978

First published 1978

Printed in the United States of America
Typeset by David E. Seham Associates, Inc., Metuchen, N.J.
Printed and bound by Vail-Ballou Press, Inc., Binghamton, N.Y.

Library of Congress Cataloging in Publication Data
Erwin, Edward, 1937–
Behavior therapy.
1. Behavior therapy.   2. Behavior therapy – Philosophy.
3. Psychiatric ethics.   I. Title.
RC489.B4E77   616.8'914   78–17623
ISBN 0 531 22293 1 in hard covers
ISBN 0 521 29439 8 as a paperback

To Ken and Nick

Contents

Foreword

This could be the most important book yet written on behavior therapy, for in the chapters to follow, the underpinnings of that amorphous approach to human problems are critically examined and elucidated as they have never been before. It is perhaps not surprising that the field had to await the clear thinking and insightful analysis of a philosopher before such a work was produced, but the philosopher had to be one who was widely read and knowledgeable in both the clinical and the theoretical aspects of behavior therapy, as Erwin clearly is. For my own part, I can only wish that Erwin's book had been available during long and sometimes arduous board meetings of the Association for the Advancement of Behavior Therapy at which prominent psychiatrists and psychologists spent hours attempting to agree upon a definition of behavior therapy. The somewhat surprising answer to the questions raised in those interminable and fruitless discussions is contained in Erwin's first chapter and will have an impact on every psychiatrist and psychologist interested in the nature of behavior therapy. Every behavior therapist should read this book to gain a perspective on his or her own behavior.

The importance of Erwin's work, however, goes beyond its immediate focus. Many say that behavior therapy, with its emphasis on empirical demonstration and the scientific method, will lose its own identity and become the basis for a broader, more integrated approach to behavior problems which encompasses biological and pharmacological methods of attack. If this comes to pass, Erwin's statements could well provide the ultimate philosophical foundations of the new approach. Ethical issues, which we are facing increasingly as our technology becomes more successful, follow logically from philosophical foundations, and Erwin's analysis represents the most advanced thinking on this subject to date. This book is a breakthrough, containing arguments with which not everyone will agree but which everyone must confront.

DAVID BARLOW
Professor of Psychiatry and Psychology,
Brown University, and
President, Association for the
Advancement of Behavior Therapy

Preface

Why study foundations?

Behavior therapy techniques can be used and researched without commitment to any distinctive underlying theory. Why not, then, view behavior therapy simply as a technology and ignore the study of foundations? A partial answer to this question is that we want to deepen our understanding of clinical phenomena, even if that gains us no practical advantage. One can build bridges simply by using engineering principles, but that is no reason to neglect quantum theory.

An adequate theory might also provide some important practical benefits. First, if better clinical techniques are to be developed, it will be helpful to know exactly which features of our successful techniques are therapeutically productive and why. Second, the class of possible techniques is quite large: The researcher, consequently, needs some guidance concerning which are worth studying. Empirical data and sheer hunches will play some role here, but adequate theoretical principles might tell us that certain techniques have a greater antecedent likelihood of success than do others. Third, some behavior therapists are interested in explaining the origin and, more importantly, the maintenance of maladaptive behavior patterns. If we better understood the causes of alcoholism, sexual impotence, schizophrenia, and so forth, we might be able to treat these problems more effectively. The development of an adequate theoretical foundation might enhance our understanding of these matters.

Even if theory can be important, one might object, current theory is just not firm enough to support behavior therapy. This point may be correct, but that is one of the things we need to find out. Some behavior therapists hold that current principles or theories of learning can serve at least as a partial foundation (Wolpe, 1976). A systematic and careful examination of foundational claims should settle this issue. If current theory is found to be inadequate, we might begin to develop a better theory or, more plausibly, several more modest theoretical principles. The attempt may fail; but if the rewards are large, we should try.

An additional reason for discussing foundations is to eliminate misunderstanding. It is widely believed that behavior therapy developed out of a certain theoretical framework embracing operationalism, behaviorism, and learning theory (Krasner, 1971); but there has been considerable criticism of this framework (Chomsky, 1959, 1971; Breger & McGaugh, 1965). As a result, some critics are skeptical about behavior therapy because of what they believe to be its dubious theoretical presuppositions. In evaluating this skepticism, it would be useful to see to what extent behavior therapy is tied to the behavioristic – learning theory framework from which it originated.

Other critics are concerned about the misuse of behavior therapy. In the United States, for example, demands have been made to curtail the funding of some behavior therapy research (Ervin Committee Report, 1974) and to place legal restrictions on the use of token economy programs (Wexler, 1973). In assessing the merits of these demands, it is not enough to know that the technology works; we also need to become clearer about the moral basis for using it.

Paradigms and techniques

The term "behavior therapy" is used to refer to a kind of therapeutic technique and to what Kuhn (1962) has called a "paradigm." In one sense (not necessarily the one Kuhn intends), a paradigm includes: (1) exemplars, that is, one or more influential examples of a successful research strategy; (2) an empirical theory; and (3) a set of methodological and philosophical assumptions. There is a good deal of controversy about foundational assumptions, but there is enough agreement to permit talk of a distinctive behavior therapy paradigm without implying that every behavior therapist accepts every element in the paradigm. Exemplary instances of a successful research strategy might be Watson's conditioning of little Albert (Watson & Raynor, 1920); Jones's (1924) use of counterconditioning to treat a small-animal phobia; Lindsley, Skinner, and

Solomon's (1953) use of operant conditioning to treat psychotic patients; and Wolpe's (1958) use of desensitization to treat neurotic clients. The most commonly accepted empirical theory is some type of learning theory, for example, Skinner's or Pavlov's, or some set of conditioning principles, including the law of effect. The most widely accepted philosophical and methodological assumptions include a commitment to experimental testing of therapeutic claims, some form of behaviorism (Eysenck, 1972), and a rejection of the idea that most behavior disorders are diseases.

It would be difficult to determine exactly how many behavior therapists accept the preceding paradigm. First, it is not clear who counts as a behavior therapist. Should we count everyone who uses behavior therapy techniques or just those who embrace certain theoretical ideas? Or should we use some other criterion? Second, positions are constantly changing. For example, some writers who once contended that behavior therapy is based solely on learning principles would now qualify that thesis; others have abandoned it altogether. For these two reasons, at least, I make no claim concerning how many behavior therapists now accept the paradigm in question. Such a claim would not be especially relevant to my concerns. I am interested, for example, in the connections between behavior therapy and conditioning principles; in whether or not behavior therapy either is or ought to be behavioristic; in whether or not behavior disorders are illnesses. These issues are important partly because certain shared assumptions about modern learning theory, behaviorism, and a medical model have been influential; but the issues remain important even though many of the original assumptions are now questioned by many behavior therapists.

Cognitivism and behaviorism

A cognitivist point of view is defended in this work, but that is hardly novel. It is now difficult to find many behavior therapists who are not cognitivists in some sense. What might be different here is the nature and grounds of the cognitivism. First, some behavior therapists are willing to use cognitive concepts only if rather austere behavioristic constraints are satisfied. For example, some will use such concepts only to denote dependent variables; mentalistic causes are ruled out (Thomas & Blackman, 1976, p. 142). Others use cognitive concepts only if they are operationally definable in terms of observables or if the sentences in which they appear can be given a behavioristic translation (Waters & McCallum, 1972; Eysenck, 1972, 1976). I have rejected these behavioristic constraints in this work (Chapter 2): In this respect, the cognitivism is more radical than that which is acceptable to some behavior therapists. Second, I have tried to connect the philosophical and empirical ideas constituting the rival behavioristic positions including analytical and methodological behaviorism, operationalism, and certain empirical theories and principles of learning. These strands reinforce one another, making the resulting interlocking system highly resistant to piecemeal attack. A unified criticism of this entire system of ideas, as is attempted here, can help to place a cognitive viewpoint on a more secure foundation.

Although the issues in this work should be of interest to psychologists and philosophers, it is difficult to write for both groups without creating insurmountable stylistic problems. Psychologists may think I am traveling recklessly fast around some dangerous curves and coasting too slowly through some flat, arid areas. Philosophers may think the same, but they are likely to disagree about the location of the curves. I am aware of the risks but have been willing to take them because of the nature of the issues: They are important, and they do crisscross several disciplines.

A number of people were kind enough to comment on parts of the manuscript. I would especially like to thank Noam Chomsky, Sidney Gendin, George Graham, Lowell Kleiman, Howard Rachlin, Michael Slote, and Bruce Winick. I would also like to thank the philosophy graduate students and faculty at the University of Miami for their instructive comments and the Office of Research Coordination at the University of Miami for a typing grant. Susan Milmoe read the entire manuscript and made useful suggestions for improving each chapter. Gerald Davison encouraged me in pursuing the project and made several helpful suggestions. Most of all, I would like to thank Patricia Erwin.

E. E.

1. What is behavior therapy?

Some basic issues

Is it possible to give an adequate definition of *behavior therapy*? Why do we need one? How will we know if we have found one?

First, we will sketch (in Section I) a brief history of the behavior therapy movement and then describe (in Section II) techniques used by behavior therapists. We will then be in a better position to say (in Section III) what behavior therapy is. (Discussion of theoretical issues begins in Section III; the reader familiar with the behavior therapy literature may want to start with this section.)

I. Origins

Although it would be arbitrary to fix the beginning of the behavior therapy movement at any precise time, there is some reason to trace its origins to the work of John Watson. In several important works, Watson developed and defended principles of behaviorism, including the ideas that psychologists should use experimental techniques and not rely on introspection and that they should study behavior and not the mind (Watson, 1913, 1919, 1924). His opposition to any kind of mentalistic psychology was sometimes based on the premise that the mind does not exist and sometimes on methodological arguments. The methodological arguments have had an important impact on the development of twentieth-century psychology, at least in the United States, and have influenced many leading behavior therapists.

Besides founding the school of behaviorism, Watson, together with his wife Rosalie Raynor Watson, performed a famous experiment in which a fear of rats was induced in a child, little Albert (Watson & Raynor, 1920). Albert initially displayed no fear of rats, but subsequently did so after a loud noise and a rat were presented together. The repetition of this pairing soon made the child afraid of the rat alone. Later, the child reacted fearfully to a white rabbit and to other furry objects.

1

Watson and Raynor did not prove, of course, that all neurotic behavior results from conditioning, but they did demonstrate how *one* phobic reaction *could* develop in this way. Furthermore, their work suggested that in a case of this kind a counterconditioning technique, such as the use of an extinction procedure, could eliminate the problem. One of Watson's students, Mary Cover Jones, was one of the first to use such a technique, in treating a small-animal phobia (Jones, 1924, 1975).

There is an obvious analogy between the procedure of Watson and Raynor and the techniques used by Pavlov to condition a salivating response in dogs. This is not surprising, because Pavlov's work influenced Watson and his colleagues. For this reason and because of his work on the production of neuroses in dogs, Pavlov's contribution to the behavior therapy movement is significant (Franks, 1969).

Despite the work of Watson, Pavlov, and others, the behavior therapy movement did not develop in any significant way until the 1950s. Some of the important papers in this period are Lindsley, Skinner, and Solomon's (1953) study of operant conditioning in the treatment of psychotic patients; Wolpe's (1958) report of a successful treatment of neurotics by the use of (what is now called) *systematic desensitization*; and Lazarus's (1958) paper entitled "New Methods in Psychotherapy: A Case Study." In the 1960s two behavior therapy journals were begun: *Behaviour Research and Therapy* (begun in 1963) and *The Journal of Applied Behavior Analysis* (begun in 1968). In addition, several influential anthologies were published, including Eysenck's *Behavior Therapy and the Neuroses* (1960) and *Experiments in Behavior Therapy* (1964) and Ullmann and Krasner's *Case Studies in Behavior Modification* (1965). The work reported in these journals and anthologies in the 1960s is somewhat varied, but the following points seem particularly salient:

The influence of modern principles and theories of learning is strong. One may or may not agree with Wolpe's (1976) contention that behavior therapy has been *based* on principles and paradigms of learning, but even a cursory review of the relevant literature shows that there are several important connections between the practice of behavior therapy and research on learning. Some of these connections are explored later (Chapter 3).

Some writers contend that the development of behavior therapy has been strongly influenced by the philosophy of behaviorism (Krasner, 1971a; O'Leary & Wilson, 1975). This contention is difficult to prove by appeal to any direct historical evidence, but it is plausible. One difficulty in obtaining direct evidence is that before 1970 there is relatively little discussion of behaviorism in the behavior therapy literature. Some writers referred to themselves as behaviorists but did so because they accepted the learning theories of Thorndike, Pavlov, Hull, or Skinner; they were not necessarily endorsing any particular philosophical doctrine. It is true, however, that in behavior therapy research and practice, the primary focus was on behavior, not on the mind or psyche. That has been one of the important differences between behavior therapy and traditional psychotherapy. It is not implausible to think that this difference was partly due to the influence of behaviorism. What exactly is meant by behaviorism and how it relates to behavior therapy is discussed in more detail in Chapter 2.

The so-called "disease model" of mental illness is often explicitly rejected (Ullmann & Krasner, 1969, 1975; Bandura, 1969; Rimm & Masters, 1974). There are several reasons. The conceptual arguments of such provocative nonbehavior therapists as Szasz (1961) were purporting to show that the idea of a "mental disease" is incoherent. Doubts about the utility of the medical classifications traditionally used to categorize so-called mental illnesses were becoming increasingly prevalent in clinical circles. A rejection of the medical model accorded well with ideas about behaviorism and modern learning theory. Although a behaviorist can agree to the use of certain mentalistic concepts, it is not surprising if he is somewhat skeptical of classifying behavioral problems as *mental* illnesses. He is also not likely to see such problems as *illnesses* if he believes that laws of learning can explain the origin and maintenance of so-called abnormal as well as normal behavior. All these ideas are discussed and employed in Ullmann and Krasner's (1969, 1975) defense of a psychological model for behavior therapy. The defense of a psychological model and a rejection of the medical model are discussed in Chapter 4.

An important characteristic of most early behavior therapy writings is a skepticism about psychoanalysis. One of the main grounds for this skepticism was Eysenck's influential reports (1952, 1966) that the percentage of remissions of symptoms in untreated neurotics after two years was at least as great as that in patients treated by psychoanalysts or eclectic psychotherapists. Eysenck's arguments are now controversial. They have been vigorously criticized (Bergin, 1971; Bergin & Suinn, 1976) and defended (Rachman, 1971), but during the 1960s they served as stimulants to behavior therapists to develop alternative therapeutic techniques (Ullmann & Krasner, 1975).

It would be a mistake to assume that all early behavior therapists agreed about modern learning theory, behaviorism, and the belief that mental illness did not exist; there has always been some disagreement about these matters. More recently there have even been attempts to reconcile behavior therapy and psychoanalysis (Wachtel, 1977). However, there has been at least one doctrine that appears to be acceptable to all behavior therapists, early and late: Claims of therapeutic effectiveness need to be subjected to rigorous experimental tests. Behavior therapists have not been alone in agreeing to this demand, but in the fields of clinical psychology and psychiatry they have been more consistent than any other group in urging the need for experimental rigor.

Conclusion. The preceding discussion of origins is intended only to highlight certain important events; it is obviously not an adequate historical account of the behavior therapy movement. More detailed accounts can be found in Franks (1969); Ullmann and Krasner (1975); Krasner (1971a); Yates (1970); and Eysenck and Beech (1971). We should not expect, however, to gain too much even from a relatively complete account of the study of origins. It would be an egregious logical mistake to derive a conclusion about the nature of behavior therapy from a description of its origins. Behavior therapy might, for example, have originated out of learning theory experiments on rats, cats, dogs, and pigeons without having any logical ties to learning theory; it might have had behavioristic beginnings and yet not be, in any interesting sense, behavioristic. A better guide to the nature of behavior therapy would be a description of behavior therapy techniques. It is to this subject that we now turn.

The descriptions that follow are brief, elementary, and incomplete in important respects. Their function is to help determine the sorts of techniques we discuss in Section III. More complete descriptions can be found in standard behavior therapy textbooks (e.g., O'Leary & Wilson, 1975; Rimm & Masters, 1974).

II. Techniques

In attempting to describe therapeutic techniques, we must be careful not to beg two important theoretical questions: (1) Is there such a thing as a *behavior therapy technique*? (2) If question 1 has an affirmative answer, which techniques qualify? To most behavior therapists it will seem obvious that there are behavior therapy techniques, but not everyone agrees (Bergin, 1970). One possibility is that the techniques used by behavior therapists have no theoretically interesting properties in common, except possibly for their being used and studied by therapists who share common methodological and philosophical assumptions. To avoid ruling out this possibility prematurely, the term *behavior therapy technique* will be used in the present section to refer to techniques commonly described as such by behavior therapists; no judgment will be made now about the accuracy of this description.

This leads to our second question: Because behavior therapists disagree in their classifications, which techniques should we include? Some writers, for example, include cognitive techniques (Rimm & Masters, 1974), but others do not (Beck, 1970). If we take sides on this issue now, we are likely to bias our inquiry into the nature of behavior therapy. To avoid doing that, let us distinguish between *paradigmatic* and *nonparadigmatic* behavior therapy techniques. The former term will be applied to techniques concerning which there has been widespread agreement and little or no disagreement about their classification, techniques that have been most thoroughly researched by behavior therapists and that are often used to illustrate what is meant by *behavior therapy*. Using these criteria, at least four procedures qualify as paradigmatic instances of behavior therapy techniques: (1) systematic desensitization; (2) aversion therapy; (3) operant conditioning; and (4) modeling. This list may not be exhaustive, but no harm will result if some techniques that might qualify as paradigmatic are classified as nonparadigmatic.

Paradigmatic techniques

Systematic desensitization

When using systematic desensitization (or reciprocal inhibition therapy), a therapist usually describes a set of threatening situations, sometimes called an *anxiety hierarchy*. With the help of the client, the potential situations are ranked from least threatening to most threatening. For example, someone with a snake phobia might rate the picking up of a live snake as more threatening than simply being in a room with a snake, which in turn might be considered more threatening than seeing a snake in the zoo. The next step is to train the patient to relax by using a relaxation training procedure, such as that developed by Jacobson (1938), although some therapists consider this step unessential (Paul, 1969). The subject is then told to imagine as vividly as possible the least threatening scene in the anxiety hierarchy. If the patient remains relaxed, he moves up the hierarchy. If anxiety is exhibited at a certain level, either the scene is repeated or the patient goes back to imagining a less threatening situation. The goal is to have the patient run through the hierarchy in a relaxed state. One important advantage of using imagined rather than actual scenes is that the therapist is given greater flexibility. For example, if a patient has a fear of flying, the therapist cannot bring an airport or a jumbo jet into his office, but he can ask his patient to imagine these things.

Desensitization has been used to treat a wide variety of problems, including agoraphobia, claustrophobia, social anxiety, reactive depression, fear of public speaking, stuttering, frigidity, fear of atomic attack, impotence, and asthma (Paul, 1969; Wolpe, 1973). Although most of the original studies of desensitization were uncontrolled case reports, Lang and Lazovik published a controlled study, the first of its kind, in 1963. Subsequent studies, some having an extremely sophisticated experimental design, provided fairly firm evidence for the effectiveness of desensitization, at least for certain types of disorders and for certain types of patients (Lang, 1964; Paul, 1966; Davison, 1968; Moore, 1965). Paul (1969) carefully reviews these and other studies and concludes that at least eight are sufficiently well controlled to establish a causal relation between the therapy and the therapeutic benefits, the first time in the history of psychological treatment, according to Paul, that this has been accomplished.

Many of the subjects in the studies discussed in Paul's review were college students with rather mild phobias, but that is not true of some of the more recent studies. In one well-controlled study (Gelder et al., 1973), desensitization and another behavior therapy technique, flooding, were used with psychiatric outpatients having a mean age of thirty-five. Some of these patients had relatively severe phobias. The authors concluded that both systematic desensitization and flooding were effective. In another controlled study comparing various techniques, Hedberg and Cambell (1974) found desensitization to be "highly effective" in treating alcoholics, although not as effective as another behavior therapy technique described as "behavioral family counseling."

Assessment. It would be extremely difficult in a brief space to give an adequate analysis of the evidence for the effectiveness of either desensitization or the other behavior therapy techniques to be discussed later. The following is not intended to be such an analysis, but it may highlight some of the main issues.

For any complex therapy, it is possible to distinguish at least three separate questions: (1) "Is it effective in producing therapeutic benefits?" (2) "Exactly which components of the therapy contribute to the production of such benefits?" (3) "For those components that do make a causal contribution, why are they productive?" If we know that a certain therapy is not effective, there may be no point in asking questions 2 or 3; but suppose that that is not true. Suppose, for example, that we have some reason to believe that psychoanalysis is effective. We may then be motivated to ask if specific components, such as the use of free association or dream analysis, make any difference, singly or in combination, to therapeutic outcome. If the answer is positive for both components, then we may go on to ask question 3: Does psychoanalytic theory or some rival theory best explain why these components make a difference?

The preceding distinctions should be kept in mind when discussing systematic desensitization. With respect to this therapy there have been attempts to answer our second and third questions (Rosen et al., 1972; Gaupp et al., 1972; Murray & Jacobson, 1971; Davison & Wilson, 1973; Bandura, 1977), but the evidence is still inconclusive. For this reason we will deal only with question 1: Is the therapy effective? Even this question may be too difficult to answer, depending on how it is interpreted. To circumvent some of the problems, we can stipulate the following. In asking if the therapy is effective, we will mean: "Does its use sometimes make a significant causal contribution to the production of beneficial therapeutic change?" (We could also specify what is meant by "significant" and "beneficial," but we will assume that these terms are sufficiently well understood to get on with the discussion.) If we answer yes to question 1, we will be making a relatively weak causal claim; one that does not imply that in any given therapy situation, it is the systematic desensitization alone that accounts for any therapeutic change, nor that the therapy will be effective with any clinical problem, any client, or any therapist.

Understood in this minimal way, the claim that systematic desensitization (hereafter, SD) is effective is widely accepted and is said to have been empirically demonstrated (Paul, 1969; Franks & Wilson, 1975, p. 66). Has it been empirically demonstrated? Despite a wide body of supporting research, there are still some grounds for skepticism. For example, Wolpe (1977) has recently raised an issue about misconception-based fears and has concluded that because of a neglect of the issue hundreds of research studies of SD lack the significance that is commonly attributed to them. Wolpe's point depends on the seemingly plausible assumption that phobic patients will respond differently to different treatments, depending on whether their phobia stems from a belief that the object of their fear is dangerous or arises from an automatic reaction to the phobic object. It seems plausible to think that some type of cognitive therapy will be more effective if a false belief is at the root of the client's problem and that systematic desensitization will work better where the fear response is automatic. If that is right, then there is need to control for the source of the client's problem when testing therapeutic claims; most studies have not done that. For example, suppose we find that a greater percentage of clients treated with SD improve compared to a control group receiving a pseudo-therapy. If cognitive-based problems are more likely to be affected by nonspecific factors, such as the expectation of being cured, then the mean differences between the two groups might have arisen because more clients in the treatment group have problems that are cognitively based. Wolpe (1977) is not suggesting that all previous research on SD is worthless; but he does contend that many of the experiments will have to be done again because of a failure to control for differences in the bases of phobias. The exact importance of this variable is difficult to determine without hard evidence about how clients with misconception-based fears react to different treatments, but there is some reason to be concerned that some of the evidence commonly presented for the effectiveness of SD is irremediably contaminated.

A second, and more important, reason to be skeptical concerns the operation of factors in the therapeutic situation that are not specifically part of the desensitization package. One of the most important of these is the client's expectation that he will be helped by the therapy. There is evidence that this variable can account for some of the improvement that typically follows the use of SD (Rosen, 1974; Tori & Worrel, 1973; Lick, 1975). Can it account for all such change? It might seem that the answer is clearly no: There have been many controlled experiments in which a SD treatment group has shown superior improvement to a pseudo-therapy group in which expectancy for improvement was induced by the experimenter (Paul, 1966; Lick & Bootzin, 1970; Miller, 1972; Davison, 1968; Hyman & Gale, 1973; Nawas, Fishman, & Pucel, 1970). However, much of the research in this area is difficult to interpret because of doubts as to whether or not the pseudo-therapy and SD were equally credible as viewed by the subjects (Borkovec & Nau, 1972; Nau, Caputo, & Borkovec, 1974). Newer studies have attempted to solve this problem by using more adequate methods to assess the subjects' expectation of therapeutic gain; the findings, however, have been inconsistent. Some of these studies (Brown, 1973; Steinmark & Borkovec, 1974) have found SD to be superior to an equally credible placebo therapy, but others have not (Lick, 1975, McReynolds et al., 1973).

One reaction to evidence about expectancy is to say that it bears not on the efficacy of SD, but on the explanation of why the therapy works; that is, it is relevant to answering our second or third questions but not the first (Lick & Bootzin, 1975, p. 928). This raises an interesting conceptual issue. Suppose that the use of the therapy is especially effective in establishing and maintaining expectancies that are therapeutic. Should we say (1) that the therapy causes the therapeutic change but does so through the operation of cognitive factors or (2) that the cognitive factors cause the change? The second option seems more plausible, although it may not matter to the client which option is correct. Suppose, for example, that psychoanalysis is useless in treating phobias but that psychoanalysts can be convinced that they will be helped with their own phobias only if they are given genuine psychoanalytic therapy; if we give them a pseudo-therapy resembling psychoanalysis, they will detect the difference and lose faith in the therapy.

Assuming that belief in the therapy is efficacious, it seems plausible to say that the psychoanalysis is not causing the therapeutic change, even though undergoing it is a necessary condition for the expectancy factor to become operative in phobic psychoanalysts. If this is right, then even if SD is particularly useful in inducing therapeutic expectancies, it might still be false that the therapy itself is effective. In any event, it is not clear that SD is more useful than certain pseudo-therapies in inducing an expectation of cure. In studies by Wilson (1973), Lick (1975), and McReynolds et al.

(1973), there was evidence that the pseudo-therapies and SD were seen as equally credible.

Assuming that expectancy of cure can sometimes facilitate therapeutic change, how it does so is still unclear. One possibility is that the client who believes he is being helped may be motivated to test his belief by exposing himself to the phobic stimulus; another possibility is that the subject is "under more demand" to show improvement than is a client who does not expect to be helped (Nisbett & Valins, 1971; Lick & Bootzin, 1975). There are other possibilities. For some it may be more plausible to say that the therapy is effective but works partly because of the client's beliefs; for others, that the belief and not the therapy causes the therapeutic change. Even without knowing how expectancy of cure works, however, we can say this: If *none* of the improvement that follows SD is caused by the therapy, if all of it is caused by the operation of nonspecific factors, including the client's belief that he will be helped, then the therapy is not effective; the "nonspecific" factors, by definition, are not part of the therapy. It is not true, then, that data concerning expectancy do not bear on the issue of the effectiveness of SD. On the contrary, if it is true, as argued by Kazdin and Wilcoxon (1976), that the overwhelming majority of SD studies have failed to rule out differences in expectancies of success in clients in treatment and control groups, and if the relatively few studies that have done this have produced inconsistent results, then an important rival hypothesis has not yet been ruled out: that the apparent success of SD is caused by nonspecific factors. If this is true and if we add in the uncertainty generated by the almost universal failure to control for the source of the client's problem, then there is good reason to doubt that the effectivess of SD has been empirically demonstrated. Although some of the uncertainties are likely to be removed by research that is already in progress, it is still sobering to realize that in 1976 (the year in which Kazdin and Wilcoxon's report was published), reasonable doubts could still be raised about the most heavily researched of all behavior therapy techniques. The issues have simply proved to be much more complex than was once thought. The doubts, however, concern not the effectiveness of the therapy, but the demonstration of that effectiveness. First, the total evidence provides no support for the hypothesis that SD is not effective. There have been some reports of SD failure (e.g., Gelder & Marks, 1966), but they are counterbalanced by hundreds of apparent successes (Paul, 1969; Wolpe, 1973; Paul & Bernstein,

1973). Second, the evidence supports a stronger claim, although we will not try to prove it here: If we try to fit to the total relevant evidence two competing hypotheses – (1) SD is effective (in the sense indicated earlier) and (2) expectancy of success (in combination with other nonspecific factors) has caused all the improvement reported in SD studies – then (1) will fit the evidence better. To make (2) fit, we have to assume crucial differences in expectancies between treatment and control subjects in very many experiments; although that assumption may not have been falsified, it has not been empirically confirmed. Even if we cannot say, then, that the effectiveness of SD has been demonstrated, the hypothesis that it is effective is more plausible than any rival. In sum, there is still reason to be cautious, but it is more reasonable to believe, from current evidence, that SD works than to believe that it does not.

Aversion therapy

Described abstractly (and somewhat loosely), an aversion technique involves the use of noxious physical stimulation to eliminate or reduce the frequency of unwanted behavior. Sometimes the unpleasant stimulation is presented simultaneously with the behavior; sometimes it follows, and is made contingent on, the occurence of the behavior. Some writers classify the former as classical or respondent counterconditioning and the latter as operant counterconditioning. The use of such classifications, however, can suggest that aversion therapy results can be best explained in terms of either classical or operant conditioning principles; and this suggestion is controversial (Bandura, 1969, Chap. 8).

Included in the category of aversion therapy are a wide variety of specific techniques used to treat a number of different types of clients and problems. An interesting example is the treatment by Lovaas and his associates of autistic and schizophrenic children. Prior to treatment, many of the subjects had engaged in self-destructive behavior that threatened to maim or kill them and that apparently could not be eliminated by traditional psychotherapy. In one case, a seven-year-old boy would beat his head when not restrained. His head was covered with scar tissue and his ears were swollen and bleeding. An extinction procedure was tried: the boy was allowed to sit in bed with no restraints and with no attention given to his self-destructive behavior. After seven days, the rate of injurious behavior decreased markedly, but in the interim the boy had engaged in over ten-thousand such acts, thus making the therapists fearful for his safety. A punishment procedure was subsequently introduced in the form of one-second electric shocks. In a brief time the shock treatment dramatically decreased the unwanted behavior.

An even more severe case is that of Marilyn, a sixteen-year-old diagnosed as moderately retarded with psychotic features. She had been hospitalized for two years previous to the treatment and had been kept in a camisole to prevent her from injuring herself. When freed from the camisole, she would bite her hands, use her teeth to remove her nails from their roots, and bang her head violently. One finger had to be amputated because it had been severely mutilated, and her scalp was covered with scar tissue. A total of five shocks brought her biting and headbanging to zero, where it remained for the rest of the session (Bucher & Lovaas, 1968). Similar results were found by Risely (1968), when he punished an autistic girl with electric shock for climbing in high places, and by Tate and Baroff (1966).

Unwanted sexual behavior has also been treated by the use of aversion therapy. One of the early reports (Raymond, 1956) concerns a thirty-three-year-old man who had had a handbag and baby carriage fetish from the age of ten. He was referred for treatment after being arrested for "attacking" a baby carriage. The patient was shown a collection of handbags, baby carriages, and colored illustrations after he received an injection of apomorphine and just before nausea was produced. Eight days later, treatment was suspended and the patient reported having sexual intercourse with his wife without making use of his usual fantasies about handbags and baby carriages. After several days of renewed treatment, he reported that the sight of baby carriages and handbags made him sick. He received a booster treatment six months later, although it was apparently unnecessary; fifteen months later, a follow-up showed a cessation of the troublesome behavior. He was also able to have sexual intercourse with his wife without utilizing his formerly favored images.

Subsequent studies have reported the successful use of electric shock for treatment of transvestism (Blakemore et al, 1963; Marks & Gelder, 1967); paedophilia (Bancroft, 1966); and exhibitionism (Kushner & Sandler, 1966). In 1971 Feldman and MacCulloch published an important controlled study of the use of shock therapy for homosexuality. Although not all the patients were helped, more than half of the first forty-three were judged to have become significantly more heterosexual after an average of twenty sessions. Each subject was asked to rate pictures of males and females in terms of attractiveness. He was then shown, for a period of eight seconds, a slide of the male judged to be least attractive. During that time he had the option of pressing a button to remove the slide and thereby avoid a painful electric shock. If the male slide was removed, a photo of a previously highly rated female was then substituted. The procedure was then repeated until the patient would avoid staring at the most appealing male slides.

Birk et al. (1971) used a modified version of the Feldman and MacCulloch technique to treat homosexual behavior and found evidence of substantial therapeutic effects that endured at least one year after termination of all conditioning treatments. The study was well controlled but, as the investigators note, the absence of double-blind procedures makes it possible that the differences perceived between treated and placebo patients may have been due to patient or experimenter expectation.

Aversion therapy has also been used to reduce or eliminate alcoholism and smoking, apparently with mixed results. In an early review of the literature, Rachman and Teasdale (1969) conclude that there is "strong evidence" that aversion therapy is frequently effective in terminating alcoholism, but that the evidence is not definitive. In well-conducted studies, they suggest, the abstinence rate observed one year after treatment is in the region of 60 percent; the relapse rate, however, is a continuing problem.

Schmahl, Lichtenstein, and Harris (1972) point out that electric shock has been used to eliminate cigarette smoking in several sophisticated studies (Powell & Azrin, 1968; Steffy, Meichenbaum, & Best, 1970) but that the lasting effects of such treatment have been unimpressive. As a substitute for electric shock, Schmahl and his colleagues used warm, smoky air or warm, mentholated air as an aversive stimulus. The warm air was blown by a special apparatus into the faces of the subjects while they smoked. Each trial was terminated when the subject signaled his inability to tolerate further inhalation by crushing his cigarette and saying something, such as, "I don't want to smoke anymore." The results included a 100 percent rate of cessation of smoking at termination of the experiment and a 64 percent rate at a six-month follow-up (or a 57 percent rate if those not contacted are classified as failures). Although these results are impressive compared with those of other investigators, the authors point out that their treatment program included other components besides aversive stimulation. These additional components, such as social reinforcement, might account for at least some of the results.

Assessment. Aversion therapy has probably generated more controversy than any other behavior therapy technique. Because of the influence of certain popular writings and the movie *A Clockwork Orange,* it is likely that to some critics behavior therapy *is* aversion therapy. If this conjecture is correct, it is useful to place the facts in perspective. Aversion therapy has been widely used, but it is only one of a set of behavior therapy techniques, and not the one used most extensively. Based on published studies, Eysenck and Beech (1971, p. 576) estimate that for every 100 patients treated by desensitization, for example, only one is treated by aversion therapy.

It is also useful to distinguish issues that, although connected, are best discussed separately. One set of issues concerns the morality of using aversion therapy. Given that this type of therapy is invariably painful or at least unpleasant, should it be used even if it is effective? If it should be used, what conditions should be present? For example, should it be used in certain institutional settings, such as prisons; with patients incapable of consenting, such as small children or adult psychotics; or in the modification of, for example, homosexual behavior? These moral issues are discussed in Chapter 5.

A second set of issues concerns the nature of aversive techniques: Are they instances of classical or respondent conditioning, do they contain elements of both kinds of conditioning, or are their effects to be explained primarily in terms of cognitive factors (Bandura, 1969; Hallam, Rachman, & Falkowski, 1972; Rachman & Teasdale, 1969; Carlin & Armstrong, 1968; Wilson & Davison, 1974)?

Finally, we can ask simply: Is aversion therapy effective? If we interpret this question as we did earlier (i.e., does use of the therapy with some clients sometimes make a significant causal contribution to the production of beneficial therapeutic change?) the answer is probably yes. For example, the work of Lovaas & Simmons (1974) and others (Risely, 1968; Nedelman & Salzbacher, 1972) provides impressive evidence that electric shock can be effective in modifying the self-destructive behavior of some autistic children, even if such changes do not consitute a cure for autism and even if the changes are only temporary in some severe cases (e.g., Romanczyk & Goren, 1975). The evidence is impressive in such cases because the changes occur very rapidly, and, in contrast to the use of SD, appeal to expectancy of cure to explain the results with autistic children is not credible. Aversion therapy also contrasts with SD, however, in that it is not a unitary therapy; as noted earlier, the term *aversion therapy* denotes a number of different pain-producing techniques. For this reason it is even less informative than before to say that aversion therapy is "effective," if we interpret this claim as we did earlier. It would be more instructive to talk about specific types of aversive techniques as used to treat specific types of problems; the evidence is different for different types. For example, the use of electric shock in modifying some types of homosexual behavior may be effective in some cases (Feldman & MacCulloch, 1971), but the evidence is less firm than that supporting the modification of self-destructive behavior and there remains reason to be skeptical (Barlow, 1973; Wilson & Davison, 1974). The use of electric shock in treating alcoholism has had mixed results, depending on the type of technique used. For example, Wilson, Leaf, and Nathan (1975) found electrical escape conditioning to be relatively ineffective but obtained much better results with the use of an operant punishment procedure in which the shock was made contingent on the patient's drinking alcoholic beverages. Despite the guarded optimism in Rachman and Teasdale's earlier review (1969), the use of electric shock alone has not proved to be generally effective in the treatment of alcoholism (Nathan, 1976). The use of electric shock to treat cigarette smoking, as noted earlier, has had relatively poor results. Other aversive techniques, such as the use of warm, smoky air, might be more promising (Schmahl et al., 1972); but the warm, smoky air method was tried earlier and the gains were short-lived (Wilde, 1965).

Operant conditioning

A third kind of technique involves the systematic manipulation of the consequences of a behavior so as to modify subsequent behavior of the same type. This may involve the removal of rewards that customarily follow a maladaptive response or the provision of a reward following the emission of a desirable response. An example of the first might be the elimination of attention-paying behavior on the part of nurses who respond to the head banging of an autistic child. An example of the second might be the giving of candy to retarded children as a reward for feeding themselves. This category includes a wide variety of specific techniques, only a few of which need be mentioned here.

One early and influential use of an operant technique is reported by Bachrach, Erwin, and Mohr (1965), who treated a severe case of anorexia nervosa. The patient, age thirty-seven, had begun losing weight in September of 1943; by 1945 her weight had fallen from 118 pounds to 95 pounds. By 1960, the time of her admission to the University of Virginia Hospital, her weight had fallen to 47 pounds. At the instructions of the behavior therapists, the woman was removed from a rather pleasantly decorated room to a barren one, where amenities were provided only if she ate. Each of the three authors ate one meal a day with the patient and verbally reinforced any movements associated with eating. At first, any portion of the meal that was eaten was a signal for a reward; a radio, TV set, or phonograph was brought into her room by a nurse. Later, rewards were made contingent on her eating everything on her plate. By the end of two months, she had gained 14 pounds and was discharged from the hospital. Reinforcement for eating was then provided at home with the cooperation of her family. Her weight later increased to 88 pounds and apparently stabilized at that level. Upon reexamination eighteen months later, she still weighed 88 pounds.

An influential use of operant techniques is reported by Allyon (1963), who conditioned a forty-seven-year-old schizophrenic woman to stop wearing excessive amounts of clothing. At the beginning of treament she wore 25 pounds of clothing, including as many as eighteen pairs of stockings at once. The woman was initially allowed to wear no more than 23 pounds of clothing and was weighed prior to eating to determine whether the limit was exceeded. If it was exceeded, she was denied her meal. Although she missed a few meals, she eventually began to discard more and more clothing as the weight limit was gradually decreased. At termination of treatment, her clothing weighed only 3 pounds.

Another important kind of operant technique involves the use of a token economy program. Krasner (1971b) details three aspects of such programs. First, the institutional staff designates certain specific patient behaviors as "good" or "desirable," Second, a medium of exchange is chosen, consisting of a token that may be exchanged at a designated rate for back-up reinforcers. The token might be a plastic rectangle, a small coin, a poker chip, or a mark on a piece of paper. Third, primary reinforcers are designated and may consist of such items as food, play time, candy, cigarettes, or anything the patient desires. The tokens are then used to reward the set of target behaviors that have been judged to be desirable. The tokens may later be exchanged for the back-up reinforcers.

One of the first applications of such a program was by Staats (1965) to train reading discrimination in children. Allyon and his colleagues (Allyon, 1963; Allyon and Haughton 1962, 1964; Allyon and Michael, 1959) used a similar program to change the behaviors of patients in a psychiatric patient ward. Another token economy program (Atthowe & Krasner, 1968; Krasner, 1968) was used with chronic schizophrenics in a veterans hospital in California. A number of such programs have been now instituted in mental hospitals around the country and many have apparently been successful in changing selected behaviors of psychotic patients (Krasner, 1971b).

Assessment. Operant conditioning, insofar as it involves giving rewards, is less likely to raise certain controversial issues generated by the use of aversive techniques. However, insofar as such programs involve a captive audience, as in a school or hospital ward, certain ethical issues can be raised (O'Leary et al., 1972; Winett & Winkler, 1972; O'Leary, 1972). Furthermore, such programs sometimes involve withholding certain items, such as food or clothing, when target behaviors are not exhibited; and this has raised certain moral and legal issues (Wexler, 1973). The discussion of these issues will again be postponed until Chapter 5.

The empirical record for operant techniques has been encouraging in some areas but discouraging in others. In a major review of the literature on token economy programs, Kazdin and Bootzin (1972, p. 367) conclude: "The extensive literature that has developed on token economies indicates clearly that a wide variety of behavior can be changed in many different populations of subjects using conditioned reinforcers." In a second major review, Carlson, Hersen, and Eisler (1972) reach a similar conclusion. However, both reviews point to a major difficulty in many token economy studies: the failure to provide evidence of maintenance of the acquired behaviors after the patient leaves the token economy program. Efforts are now being made to overcome this difficulty, and some success is reported by Atthowe (1973); Jones and Kazdin (1975); and Hollingsworth and Foreyt (1975). Investigators are also trying to identify those variables likely to facilitate generalization of behavioral change to conditions outside of the token economy setting. O'Leary and Drabman, in their (1971) review of token economy programs in the classroom, offer some useful suggestions as to how this might be done.

Many token economy programs have been used in hospital wards to modify specific behavior patterns of schizophrenic patients; where these programs have been successful, the main benefit has been the improvement of the patient's existence in the hospital. There have been some reports of increases in discharge rates, but the evidence so far has been inconsistent (e.g., Heap et al., 1970; Birky et al., 1971) and inconclusive. There is little or no direct evidence that operant techniques can permanently eliminate disordered thought processes or hallucinations, or in any sense "cure" schizophrenia (Stahl & Leitenberg, 1976).

The use of operant techniques in another area, the treatment of obesity, has often led to disappointing results. Franks and Wilson (1975) point out that in most successful studies, the weight loss has been modest ($\pm$ 10 pounds) and the follow-ups have been nonexistent or brief, usually less than six months. An exception to the latter generalization is the study of Levitz and Stunkard (1974), who compared behavior treatment therapy to a program of nutrition education conducted by a leader of TOPS (Take Off Pounds Sensibly) and to a third treatment, the usual TOPS program. Although the weight losses were relatively modest (20 pounds or less; for most, less), those in the two behavior therapy groups lost significantly more weight than those in the other two groups; a nine-month follow-up showed the differences to be even greater.

Modeling

In using a *modeling* procedure, the therapist attempts to facilitate behavioral change by having a subject or patient witness the performance of another person, the model. In some cases the patient learns how to perform new responses; in others, to refrain from making old, unwanted responses; and in still others, to make certain responses more frequently.

That human beings sometimes learn by imitating others is hardly a novel suggestion; the experience of the race has long ago confirmed that fact. In recent years, however, social scientists have learned a great deal about the mechanisms involved, the kinds of behavioral changes that can be brought about by this kind of procedure, and the kind of conditions most propitious for facilitating such changes (Bandura, 1969, 1971). As a result of these discoveries, modeling procedures are now being used to treat various kinds of maladaptive behaviors. They have been used, for example, to teach complex linguistic behavior to autistic and schizophrenic children. As described by Bandura (1971), Lovaas and his associates have used the following method, which combines both modeling and shaping techniques.

First, the therapist sits directly in front of the child so that the responses being modeled cannot be ignored. Second, the child is not permitted to withdraw or to exhibit the kind of disruptive, bizarre behavior that is characteristic of such children. If necessary, the child is physically restrained or slapped on the thigh. If the child lacks all or most of the required responses, the therapist breaks down the behavior to be imitated into incremental steps that can be easily followed.

When the child responds properly, a reward is given to encourage further imitations. For example, at first the therapist may reward any random sounds made by the child, but later, only if vocalization occurs within a certain time. Later still, the therapist exhibits progressively more complex verbal responses and rewards only those responses that approximate those of the therapist. After the child is able to learn new words by imitating the model, he is taught what the words mean by the pairing of a phrase, such as *glass of milk,* with its referent. Finally, the child is taught the use of both abstract words and complex grammatical strings. Similar methods have been used with some success by a number of investigators (Risely & Wolf, 1967; Sloane, Johnston, & Harris, 1968; Lovaas, Berberich, Kassorla, Klynn, & Meisel, 1966; Lovaas, Dumont, Klynn, & Meisel, 1966).

Modeling techniques have also been used to reinstate and modify speech behavior in mute or near-mute adult psychotics (Sherman, 1965; Wilson & Walters, 1966).

Less seriously disturbed children and adults have also been treated by the use of modeling procedures. For example, hyperaggressive and extremely withdrawn children have been helped in this way (Gittleman, 1965; O'Connor, 1969). Patients with various kinds of phobias have also been treated by having them observe a model deal calmly with a situation or object the patients find threatening. In one controlled study (Bandura, Grusec, & Menlove, 1967), children who were afraid of dogs were assigned to four different groups. Children in the first group participated in eight sessions during which they observed a fearless peer model exhibit progressively more fear-provoking interactions with a dog.

This was done in what Bandura describes as a "highly positive party context" (Bandura, 1971). A second treatment group was exposed to the model and the same performance, but in a neutral context. The third group observed the dog in the partylike context with the model absent. The fourth group participated in the party activities but was not exposed to the dog or the model. The children in the first two groups, those subjected to the modeling, displayed significantly greater approach behavior toward both the dog used in the experiment and an unfamiliar dog than children in the other two groups. Of those in the first two groups, 67 percent were able to remain alone in a room confined in a playpen with the dog; relatively few of the children in the control groups were able to complete this demanding task.

Modeling has also been used to treat successfully both children and adults with snake phobias (Bandura, Blanchard, & Ritter, 1969; Ritter, 1968) and with various other phobias, including a dissection phobia (Ritter, 1965), a street-crossing phobia (Ritter, 1969a), and acrophobia (Ritter, 1969b).

Assessment. Some investigators (Melnick, 1973; McFall & Twentyman, 1973) have reported failures in the use of modeling, but the vast majority of well-designed studies have provided evidence of its efficacy. That is true of the controlled studies considered in Bandura's major review (1971) and of newer studies (Rachman, Hodgson, & Marks, 1971; O'Connor, 1972; Bandura, Jeffery, & Wright, 1974; Denny & Sullivan, 1976; Horne & Matson, 1977). On balance, there is fairly firm evidence that modeling is a useful therapeutic technique for certain types of problems. It is probably best suited, concludes Bandura (1971, p. 703), to the treatment of anxiety conditions in which the absence of anticipated aversive consequences can be easily and repeatedly demonstrated to the client.

Nonparadigmatic techniques

In addition to the techniques considered so far, there are others we might classify as nonparadigmatic, either because they have not been as thoroughly researched by behavior therapists or because they are less obviously instances of a "behavior therapy technique." To avoid begging certain theoretical questions, only the paradigmatic techniques will be appealed to in our attempt to define behavior therapy. For this reason only a brief description will be given of some of the nonparadigmatic techniques; more complete descriptions can be found in Wolpe (1973), Rimm and Masters (1974), Lazarus (1971), and O'Leary and Wilson (1975).

Assertive training, implosive therapy, and flooding

The term *assertive training* is sometimes applied to any technique aimed at increasing the client's ability to exhibit *assertive behavior* in a socially appropriate manner (e.g., Rimm & Masters, 1974, p. 81). When defined this loosely, the term can apply to almost any therapeutic technique, including psychoanalytic procedures, because almost any technique can be used for the preceding purpose. There is, furthermore, some difficulty in explaining what is to count as assertive behavior. Rimm and Masters (1974, p. 105) define this concept so that it applies to behavior marked by the appropriate expression of feeling. Such a definition requires additional clarification, unless we already possess a clear idea of what is an "appropriate" expression of feeling. The same behavior, such as interrupting a sales clerk or repeatedly asking a female college student for a date, will be seen as both appropriate and not appropriate, depending on the context and the viewer's assumptions about morality, etiquette, standard procedures, and so on. In practice, these conceptual difficulties are circumvented by applying the term *assertive training* to a specified set of procedures used to increase the frequency of behavior *judged* to be assertive by the client, the therapist, or both. The most widely used of these procedures is *behavior rehearsal,* in which the client and therapist typically practice some desired activity, such as asking an employer for a raise or expressing affection to one's spouse. The therapist, for example, might play the role of the employer and respond to the client's request. The therapist may then offer suggestions to improve the client's performance and may show by example what an adequate performance looks like. The therapist and client may then reverse their roles: The therapist will exhibit the appropriate behavior and the client will respond. Homework assignments may then be given requiring the client to practice acting in the desired manner.

Flooding and implosive therapy are similar to each other. The client is exposed, in imagined or aversive real-life scenes, to material that is usually anxiety-provoking. The main difference is that in implosive therapy, but not flooding, psychodynamic material is often included.

When these procedures are used, the client is confronted suddenly with the phobic material, in contrast to desensitization, where the introduction is gradual. For example, Gelder et al. (1973) point out that an agoraphobic patient having a neurotic fear of leaving his house might be asked to imagine the following scene as vividly as possible: He experiences a dreadful panic in a crowded supermarket, surrounded by an unsympathetic crowd; he then faints and is taken by ambulance to a mental hospital. A patient with a snake phobia might be asked to imagine her body and face covered with crawling snakes. It is hoped that by being confronted with such extreme anxiety-provoking situations, while additional aversive consequences are absent, the patient's anxiety will extinguish (Stampfl & Levis, 1967).

Assessment. Assertive training has not been studied as extensively as other behavior therapy techniques, but there are several controlled studies providing some evidence of its effectiveness (Young, Rimm, & Kennedy, 1973; McFall & Lillesand, 1971; McFall & Twentyman, 1973).

The evidence concerning flooding and implosive therapy has been mixed: Many of the favorable studies have methodological defects; some of the better-designed studies have been unfavorable (Rachman, 1966). Thus many writers have expressed reservations about the use of these techniques (Rimm & Masters, 1974; Morganstern, 1973). Some newer studies, however, strongly suggest that these techniques may be effective with certain severe phobias, especially agoraphobia (Everaerd, Rijken, & Emmelkamp, 1973; Emmelkamp, 1974; Hand, Lamontagne, & Marks, 1974).

Cognitive techniques: covert sensitization, cognitive restructuring, and self-control

Covert sensitization is similar to aversive therapy in that aversive stimulation is paired with an unwanted behavior; in the former, however, the stimulation is not a drug or an electric shock but a scene *imagined* by the client. Cautela (1967) describes the use of such a technique to treat alcoholism. The client is taught how to relax and is told to raise his finger when he does not feel tense. He is then told that he must learn to associate drinking alcohol with some unpleasant situation. The therapist then describes in vivid detail some scene such as the following: The client is at a table with his friends and is about to bring a glass of liquor to his lips. He begins to feel sick and vomits all over himself, on his companions, on his glass, and on the floor. The patient is then asked to visualize the entire scene, raising his finger when he can both picture it and feel nauseous when, in the imagined scene, he has the intention of drinking. He is then told to imagine a feeling of relief when he runs away from the table out into the fresh air. The client is then given a homework assignment of ten to twenty repetitions of imagining the same scene. He is also instructed to imagine vomiting on his drink whenever he is tempted to drink.

In one case study, Anant (1967) used a similar procedure to treat twenty-six alcoholic patients, ages nineteen to fifty-five. One client left before treatment was completed. The remaining twenty-five patients abstained completely from drinking during the follow-up periods, which ranged from eight to fifteen months. Although this study is suggestive, longer-term follow-ups are needed to learn about relapses.

Cognitive restructuring, or rational emotive therapy, has developed largely out of the work of Albert Ellis (1962). One of the key assumptions underlying this therapy is that the emotional reactions and maladaptive behavior patterns of some clients are caused, in part, by the holding of irrational beliefs. One such belief suggested by Ellis (1962) is that it is necessary for an adult human being to be loved or approved of by virtually every significant person in his community. Another is the belief that one has virtually no control over one's emotions and that one cannot help feeling certain things. The therapist who uses cognitive restructuring helps the client to identify those irrational beliefs that are causally responsible for the maintenance of a specific maladaptive behavior pattern. The next, and sometimes more difficult, step is to help the client eliminate those beliefs. In one case, described by Rimm and Masters (1974, p. 426), Ellis (1971) treated a twenty-three-year-old girl who suffered severe guilt feelings because she failed to adhere to certain rigorous rules dictated by her parents and supported by her religious beliefs. One consequence was her inability to engage in creative writing; another was her difficulty in maintaining successful relationships with men. She was encouraged by Ellis to examine critically her views on religion, sexual behavior, perfection, and the need to be loved. At the end of four treatment sessions, the client reported that she could now manage without additonal help. A twelve-year follow-up showed that she had maintained a successful marriage and writing career.

Even if some irrational beliefs are pervasive, it is doubtful that we could draw up a small, manageable list of irrational beliefs that every therapist could appeal to in his use of cognitive restructuring; the number of propositions that might be irrationally believed is, in fact, infinite. One way to get around this difficulty is to devise a useful classification scheme of *kinds* of irrational beliefs; another is to classify irrational inference patterns. This last way out is taken by Beck (1970) and Lazarus (1971), who give "overgeneralization" and "dichotomous reasoning" as examples. In the former, one infers a general conclusion from a single instance; in the latter, one infers that an event or object must have only one type of evaluation, such as "good or bad," "right or wrong," and so on. The use of these classifications of faulty inference patterns suggests that in the future, therapists may find it useful to draw on the work of logicians, particularly on recent work on informal fallacies. There are also interesting similarities between cognitive restructuring and what has been called *therapeutic positivism.* A key idea of the therapeutic positivists (Wisdom, 1952; Wittgenstein, 1953) was that most philosophic puzzlement is produced by conceptual confusion analogous in certain respects to a neurosis. The main, if not only goal, of doing philosophy, on this view, is not to provide new information but to cure the philosophically puzzled by rooting out their fundamental confusions. Despite these and other suggestive similarities, however, there are also important differences: The therapeutic positivists were philosophers, not psychologists; they did not do empirical studies of their techniques; and they were not explicitly trying to change maladaptive behavior patterns.

The use of self-control procedures often involves the manipulation of cognitive elements, such as the client's awareness of the rate at which he emits a certain response. Although some writers (Meichenbaum, 1971a) classify at least some of these procedures as "cognitive techniques," others (Kanfer and Karoly, 1972) try to fit them into a behavioristic framework. The inclusion of self-control in the present section is not intended to prejudge the issue of how such techniques are best classified. A related issue is whether *self-control technique* denotes a specific kind of procedure. Many different techniques could be used by clients to control their behavior; in fact, a behavior therapist might become his own client and attempt to use desensitization or aversive therapy or some other form of behavior therapy to modify his own behavior. Despite this difficulty, we will follow the practice of other behavior therapists and talk as if there are such specific techniques, without judging the correctness of this practice.

In many self-control programs the client is instructed to determine how often the target behavior occurs and under what conditions. Some effort is usually made to alter those conditions that, it is hypothesized, are helping to maintain the behavior. Finally, the client, with the therapist's help, will attempt to program his environment so that the unwanted behavior will be punished or its absence rewarded. Alternatively, some behavior that interferes with the undesirable response might be systematically rewarded. Usually, little reliance is placed on the attempt to control the unwanted response by the use of "will power." Some of these features are found in the self-control program used by Penick et al. (1971) to treat obesity. Thirty-two patients were assigned to two groups consisting of welfare patients and private patients. Patients in each of these groups were then randomly assigned to a behavior therapy group or a control group. Those in the two control groups received supportive psychotherapy, instruction about dieting and nutrition, and, infrequently, appetite suppressants. The patients in the two behavior therapy groups were first asked to keep records of the amount, time, and circumstances of their eating. Second, they were encouraged to change the stimuli associated with their eating. For example, they were told to eat in one room only and not to do such things as read or watch television while eating. Third, they were instructed to perform certain actions while eating, such as counting each mouthful of food and placing utensils on the plate after every third mouthful until that mouthful was chewed and swallowed. Fourth, a point system was devised to reward the use of these control procedures. The points were converted into money, which was given the group and then donated to charity. In addition, the patients doctored some of their favorite snacks with castor oil or something else having an unpleasant taste. Treatment lasted for three months. Although patients in all four groups lost weight, those in the two behavior therapy groups did better, with 13 percent losing more than 40 pounds. In the control groups, no one lost more than 40 pounds; 24 percent lost more than 20 pounds.

Assessment. Franks and Wilson (1975, p. 73) point out that an emphasis on cognitive or mediational variables characterizes much of the current behavior therapy literature. We might take this as evidence of apostasy, that behavior therapists are now using and studying nonbehavioral techniques; or we might conclude, depending on our definition of *behavior therapy*, that some of the new behavior therapy procedures are cognitive techniques. Whatever option we take, the development of these new techniques is intriguing. That people can be taught to eliminate some of their maladaptive behavior patterns without simply relying on will power; that the attack on irrational beliefs and faulty logic can be therapeutically efficacious; that problem behaviors can be changed by associating them with painful imagery – all of this is exciting, if it is true. What does the evidence show? There are studies supporting the use of covert sensitization (Cautela, 1972, 1973; Wisocki, 1973; Levine, 1976), but there have also been studies with negative results (Elliot & Denney, 1975; Foreyt & Hagen, 1973; Diament & Wilson, 1975). There is still a paucity, moreover, of well-designed studies with positive results (Wilson & Tracey, 1976).

A number of case reports and some controlled studies of cognitive restructuring (or rational emotive therapy) have now been reported and the results, although inconclusive, have generally been favorable (Goldfried & Goldfried, 1975; D'Zurilla, Wilson, & Nelson, 1973; Lazarus, 1971; Ellis, 1971; Goldfried & Sobicinski, 1975; Goldfried, Decenteceo, & Weinberg, 1974; Moleski & Tosi, 1976).

The utility of self-control techniques for the treatment of certain sorts of problems, including obesity, has been supported by several controlled studies (Penick et al., 1971; Meichenbaum & Cameron, 1974; Stuart, 1971; Hall, 1972; Mahoney, Monra, & Wade, 1973). Less favorable results have been reported for the treatment of cigarette smoking, although an exception is Delahunt and Curran's (1976) use of self-control and negative practice procedures. At the end of a six-month follow-up, the combined treatment group showed superior improvement compared to cigarette smokers in a wait-list control group. Interesting results are also reported by Rosen, Glasgow, and Barrera (1976). Highly fearful snake phobics received either therapist-administered or self-administered desensitization. Both groups improved to the same extent and did somewhat better than controls.

Although there have been many case studies and some controlled studies of cognitive techniques, there is reason to be skeptical even where the evidence is consistently favorable. Too little is known about the nonspecific variables that sometimes cause therapeutic change and that might explain some of the apparent successes; too little is known about the specific ingredients of these techniques; too many of the studies suffer from methodological defects. Many more replications of well-designed studies will be needed before the evidence supporting the effectiveness of these techniques will compare favorably with, for example, systematic desensitization and modeling. Despite these reservations, some of these techniques appear promising; their continued use is likely to widen greatly the scope of behavior therapy, assuming that they qualify as behavior therapy techniques.

III. Definitions

Providing an adequate definition of *behavior therapy* has proved to be difficult. Many definitions have been proposed and no way has been found to demonstrate the superiority of any one of them. To impose some order on what has become a chaotic situation, we should begin by asking two logically prior questions: (1) "Why seek a definition?" and (2) "How we will we know if we have found one?"

Theoretical goals

One purpose for finding a definition is for its own sake, just as philosophers try to define basic concepts, such as *causation* or *explanation*. There need not be any practical or theoretical need served; we might simply want to know: What is explanation, causation, or behavior therapy? This goal, however, is not likely to appeal to most behavior therapists, who are likely to ask what *they* will gain from an acceptable definition.

A second goal is to facilitate testing of general claims about behavior therapy. For example, in justifying the funding of a certain Ph.D. program, we might wish to compare behavior therapy with some other type of therapy. Such comparisons need not be pointless or untestable, as some writers suggest (Brown & Herrnstein, 1975, p. 610); for some rival therapies there is no hard evidence that they are ever effective. It is often more illuminating to talk not about behavior therapy in general, but about a particular type of behavior therapy with a certain class of patients having a specific kind of problem, but that is not always true. Causal claims can vary along a continuum of abstractness from the very general ("Smoking causes cancer") to the very specific ("The smoking of *this* type of cigarette probably caused *this* type of cancer under these conditions in *this* individual"). The degree of abstraction we can sensibly choose will depend partly on our purposes, on the available evidence, and on the context of our utterance. If we do find it useful to talk about behavior therapy in general (as we sometimes will in the present work), it may be helpful (some would say it is necessary) to have an adequate definition in hand.

A third goal is to resolve skeptical doubts about the existence of behavior therapy as a kind of therapy. As suggested earlier (Section I), it is possible that behavior therapists simply share a common paradigm; the techniques they use and study may not have any interesting properties in common not shared by other therapies. Part of the disagreement over definitions may, of course, be caused by disagreement over this very issue, but we might be able to resolve the disagreement if we could demonstrate the superiority of a single definition.

A fourth goal is to be able to classify new techniques. This can be particularly important in a rapidly growing discipline that is in danger of fragmentation. Suppose, for example, that a new technique possesses characteristics X, Y, and Z. Even if we know what the characteristics are, how do we tell whether or not the procedure is a behavior therapy technique? An adequate definition may not help us in all cases (there may be undecidable borderline cases); but it may help in some.

A fifth goal is linked to our inquiry into foundations. To avoid begging any important theoretical questions about underpinnings, we should begin by characterizing behavior therapy in a relatively theory-neutral fashion. We should not define it in terms of classical conditioning, for example, before determining that this is its theoretical basis.

Constraints

Now that we know why we want a definition, we can more easily answer our second question: We can partly judge a proposed definition by seeing how well it serves our theoretical goals, assuming that the definition is correct. Are definitions correct or incorrect, however, or are all definitions arbitrary? Here we must distinguish between a symbol and what it expresses. It may be arbitrary that we select a given symbol, a certain configuration of letters, to express a certain concept; but once we do, it is either true or false that a proposed definition fits that concept. It may be arbitrary, for example, that the term *reinforcer* is sometimes used by operant theorists to mean *an event that increases the probability of a response;* but it is not arbitrary to say that a definition does not correctly fit this usage if it allows any reward, even an ineffectual one, to qualify as a reinforcer. What we are seeking, then, is not just any arbitrary definition of *behavior therapy,* but one that fits the usage of most behavior therapists. If there is more than one such usage, then we may need more than one definition.

We can now lay down the following constraints: a definition of *behavior therapy* must not (1) be too unclear or uninformative to be useful; (2) apply to anything not an instance of behavior therapy; (3) fail to apply to any instance of behavior therapy; (4) include any property that (at best) is only contingently a property of behavior therapy.

Condition 1 is somewhat obscure, but can be made clearer by referring back to our theoretical goals. For example, the term *behavior modification* is sometimes used in a wider and a narrower sense. In the narrower sense it is synonymous with the term *behavior therapy.* In this sense it would be correct, but not very illuminating, to say that behavior therapy is behavior modification. Unless we can independently clarify the term *behavior modification,* this definition offers no guidance on how to determine whether or not something is an instance of behavior therapy. It is not sufficiently informative to be useful, at least not for our purposes.

The justification of conditions 2 and 3 is that they are needed to avoid contradiction, assuming that our definition is to capture the meaning of the phrase *behavior therapy.* Suppose, for example, that we correctly define it as "therapy having the properties X, Y, and Z." If something not an example of behavior therapy could have these properties, it *would not* and, given the definition, *would* be behavior therapy. Conversely, if an instance of behavior therapy lacked one or more of these properties, it both would and, given the definition, would not be an example of behavior therapy. Both of these results are self-contradictory.

How do we tell if conditions 2 or 3 are violated unless we can independently identify a behavior therapy technique? If we need a definition to do that, how can we get started? We will need to know that a certain definition of *behavior therapy* is correct before we know that any definition is correct, and that is logically impossible. The way around this difficulty is to appeal to *paradigmatic* techniques, techniques that are obvious examples of behavior therapy if there are any behavior therapy techniques at all. For reasons given in Section II the following qualify as paradigmatic: systematic desensitization, aversion therapy, operant retraining, and modeling. If a definition implies that one of these is not a behavior therapy technique, then, in the absence of some special explanation, we have reason to believe that condition 3 is violated.

What about condition 2? Are there any clear instances of non-behavior therapy procedures? There are. As Stolz, Wienckowski, and Brown (1975) point out, according to the usage of most behavior therapists, psychosurgery and electroconvulsive therapy (of the kind used to treat severe depression) both fail to qualify as behavior therapy. That is also true of the attempt to cure neuroses or psychoses by simply giving drugs to the patient. In addition, psychoanalysis, client-centered therapy, gestalt therapy, and existential psychiatry also fail to qualify, as is evidenced by the kind of research reported on in the behavior therapy textbooks (Rimm & Masters, 1974; O'Leary & Wilson, 1975). If a definition entails that one of the preceding is a behavior therapy technique, then, in the absence of some special explanation, we have reason to believe that condition 2 is violated. In saying this we are not prejudging such questions as "Should behavior therapists use some of the preceding techniques?" and "Are some of the elements of one or more of the preceding therapies explainable by some of the same principles that explain the workings of behavior therapy?" An affirmative answer to either question is compatible with saying that none of the preceding *is* a behavior therapy technique.

The rationale for condition 4 may be less clear; hence less use will be made of it. To illustrate what it means, let us suppose it is a property of all behavior therapy techniques and of them only that they are employed in South Africa, Canada, Sweden, England, Australia, and America. If this were true, we would still not want to include that as a defining property. If, for example, aversion therapy were later banned in Australia, we would still want to count it as a behavior therapy technique. In general, we do not want to build into the definition some property that for accidental and transient reasons just happens to be possessed by all instances of behavior therapy, and only by them.

Although additional definitional constraints might be imposed, the gain in number might be offset by a loss of obviousness. The preceding conditions, with the possible exception of condition 4, should be relatively uncontroversial and yet of sufficient strength to test most of the definitions that have appeared in the literature. We now turn to some of these definitions.

Current research definitions of behavior therapy

We should distinguish at the outset two very different uses of the term *behavior therapy*: to refer to a certain paradigm (roughly, a set of theoretical and methodological assumptions shared by most behavior therapists) and to a kind of therapy (to a technique or set of techniques). The same kind of ambiguity infects the term *psychoanalysis*, as used to refer to a theory and to a kind of therapy based on that theory. Confusion is likely to result if we mix the two uses, as many writers do. For example, Brown and Herrnstein (1975, p. 602) contend that the main thing shared by all or most behavior therapies is a rejection of Freud's "disease" concept of neurosis. This could not possibly be true, because a therapeutic technique cannot reject anything. What is true is that most behavior *therapists* reject the disease concept. It is also not true of any behavior therapy *technique* that it assumes that maladaptive behavior is usually learned or that learning principles can be used in modifying maladaptive behavior (Rimm & Masters, 1974, pp. 10–11). These assumptions are shared by many behavior therapists; they are not shared by and are not a property of behavior therapy techniques. The point might not be worth stressing except that it is exceedingly difficult to find interesting properties shared by all behavior therapy techniques and only by them. If we follow the practice of many writers and simply list assumptions of behavior therapists or mix such assumptions with characteristics of techniques (O'Leary & Wilson, 1975, pp. 16–17), we can easily deceive ourselves into thinking that we have said what a behavior therapy technique is when we have at best defined a behavior therapy paradigm.

Why not combine talk of paradigms and techniques as in the following definition: Let us say that a behavior therapy technique is simply one used by someone in the behavior therapy paradigm? This will not work for at least two reasons. First, some behavior therapists (e.g., Lazarus, 1971) sometimes use what are clearly not behavior therapy techniques, assuming that there is a distinction to be drawn between kinds of techniques. In fact, there is no reason why someone in a behavior therapy paradigm could not use psychoanalysis, client-centered therapy, or any technique if only to compare it with behavior therapy. Second, to give the preceding definition is not to answer the skeptic who doubts that the behavior therapies share any interesting distinguishing properties other than their being used by people having common assumptions. Suppose, for example, that certain eclectic psychiatrists share a distinctive set of theoretical assumptions but use a wide variety of techniques. No matter how different the techniques are, they might possess one distinctive property: being used by the eclectic psychiatrists. Citing this property is no answer to the skeptic who argues that the techniques used by these eclectic psychiatrists are very different. The same point applies to attempts to define "behavior therapy technique" by talking about a behavior therapy paradigm. In the rest of this chapter we will use the term *behavior therapy* to refer to a kind of therapy. It should not be assumed, however, that all the definitions to be considered were originally intended to reflect this usage or that their authors would necessarily defend today what, in some cases, were meant to be tentative formulations. In subsequent chapters we will consider some elements of a behavior therapy paradigm, such as the assumption that we should reject the disease concept of neurosis. Even then it should not be inferred that all behavior therapists accept the assumptions in question. Where there is disagreement, which is almost everywhere, that will be made clear.

Apart from those that specify assumptions of behavior therapists, most definitions of *behavior therapy* fall into one or two classes: doctrinal or epistemological. Doctrinal definitions link behavior therapy to certain doctrines, such as certain theories, laws, or principles of learning. Epistemological definitions characterize behavior therapy in terms of ways of studying clinical phenomena.

One of the most influential doctrinal definitions is that given by Eysenck (1964): "Behavior therapy may be defined as the attempt to alter human behavior and emotion in a beneficial manner according to the laws of modern learning theory." Similar definitions are given by many writers, although some speak of learning laws or principles but make no reference to learning *theory* (Wolpe, 1976; Franks, 1969; Meyer, 1970; Levis, 1970). This kind of definition offers several important advantages. It is relatively clear, or at least can be made clear if the learning doctrines can be easily specified. It offers guidance as to how a new technique can be classified: Simply see if the therapy bears the right logical connection to the right learning doctrine. Most important, the definition offers us a way of unifying the field of behavior therapy and of meeting the challenge of the skeptic who doubts the existence of behavior therapy.

Despite its merits, the learning doctrine definition is unacceptable. Even if correct, it is not suitable for at least one of our purposes. We want to specify what behavior therapy is in a relatively neutral way so that we can ask about its foundations. In particular, we want to ask if behavior therapy is based on learning theory. If we build an affirmative answer into the very definition of *behavior therapy*, then, of course, an affirmative answer will follow; but that will be a trivial consequence, of no theoretical interest.

It might be replied that the preceding consideration does not show a learning theory definition to be incorrect, or even unsuitable for someone with different goals. This reply is correct, but there are other objections. It will be argued later (in Chapter 3) that at least some paradigmatic behavior therapy techniques are *not* based on learning theories, laws, or principles. If these arguments are sound, then the learning definition violates condition 3: It does not fit some behavior therapy techniques. This is a decisive reason for rejecting it. There is also some reason to believe that condition 4 is violated. Even if it were true that all paradigmatic behavior therapy techniques were based on current learning doctrines, how likely is it that this would be anything more than a contingent feature, the presence of which would be explainable by reference to the tradition out of which behavior therapy developed? If a tie to modern learning doctrines is at best a contingent feature, it would be a mistake to build it into our definition.

Someone might reply to this last objection as follows: Let us forget about capturing the sense in which most behavior therapists use the term *behavior therapy* and simply stipulate that, as we will use it, a commitment to certain learning doctrines will be a defining feature. This reply cannot be rejected as false, because it makes no claim to truth. Anyone is free to stipulate that he will use the term *behavior therapy* as he pleases, but if he does not also claim that his definition fits the usage of most behavior therapists, he is not doing anything relevant to our present concerns. There is also reason to question the wisdom of making such a stipulation. Who can foresee what the techniques used by behavior therapists twenty years from now will look like or what principles or theories will have to be invoked to explain their workings? If we make it true by definition that a behavior therapy technique must be based on current theories or principles of learning, then it may well turn out that most of the techniques used and studied by behavior therapists in the future will fail to qualify as behavior therapy (in the stipulated sense).

Some of the preceding problems are avoided by more recent

doctrinal definitions that speak simply of procedures employing psychological principles (Rimm & Masters, 1974, p. 1) or principles derived from research in experimental and social psychology (Franks & Wilson, 1975 p. 1). These definitions do not explicitly tie behavior therapy to principles of learning, or indeed to any specific principles. The narrowness of the earlier definitions is thus avoided. The gain in scope is offset, however, by a loss of clarity. Unless some hint is given as to the specific principles being referred to (if any), such definitions violate condition 1: They are too unclear to be useful. Imagine, for example, someone challenging our description of a new technique as an example of behavior therapy. How could we use such a definition to meet the challenge without some specification of what psychological principles are relevant? It is also doubtful that such open-ended doctrinal definitions will provide any cohesion for behavior therapy, unless the underlying principles themselves form some coherent whole. Suppose, for example, that such disparate techniques as psychoanalysis, gestalt therapy, and phenomenological therapy were all based on psychological principles; that would not be sufficient for binding them together if the underlying principles were themselves very different.

We might try to avoid the preceding difficulties by linking behavior therapy to a specific set of homogeneous psychological principles. It is not clear what these principles might be if they are not learning principles, but even if they are found, we are likely to violate condition 3. It will be argued later (in Chapter 3) that at least some behavior therapy techniques have no adequate theoretical foundation of any kind, at least for the present. If these later arguments are sound, then any doctrinal definition that refers to specific principles will violate condition 3. Alternatively, the underlying principles may be left completely unspecified, but once again the definition violates condition 1: It will be too unclear to be useful.

Assuming that no doctrinal definition is likely to work, let us turn to epistemological definitions. Davison and Neale (1974) point out that behavior therapy is characterized more by its epistemological stance – its search for rigorous standards of proof – than by allegiance to any particular set of concepts. They conclude that behavior modification (i.e., behavior therapy) is "an attempt to study and change abnormal behavior by drawing on the methods used by experimental psychologists in their study of normal behavior" (Davison & Neale, 1974, p. 485). This definition reflects an important, perhaps the most important, feature of a behavior therapy paradigm: the commitment to the use of experimental methods. What is doubtful is that this characteristic also defines a kind of therapy. Those who favor psychoanalysis or client-centered therapy, for example, can also insist on rigorous standards of proof; they too may draw on the methods used by experimental psychologists. Indeed, in doing comparison studies, behavior therapists are now using experimental techniques to study nonbehavioral techniques. The preceding epistemological definition therefore violates condition 2: it applies to some non-behavior therapy techniques. That is true even if we add an additional requirement: that the therapy be employed in the experimental investigation of the single case (Yates, 1970). There is no reason why psychoanalysis, for example, cannot be studied by the experimental investigation of the single case. This is not to deny that the Yates definition (1970, p. 18) may fit the practice of behavior therapy as it developed in Maudsley Hospital in London; what is doubtful is that it fits the usage of most behavior therapists.

The key advantage of epistemological definitions is that they free behavior therapy from allegiance to any particular theory or set of principles. The fatal disadvantage is that such definitions capture at best a central characteristic of the methods of research characteristically used by behavior therapists: They do not define a kind of therapy. The objection might be made that behavior therapists use experimental techniques not just in the evaluation but also in the very practice of behavior therapy: They take a base rate, specify specific treatment goals, and so on. This comment is correct but not decisive. A psychoanalyst or gestalt therapist can use experimental techniques in both the practice and the study of their therapy yet still not be practicing behavior therapy.

Doctrinal definitions are too narrow, because they do not fit all behavior therapies; epistemological definitions are too wide, because they fit some nonbehavior therapies. It might be thought that we could steer between these two difficulties by combining the best elements of each type of definition. This approach is illustrated by the following definition, which has been tentatively accepted by the Association for the Advancement of Behavior Therapy:

> Behavior therapy involves primarily the application of principles derived from research in experimental and social psychology for the alleviation of human suffering and the enhancement of human functioning. Behavior therapy emphasizes a systematic evaluation of the effectiveness of these applications. Behavior

therapy involves environmental change and social interaction rather than the direct alteration of bodily processes by biological procedures. The aim is primarily educational. The techniques facilitate improved self-control. In the conduct of behavior therapy, a contractual agreement is usually negotiated, in which mutually agreeable goals and procedures are specified. Responsible practitioners using behavioral approaches are guided by generally accepted ethical principles. [Franks & Wilson, 1975, p. 2]

The preceding definition obviously reflects a thoughtful attempt to move beyond overly restrictive doctrinal definitions and to take account of recent developments in the field of behavior therapy; it is so flexible, however, that it is likely to fit some nonbehavior therapy techniques and thus violate condition 2. Suppose, for example, that a new psychodynamic, nonbehavioral technique, somewhat similar to psychoanalysis, is derived from research in social psychology. Any such research will do, regardless of its quality. If the technique involves environmental change and social interaction is used to alleviate human suffering and facilitates self-control, then it will meet the conditions of the preceding definition, provided that it is systematically evaluated for effectiveness. All we need add is that psychiatrists who use the technique (1) usually negotiate a contractual agreement with their clients and (2) are guided by generally accepted ethical principles. Meeting all these conditions would not guarantee that the technique is a form of behavior therapy; by hypothesis it is not. Yet it would qualify according to the preceding definition. In fact, it is not clear how the definition would disqualify gestalt therapy or client-centered therapy, and many other nonbehavior therapies, if these therapies are subjected to systematic evaluation for their effectiveness and are used by therapists who share many of the goals of behavior therapists. In brief, the combination of an epistemological element (a commitment to systematic evaluation) and a reference to unspecified experimental and social psychology research is too weak, even when combined with other elements of the definition, to rule out certain nonbehavioral therapies. The same weakness is present in other definitions that mix an epistemological element with a reference to unspecified psychological research, such as that suggested, in a tentative and cautious spirit, by Mahoney, Kazdin, and Lesswing (1974, p. 14).

Conclusion. We have spent some time assessing definitions partly because assumptions about the nature of behavior therapy can determine conclusions about its foundations, and partly because we are taking seriously the skeptical thesis that behavior therapy, as a kind of therapy, simply does not exist.

Unfortunately, our results have been negative. We have confined our attention to the most important and influential definitions proposed in the behavior therapy literature. If instead we had examined every single proposal that has appeared in the literature, our results would not have been different. There is as yet no adequate definition available, certainly none that has won uniform approval from behavior therapists. It is now time to try a different approach.

Is a definition possible?

If a general term applies to a variety of items, they must have defining properties in common; at least, that has often been assumed to be true. How else could we explain how a general term X can be correctly applied to X's and withheld from non-X's? It must be that X's share certain properties and non-X's lack at least some of them. These distinguishing properties constitute the meaning of a general term and should be captured in an adequate definition.

This widely shared view of general terms has often sustained the attempt to define even in the face of repeated failure; this is especially true in philosophy, where attempts to give illuminating definitions of fundamental concepts, such as *truth, justice, evidence, knowledge,* and so on, have met with limited success. The defining properties must in some sense be there, it is thought; we just have to work harder at discovering them. Is this assumption true? One of the first important challenges to it was given by Wittgenstein (1953), who asks us to give necessary and sufficient conditions for something's being a *game.* He then shows how the request is not easy to meet and, more important, offers an alternative explanation of why the term *game* is applied to some items and not others. It may be that there is a family resemblance between various games, without there being any defining properties that all games share exclusively. For example, a game of one sort may possess certain important characteristics, A, B, C; a game of a second sort may resemble the first in having properties B and C, but not A; a third type might resemble the second in possessing properties C and D, but not B; and a fourth may resemble the third in sharing D and E, but not C. Games of the first and fourth type, then, may not share common properties that would distinguish them from non-games. The reason various items are correctly called games might simply be that they bear this family resemblance to one another.

Perhaps the term *behavior therapy* differs from *game* in that it *can* be defined (in a nontrivial fashion). It is difficult to prove this conjecture false, but at least we need not assume that it is true. We now have a rival explanation of why *behavior therapy* is applied to different techniques; there are important analogies between them, a family resemblance, but no set of shared defining properties. This hypothesis, furthermore, better explains some of the known facts than does the traditional assumption. It explains why no one has found an adequate definition of *behavior therapy*: No such definition is possible because behavior therapies do not share a set of illuminating defining properties. Whether or not this explanation is correct, it is sufficiently plausible to motivate us further to look for an alternative approach.

Is a definition necessary? – an alternative approach

To say what behavior therapy is, it would be sufficient to find an adequate definition, but that is not necessary. An alternative approach might consist of simply listing "important" characteristics. These characteristics need not be defining properties; they need not be part of the meaning of *behavior therapy*; some of them may even be absent from some behavior therapy techniques. However, they should be important at least in this respect: They should help to justify our grouping the paradigmatic behavior therapy techniques under a common classification. They should also have predictive power: We should be able to predict that, barring some special circumstance, such as the presence of some theoretical bias, behavior therapists will be inclined to classify a new technique as behavior therapy if and only if it possesses most or all of the characteristics listed. A further contrast with defining properties is that the latter are not affected by new empirical discoveries. For example, if *being a male* is one of the defining properties of *brother*, then it will remain so no matter what empirical discoveries are made about brothers. Empirical discoveries might motivate us to use the term *brother* in a new sense, but the status of the defining properties of the original sense will not be affected by this change. In contrast, the importance of the properties we will list may diminish as new discoveries are made about behavior therapy. Kripke's (1972) discussion of the term *gold* illustrates this point. Before physicists discovered the atomic structure of gold, its important characteristics included such items as its being yellow, metallic, malleable, and useful as a medium of exchange. These characteristics were important in that their presence or absence helped to explain why something was justifiably classified as *gold* or *not gold*, but they were not defining properties. A substance could lack one of them, such as the characteristic color, and still be gold; that is true, for example, of white gold. Furthermore, these gross properties have become less important as properties of deeper theoretical significance have been discovered.

So-called fool's gold, for example, may have most of the original important properties of gold: it is yellow, metallic, malleable, and so on, but it is still not gold. The presence of these properties is overridden by the absence of what has become a more important characteristic: the atomic number 79. We need not take a stand on Kripke's suggestion that physicists, in discovering deeper and more important properties of gold, water, and other substances, are discovering *essences*. Whether or not the suggestion is correct, what does seem plausible is that in some respects the deeper properties are more important in classifying items as samples of gold or water than are certain gross properties, such as color or taste.

One final contrast with defining properties is that the latter are always important for the same reason: They are part of the meaning of the term being defined; otherwise, they are not defining properties. Nondefining properties, in contrast, may be important in different cases for different reasons. For example, ten years ago the use of a relaxation technique was important in determining whether a given therapeutic sequence qualified as systematic desensitization. If a relaxation procedure is shown to make no therapeutic contribution, then it may lose its importance for that reason. It would be a mistake, however, to infer that this downgrading will happen in all such cases. Suppose, for example, that the use of free association in psychoanalysis is discovered to make no therapeutic contribution; it might still retain its importance in determining whether or not a therapy counts as psychoanalytic. This might happen because of the close ties between the use of free association and psychoanalytic theory or for some other reason. Why a characteristic is important for classification, then, may vary from case to case.

The kind of account previously outlined fits some recent comments by Davison and Stuart (1975). Instead of giving a definition, they simply list what they refer to as "several important unifying characteristics." The characteristics they cite are very similar to those contained in the definition accepted by the Association for the Advancement of Behavior Therapy, which we discussed earlier. In criticizing this definition, we used rather rigorous standards appropriate for definitions; but even when viewed less stringently the characteristics cited are still inadequate. By using an argument analogous to that given earlier, it could be shown that some nonbehavior therapies either do or could share the characteristics cited in the definition. Some of the characteristics are important, but they need to be supplemented if we are to explain why we should draw a distinction between behavior therapy and other kinds of therapies. Rather than run through the argument again or reassess any of the characteristics cited in other definitions, we will simply put forth our own hypothesis. Paradigm instances of behavior therapy are justifiably grouped together because they possess most or all of the following important characteristics:

1 Behavior therapy is used primarily to alleviate human suffering or to enhance human functioning (Davison & Stuart, 1975).

To stress the preceding feature is to indicate that behavior therapy is a kind of *therapy*. If, for example, we shocked an autistic child simply because we thought he deserved it or gave a nausea-inducing drug to a prisoner in order to punish him, it is not clear that we would be practicing therapy of any kind. Saying exactly what constitutes therapy is not easy, especially if we divorce the concepts of disease and therapy as behavior therapists do; but there is no need to give such a definition here. We are primarily interested in distinguishing behavior therapy from other kinds of therapy, not from other sorts of nontherapeutic activities.

2 Behavior therapy is a psychological rather than a biological form of treatment.

This characteristic is important in distinguishing behavior therapy from psychosurgery, or the use of lithium or some other drug to treat a manic-depressive, or the use of electroconvulsive therapy to treat depression. In some sense, these latter procedures are biological (or medical) treatments, whereas behavior therapy is a psychological form of treatment. We could, if we wanted greater depth, attempt to define *biological,* but that is not necessary as long as we can intuitively distinguish, in most cases, biological and nonbiological procedures.

3 Behavior therapy is usually used to treat so-called symptoms directly.

It is not always clear what item 3 means, but one contrast is with *insight* therapy. To use systematic desensitization to treat a snake phobia, for example, one need not obtain insight into the origin of the problem; one simply tries to eliminate the phobic reaction. A second contrast is with attempts to eliminate underlying causes, as when a doctor treats not the fever but the virus that causes it or when a psychoanalyst tries to strengthen the patient's ego. In contrast, behavior therapy techniques are often used without an attempt to discover or treat so-called underlying causes. However, important qualifications are needed here. If aversion therapy is used to treat alcoholism, for example, it may be used to attack the drinking behavior directly, but in addition the therapist might try to eliminate any situational variables that serve to reinforce this behavior. A therapist who uses some form of operant retraining to eliminate obesity may also help the patient to gain more insight into the causes of his or her overeating, to help eliminate these causes if possible.

It is not true, then, that in using behavior therapy, one never attacks underlying causes or never helps the patient or his family gain insight into the cause of the problem. What is true is that the primary focus of behavior therapy is usually not on either of these things. If a technique relied primarily on the gaining of insight (as with client-centered therapy) or if one generally had to get at the original, underlying cause of one's problem in order to use the therapy (as with psychoanalysis), then that would be an important (not necessarily decisive) reason for not classifying the technique as a form of behavior therapy.

4 Behavior therapy is characteristically used to modify maladaptive behavior or to teach adaptive behavior.

The contrast intended here is with those methods of psychotherapy, such as psychoanalysis, which are normally used to alter the client's psyche or personality structure. This feature is important in explaining why a technique should be classified as *behavior* therapy: The focus is on behavior. Again, important qualifications are needed. Many of those who founded and developed the behavior therapy movement accepted some version of behaviorism or at least were influenced by some of its major tenets (Krasner, 1971a). The focus, then, for theoretical as well as practical reasons was almost exclusively on the patient's behavior, but this may well change as the field expands and is infused with new theory and new techniques. For example, covert sensitization may be used to change a person's mental state, with the intention of thereby changing his behavior. In some cases behavior therapy techniques may even be used to eliminate unwanted mental states, as in Davison's (1968) use of counterconditioning to eliminate a sadistic fantasy, simply because the mental state itself is unwanted.

5   Behavior therapy is often used in an incremental rather than a holistic fashion. Problems are divided into their components and each component is treated separately.

For example, in using modeling or an operant technique to teach an autistic child how to speak, the therapist might subdivide the task into learning, first, to emit sounds; second, to use single words; third, to repeat whole sentences; and so on. In other cases the patient may have an unwanted behavioral pattern that can be broken up into smaller units and each unit can then be treated separately. For example, an obese patient might have his eating behavior broken up, for analytical purposes, into his fondly preparing food in the kitchen; carrying it into the living room; sitting down to watch television while eating; and finally, eating. Each of these component behaviors might then be modified or broken into still smaller units. This characteristic, of being applicable to discrete units of larger behavior patterns, makes behavior therapies quite flexible in their application.

6   Behavior therapy is characteristically studied and used experimentally.

Behavior therapists, probably more than any other group, have stressed the use of experimental techniques to test claims of therapeutic effectiveness. This contribution may prove to be more important and more enduring than the development of any particular therapeutic technique. One of its consequences is likely to be the increased use of experimental methods to study non-behavior therapies, if for no other reason than to compare different kinds of therapy, as in Sloane et al.'s (1975) study of short-term psychoanalysis and behavior therapy. It is likely, then, that the manner in which behavior therapy is studied and evaluated will not continue to distinguish it from other kinds of therapy.

Experimental techniques also enter into the very practice of behavior therapy, and this is probably a more important characteristic if we are trying to isolate a set of techniques rather than a paradigm. Particularly important is the practice of *operationalizing* such concepts as *anxiety, fear, depression,* and *lack of self-esteem* by linking them to specific behavior patterns. Suppose, for example, that a patient suffers from severe depression. The therapist might try to identify the ways in which the depression is expressed (e.g., in sitting mutely for extended periods in the presence of one's wife and children or retreating to one's study to sulk in the dark). The behavior therapist might tentatively target these behavior patterns as the ones to be eliminated. To take a second example, a client who suffers from deep feelings of inadequacy is likely to manifest these feelings by behaving or thinking in certain characteristic ways. For example, he may refuse to assert himself in certain types of social situations. Again the therapist can try to identify the specific behavioral or cognitive patterns and then try to eliminate them.

The practice of linking certain concepts to behavior may reflect a commitment of certain behavior therapists to operationalism or to some type of behaviorism (see Chapter 2), but that need not be so. We need not say that the depression, for example, literally *is* the behavior, just that the two are correlated. Furthermore, it need not be assumed, somewhat simplistically, that the client's problem will always vanish once the accompanying behavior is eliminated. Different cases may have to be treated differently, depending in part on what is causing the client's problem. What is important is that by "operationalizing" nonbehavioral concepts, the behavior therapist opens avenues of treatment that otherwise might be closed. He can more easily treat, say, free-floating anxiety or existential despair if he can identify specific patterns of behavior or cognition that reflect the patient's inner state. The gain in flexibility is important.

The practice of behavior therapy often involves the use of other techniques borrowed from experimental psychology, such as the establishment of a *base rate* so that the frequency at which a target behavior is emitted after treatment can be compared to its pre-treatment frequency. The therapist may also use a single-case experimental design to determine experimentally if the patient is being helped. The use of such experimental techniques is sufficiently important that there is some substance to the view that behavior therapy is simply applied experimental psychology (Davison & Neale, 1974). As noted earlier, however, psychoanalysts could use such techniques and still be practicing psychoanalysis; and a behavior therapist can fail to use such methods and yet be practicing, even if inefficiently, behavior therapy. For this reason it would be unwise to define *behavior therapy* as "applied experimental psychology." The feature is important but is not a defining characteristic; and it is not the only important characteristic.

7 Behavior therapy has had a close tie to learning theory research.

Some behavior therapists probably place behavior therapy techniques under a common rubric simply because they believe that all such techniques are based on learning theory. If that belief is false, as will be argued in Chapter 3, then we cannot appeal to it to justify our classification scheme. There are, however, important ties of some kind between most of the paradigmatic behavior therapy techniques and research by such modern learning theorists as Watson, Thorndike, Pavlov, Hull, and Skinner. The nature of these ties will be explored in Chapter 3.

Conclusion. If we need a concise way of saying what behavior therapy is, we can combine the preceding characteristics in the following way: Behavior therapy is a nonbiological form of therapy that developed largely out of learning theory research and that is normally applied directly, incrementally, and experimentally in the treatment of specific maladaptive behavior patterns. The foregoing is not a definition, for reasons given earlier. For example, one or more of the preceding characteristics may be missing from a behavior therapy technique. Furthermore, the importance of some of the characteristics may diminish in the future. For example, the tie to learning theory research is likely to become less important as new streams of experimental and social psychology begin to feed behavior therapy research. Finally, the list of important characteristics is not exhaustive.

Adequacy of our account

Assuming that we have isolated most of the important characteristics of behavior therapy, how adequate is this type of account? This question can be answered by looking at our theoretical reasons for seeking a definition. These included wanting a definition (1) simply for its own sake; (2) to facilitate the testing of general claims about behavior therapy; (3) to aid in the classification of new techniques; (4) to enable us to say in a relatively theory-neutral way what behavior therapy is, so that we may inquire into its foundations; and (5) to provide an answer to the skeptic who doubts the existence of behavior therapy. The first goal is not met. If we want a definition out of pure intellectual interest, it is likely that nothing short of a definition will suffice. With the exception of this first goal, however, all the others are met by our account. Consider the second goal. Some general claims about behavior therapy will remain difficult to test even after we say what behavior therapy is, but in any case that a definition would help, our account will do the same; that is, it will help us decide what therapeutic techniques we are talking about. It will also aid us in classifying new techniques. Consider, for example, some of the nonparadigmatic techniques described in Section II, such as covert sensitization and techniques of self-control. Some writers classify these two techniques as behavior therapies; some do not. How do we decide which position is correct? If behavior therapy is what we said – a nonbiological form of therapy that developed out of learning theory research and that is normally applied directly, incrementally, and experimentally in the treatment of specific maladaptive behaviors – then a good case can be made for classifying these two techniques as forms of behavior therapy. A therapy that is harder to classify is cognitive restructuring (rational emotive therapy). The connection between the development of this therapy and learning theory research is relatively remote; the technique originated in the work of Albert Ellis (1962). This is hardly decisive, but there are other disanalogies. Most important, in using cognitive restructuring, the therapist does not *directly* attack maladaptive behavior; instead he tries to root out underlying causes (not necessarily the original causes) and he does try to give the patient insight into what is maintaining the unwanted behavior. However, there are also important analogies. The technique is normally used in an experimental manner and the focus still is on the elimination of specific maladaptive behavior patterns. Instead of trying to weigh the positive and negative analogies too precisely, it would probably be wiser simply to say what they are. Once it is explained in what important respects a technique does and does not resemble paradigmatic behavior therapy techniques, it becomes relatively uninteresting to ask, "Yes, but is it really behavior therapy?" We should expect to find at least some borderline cases for which this question is unanswerable, and pointless. The same phenomenon (of finding unclassifiable borderline cases) can arise even where we have a full-fledged definition (e.g., a brother, by definition, is a male sibling, but there can be siblings not easily classifiable as either males or females).

For those who want to inquire into foundations, the fourth goal is particularly important. We do not want to settle by definition substantive questions about the basis of behavior therapy. Our account fares well by this criterion. Because we have managed to avoid defining *behavior therapy* in terms of any particular theory or principle, we are free to ask if it is based on behaviorism or on learning theory, on a rejection of the medical model, and so on.

What about the final goal of answering the skeptic who doubts the existence of behavior therapy? We need to examine this question a bit before answering it.

Skepticism: a rival hypothesis

Could the skeptic be right in saying that behavior therapy does not exist? On the surface this appears to be a fantastic thesis. Thousands of articles and many books have been published about behavior therapy techniques. Could all this activity be about nothing? Before we answer, consider another thesis that at first also appears somewhat bizarre: that mental illness is a myth. More has been written about mental illness than about behavior therapy. Nevertheless, Szasz (1974) and others have managed to raise serious doubts about the existence of mental illness; and at least some behavior therapists think these doubts are justified (Ullmann & Krasner, 1969). In each case the skeptic concedes that we are talking about something when we use the terms *behavior therapy* and *mental illness*, but what we are talking about, he argues, has been systematically misclassified. This concession reduces but hardly eliminates the paradoxical appearance of the skeptic's thesis. Because doubts about mental illness are discussed in Chapter 4, we will say nothing further about them now. What about doubts about the existence of behavior therapy? Is it plausible that the kind of massive misclassification the skeptic is talking about would, until now, remain undetected? How would we explain such a mistake? As a partial answer, the skeptic might point to the historical connection between learning theory research and the origin of behavior therapy. Partly because of this connection, he might argue, the idea developed that behavior therapy techniques are all based on learning theory. This idea has been further promoted by such practices as referring to thoughts and images as *behavior* and referring to any acquired behavior as *learned* and any learned behavior as a *conditioned response*.

What about those behavior therapists who are skeptical about the learning foundations of behavior therapy? Why do they tend to group so-called behavior therapy techniques under a common heading? One possibility is that such techniques, disparate though they may be, are used and studied by those who share certain epistemological and methodological assumptions (i.e., assumptions central to a behavior therapy paradigm).

Assuming that the skeptic can explain why so-called behavior therapies have been misclassified, he can make his thesis more plausible; but why is it interesting? Is not his point merely a verbal one? In a recent satirical essay Krasner (1976) mourns the "demise" of behavior modification. He is referring, presumably, not to the end of a certain type of therapeutic practice, but to the end of a linguistic practice: that of referring to behavior therapy (and certain nontherapeutic activities) as behavior modification. Although this linguistic practice has not, in fact, ended, some writers have recommended that it stop because the term *behavior modification* has taken on certain misleading connotations. Analogously, someone might take the skeptic to be simply recommending that we stop using the term *behavior therapy* to refer to a kind of therapy. This interpretation of the skeptic's point is mistaken; he is asking if there is any nontrivial distinction to be drawn between what is and what is not now called behavior therapy. That issue would remain even if we stopped using the term *behavior therapy*. To put it slightly differently, are systematic desensitization, modeling, aversion therapy, and so on, sufficiently analogous to justify grouping them together as a *kind* of therapy? This is an issue about the nature of certain techniques, not about the use of words.

One way to meet the skeptic's challenge would be to demonstrate that behavior therapy techniques have a common theoretical foundation, such as some theory, law, or principle of learning. It will be argued in Chapter 3, however, that this is not a realistic option. A second way out would be to speak of the epistemological and methodological assumptions shared by most behavior therapists. For reasons given earlier, this will not work. Therapists who share such assumptions can, nevertheless, use and study nonbehavioral therapies; and those who reject the assumptions can still use and study behavior therapies. Unless behavior therapy is based on the assumptions, they characterize a type of paradigm, not a type of therapy. A third way out, and the one we are recommending, is to list and explain the important characteristics mentioned earlier. In brief, behavior therapies are justifiably grouped together because they share most or all the following characteristics: They are nonbiological forms of therapy, most of which developed out of learning theory research and which are normally applied directly, incrementally, and experimentally to treat specific maladaptive behavior patterns. This hypothesis is at least as plausible as the skeptic's hypothesis. It is, in fact, a good deal more plausible: By accepting it we can avoid postulating the kind of massive error that the skeptic must attribute to most behavior therapists and their opponents.

Although our hypothesis is more plausible than the skeptic's, we have not proved that it is true. First, we have not proved that the characteristics listed are important; second, we are deliberately leaving open the possiblity that characteristics of deeper importance will be discovered later, which will justify changing our current classifications. For example, if we discover that the workings of aversion therapy and operant retraining procedures are explainable by a common theory and that a different theory explains the mechanism of covert and systematic desensitization, we might then be justified in distinguishing two types of therapy. Perhaps only one of these will qualify as behavior therapy. All we can reasonably say now, and all we need say, is that given the evidence currently available, our hypothesis (or one very much like it) provides the best account of what behavior therapy is. It should be conceded, however, that this account is not very deep, compared to that offered by the learning theorist. If all and only behavior therapy techniques were based on theories or principles of learning, it would be far more illuminating to use this characteristic to group such techniques rather than relying on the surface properties cited in our account. Even if one is skeptical about learning theory foundations, one can have a great deal of sympathy with what learning theorists were attempting. Had the foundations been firm, the learning theory account of the nature of behavior therapy would have been superior.

Suppose that future discoveries show that neither our hypothesis nor one like it is adequate and that so-called behavior therapy techniques have no important characteristics in common. We might then be wise to adopt the epistemological-methodological account discussed earlier, a course already taken by many behavior therapists (e.g., Hersen, Eisler, & Miller, 1975; Yates,

1970; Davison & Neale, 1974); but we should understand that to do this is to concede that the skeptic is right: Behavior therapy does not exist. On this view, there is a behavior therapy *paradigm* characterized by certain epistemological and methodological assumptions; there are behavior *therapists*, those who accept the relevant assumptions and perhaps make use of them in their clinical practice or research; but there are no behavior *therapies*.

2. Behavioristic foundations

Some basic issues

Is behavior therapy behavioristic? Can a behavior therapist consistently accept behaviorism and the use of mentalistic terms? If behavior therapy is behavioristic, is that an advantage or a disadvantage? Why?

If anything deserves to be called a philosophic foundation of behavior therapy, it is behaviorism. First, as suggested in Chapter 1, behavior therapy developed largely out of the experimental work of behaviorists, such as Watson, Thorndike, Pavlov, Hull, and Skinner. Second, in contrast to much traditional psychotherapy, the treatment is directed primarily at a person's behavior rather than his mind; the therapy is, in brief, *behavior* therapy. Third, the concepts and principles employed to explain the results of behavior therapy are said to be taken from learning theories, such as Pavlov's or Skinner's, that purport to explain behavioral change without using irreducible mentalistic concepts. Finally, many leading behavior therapists contend that behavior therapy and behaviorism have important connections. Eysenck (1972), for example, has argued that behavior therapy is behavioristic. Waters and McCallum (1973) argue that the use of mentalistic terms by behavior therapists is consistent with behaviorism and conclude that the basis of behavior therapy is behavioristic rather than mentalistic. Krasner (1971a) contends that perhaps the most important general stream feeding behavior therapy includes the concept *behaviorism*, which, following Kantor (1969), he defines as the renunciation of the doctrines of soul, mind, and consciousness. O'Leary and Wilson (1975, p. 7) point out that behavior therapy is deeply rooted in the development of behaviorism, which, they note, has as its aim the prediction and control of behavior rather than the understanding of the mind. Mahoney, Kazdin, and Lesswing (1974, p. 15) conclude that the argument of some critics that behavior therapy is not behavioristic is invalid.

In spite of the preceding considerations, some critics have questioned the thesis that behavior therapy is behavioristic. Breger and McGaugh (1965) point out that an imagined scene, of the kind employed in systematic desensitization, is not an objectively defined stimulus. Locke (1971) concludes that Wolpe's procedures are not behavioristic. At least some of these criticisms, however, depend on the assumption that the employment of mentalistic concepts is inconsistent with behaviorism. To assess this assumption, we need to determine what behavior therapists mean by *behaviorism*.

Eysenck (1972) distinguishes three kinds of behaviorism: metaphysical, methodological, and analytical; he rightly points out that neglect of these distinctions can make disputes about behaviorism merely disputes about words. These three kinds of behaviorism can be explained as follows:

1 *Metaphysical (or, radical) behaviorism* is the view that minds (or mental events or states) do not exist.
2 *Analytical (or, logical) behaviorism* is the view that all statements ostensibly about the mental can be translated into statements about behavior or behavioral dispositions.
3 *Methodological behaviorism* is the view that psychologists should, for methodological reasons, abjure completely the use of mentalistic explanations. Some methodological behaviorists say that the mind, whether it exists or not, cannot be studied scientifically; others say merely that there are sound methodological reasons for not treating mental events as independent variables, although they may be studied as dependent variables. Mental events can be effects but not causes.

Eysenck conjectures that most behavior therapists would accept one of the second two types of behaviorism but would reject the first; this position has been affirmed by behavior therapists who have written on the subject (Franks & Wilson, 1973; Waters & McCallum, 1973; Mahoney et al., 1974). If Eysenck's conjecture is correct, criticisms of a metaphysical type of behaviorism, such as that espoused by John Watson (1913), are probably irrelevant to discussions of the theoretical foundations of behavior therapy. For that reason they will not be considered here.

If we confine our discussion to logical and methodological behaviorism, then the assumption stated earlier – that the use of mentalistic terms is inconsistent with behaviorism – is false. An analytical behaviorist can consistently countenance talk of "imagined scenes," "irrational beliefs," "sadistic fantasy," and so on, so long as these locutions can be given a behavioral translation. A methodological behaviorist can consistently use such mentalistic terms provided that they do not refer to independent variables. One cannot demonstrate, then, that behavior therapy is not behavioristic simply by showing, which is obvious, that behavior therapists sometimes use mentalistic terms in describing their procedures.

Assuming that it is now reasonably clear what behavior therapy and behaviorism are, we can ask about the relationship between the two. First, what does it mean to assert that behavior therapy is behavioristic, or has a behavioristic foundation? Second, why does the assertion matter? Third, is the assertion true? We will begin with the first question.

In saying that behavior therapy is behavioristic, one might mean that behaviorism forms part of the paradigm accepted by most behavior therapists. It is this thesis that is supported by Mahoney, Kazdin, and Lesswing (1974).

A second thesis is that the *practice* of behavior therapy, including the methods of experimentation and the therapeutic techniques, is compatible with behaviorism. This thesis is defended by Eysenck (1972) and Waters and McCallum (1972). Theses 1 and 2 are likely to be connected if the paradigm accepted by behavior therapists influences their practice; but the two theses need to be distinguished to allow for the possibility that theory and practice diverge, as Locke (1971) charges.

A third interpretation is that behavior therapy is logically derivable from behaviorism. Presumably, this would mean that either analytical or methodological behaviorism, when combined with certain auxiliary assumptions, entails descriptions of behavior therapy techniques. Stated in this way, the issue is uninteresting: There is not the slightest reason to think that this type of logical relationship exists; no behavior therapist of note has claimed that it does exist. If a behavior therapist does speak of a behavioristic foundation and suggests a logical linkage of this kind, he is probably referring not to a philosophical or methodological principle, but to some version of modern learning theory. (See Chapter 3.)

Why does it matter whether or not behavior therapy is behavioristic? One thing not at issue is the effectiveness of behavior therapy techniques, which is secured primarily by empirical studies; the evidence from these studies is not likely to be seriously undermined or strengthened by the finding either that behavior therapy is not behavioristic or that it is. The empirical studies are crucial in a way that theoretical, especially philosophical, inquiry is not. It should not be inferred, however, that the issue is simply a matter of words (Eysenck, 1972) or is without theoretical interest; that need not be true if it is stated properly.

First, if we are asking about a behavior therapy paradigm, the issue is likely to be important if the paradigm influences the practice. Some of the ways this can happen are discussed in Kuhn (1962): The paradigm a scientist accepts can help determine the kinds of research problems he finds important, the kinds of solutions he deems acceptable, and the ways in which he processes and evaluates evidence.

Second, if we are asking about the practice of behavior therapy, its consistency with behaviorism is likely to matter if the latter is true. If behaviorism is true, its compatibility with behavior therapy constitutes an advantage for the latter, from a scientific point of view, relative to therapies that violate behavioristic principles. If behaviorism is false, however, its consistency with behavior therapy is not likely to matter.

Is it true that behavior therapy is behavioristic? If this question concerns a paradigm rather than a practice, we need to determine whether or not behavior therapists accept either analytical or methodological behaviorism. It is doubtful that all do (there is no single behavior therapy paradigm), but there is some evidence that one of these forms of behaviorism is accepted by many behavior therapists (Eysenck, 1972; Waters & McCallum, 1973; Krasner, 1971a; O'Leary & Wilson, 1975; Mahoney, Kazdin, & Lesswing, 1974). Assuming that behaviorism is part of the paradigm accepted by many behavior therapists, is this an asset or a liability? We will be in a better position to answer this question after we have examined the merits of behaviorism.

We also need to examine behaviorism, at least one variant of it, in order to determine if the *practice* of behavior therapy is behavioristic. As noted earlier, we cannot simply inspect the practice and see if mentalistic terms are employed; they obviously are. In describing systematic desensitization, and especially the so-called cognitive therapies (Mahoney, 1974), behavior therapists use such terms as *visual image, cognition, thought stopping, sexual fantasy,* and so on. The issue is whether these locutions are translatable, as implied by analytical behaviorism, into talk about behavior, actual or potential.

A third reason for examining behaviorism is to clear the way for our discussion of the learning foundations of behavior therapy (Chapter 3). Behavioristic theories of learning are often connected to a network of ideas, which includes some form of empiricism, operationism, macrodeterminism, and analytical or methodological behaviorism. Each interlocking strand in this network strengthens and protects the other. The result is an extraordinarily resilient system powerful enough to withstand most challenges. If one attacks the learning theory alone (Chomsky, 1959), its defenders can use other strands in the network to protect the theory (MacCorquodale, 1970). The result, as with many paradigm disputes, is often fruitless controversy. We are more likely to avoid this result if we examine now some of the ideas often used in defense of the theories of learning to be discussed later. Empiricism (roughly, the idea that most or all nontautological hypotheses require empirical confirmation) and macrodeterminism (the idea that every macro event has a cause) are accepted by many opponents of behaviorism and are not relevant to our present concerns. We do need to look, however, at the thesis of operationism to see how it serves to protect both behaviorism and various theories of learning.

I. Operationism

Operationism (or operationalism) is the thesis that all scientifically acceptable theoretical concepts (i.e., those referring to what is unobservable) must be definable in terms of measuring operations or test procedures. An early version of the thesis required that each concept be tied definitionally to a *single* measuring operation. A more flexible version allows that a *set* of operations may be employed (Davison & Neale, 1974, p. 81). For example, if a therapist uses the concept *improvement,* he may define the concept in terms of the client's performance on some objective test, such as the Minnesota Multiphasic Personality Inventory, or he may employ a whole battery of tests.

Skinner's (1945) suggestion that "behaviorism has been (at least to most behaviorists) nothing more than a thoroughgoing operational analysis of traditional mentalistic concepts" may be overstated, but there is an important connection between operationism and behaviorism. One thing that led some theorists to give behavioristic analyses was their acceptance of operationism. Furthermore, operationism is often used to rule out counterexamples to behaviorism. For example, if a given mentalistic concept cannot be defined behaviorally and no other operational definition is possible, that need not be taken as a counterexample to analytical behaviorism; instead the concept can be rejected as scientifically meaningless. Operationism is also used to support methodological behaviorism: if an explanation of behavior employs a mentalistic concept, it may be dismissed as *empty,* if the concept is operationally definable in terms of the behavior, or *nonscientific,* if it is not. Suppose, for example, that a follower of Carl Rogers uses the concept *self-actualization* to explain a patient's behavior. If the concept is defined in terms of that behavior, the explanation can be dismissed as empty: It will merely redescribe the behavior it purports to explain (Davison & Neale, 1974, p. 475). If the concept is not defined in terms of the behavior and cannot be operationally defined in some other way, an operationalist will dismiss it as being scientifically meaningless. Behavioristic theories of learning can be protected in a similar way. If a rival cognitive theory is proposed, it can be rejected as nonexplanatory if the key theoretical concepts are defined in terms of behavior, or it can be ruled scientifically unacceptable if they are not operationally definable. For example, Gerwirtz (1971, p. 303) objects to Bandura's use of the cognitive term *self-evaluation* if it is not defined in terms of independent empirical operations and suggests that it is unnecessary if it is so defined. In brief, operationism is a powerful protective strand in the network of ideas alluded to earlier; we need to discuss it before we turn to the other strands.

Fortunately, our task is made easier by the fact that a number of important objections to operationism have already appeared in the literature. These objections taken together are quite powerful and seriously undermine the operationist's thesis (Hempel, 1956; Erwin, 1970; Koch, 1964).

The first of these objections is that certain acceptable concepts of physics, such as *psi-function* and *electron,* are not operationally definable in terms of test procedures or measuring operations. This objection was first pressed by certain physicists, including the founder of operationism, P. W. Bridgman (Bridgman, 1955, p. 90; Lindsay, 1937). This objection may not be decisive if the recalcitrant concepts are few and can be isolated. The operationist might modify his thesis so as to exclude these few undefinable concepts and then try to explain why they should be treated differently from other theoretical concepts. There is, however, a second, more influential objection, first raised by Carnap (1953).

Suppose we operationally define *solubility in water* as follows.

Something is soluble in water if and only if it meets the following conditions: If the thing is placed in water, it dissolves. Anything meeting the conditions of the definition will be soluble if the definition is correct. However, something that is not soluble (e.g., a match) and is not placed in water will satisfy the conditions; consequently, the definition is incorrect. Why say that the match satisfies the definition? If it is not placed in water, then the antecedent of the conditional "If the thing (i.e., the match) is placed in water, it dissolves" is false. That is, it is false that the thing is placed in water. However, it is a rule of truth-functional logic that an indicative conditional with a false antecedent is true. Consequently, it is true of the match that if it is placed in water, it dissolves.

Consider a second example. Suppose we give the following operational definition of *retarded*. Someone is retarded if and only if he meets the following conditions: If he is given intelligence test Y, then he scores less than 75. This definition is unsatisfactory because it will apply to a nonretarded child who never takes the test. Consequently, the entire conditional – "If he is given intelligence test Y, then he scores less than 75" – is true of this particular child even though he is not retarded. The reasoning is the same as before. The conditional has a false antecedent; but an indicative conditional with a false antecedent is true.

An operationist may reply that an operational definition should use not an indicative but a subjunctive conditional. That is, it should read: "x is soluble if and only if: if x *were* placed in water at time t, then it would dissolve at time t." This definition does not obey the laws of truth-functional logic; the statement following the "if and only if" is *not* true of a match merely because the match has not been placed in water. Hence, Carnap's objection, which has been very influential among philosophers of science, does not succeed.

Although the reply of the operationist is correct, it only temporarily suppresses the difficulty raised by Carnap. Suppose we ask the operationist what he means by the phrase "if x were placed in water at time t, then it would dissolve at time t." If he replies that this means simply that "if x *is* placed in water at time t, then it will dissolve at time t," then he is back with his original definition and Carnap's original objection. Suppose, however, that he leaves the phrase undefined. Because it does not denote an observable property or measuring operation, his definition of *soluble* is not operational. He appears to be giving an operational definition but is doing this by smuggling into the *definiens* a nonoperational element. It is difficult to see a way around this problem. If there is no solution this is a serious defect in the operationist program; for the same problem will arise for other dispositional terms of more interest to the psychologist, such as *intelligent, nervous, neurotic, expectant, fearful,* and so on.

A third objection, which applies only to the original, less flexible version of operationism, is that there is often more than one way to test the applicability of a concept; this precludes the possibility of defining the concept in terms of any one of these tests. To see the point, consider the term *anxiety.* As Neale and Liebert (1973) point out, we may measure it in at least three different ways: by assessing the subjective report of an individual, by monitoring psychophysical changes, or by observing a person's overt behavior. We cannot, then, say that anxiety is nothing more than overt anxiety behavior, for anxiety can be detected by use of the second test even when no overt anxiety behavior is present. Neale and Liebert suggest that we meet this difficulty by switching to the more flexible operationist position: We can say that each test specifies only *part* of the meaning of the concept; it does not exhaust the meaning. This is more reasonable, but still objectionable even if we ignore the difficulties mentioned earlier. If *anxiety behavior* were even part of the meaning of *anxiety,* then it would be a contradiction to say that a subject is anxious, as is shown by the presence of certain physiological changes, but is not exhibiting anxiety behavior; but this is not a contradiction. It is sometimes true.

The whole attempt to equate test conditions with the meaning, or even part of the meaning, of a concept appears to be based on a confusion between meaning and evidence. To take a facetious example, the presence of certain radio signals may be evidence for the truth of "Intelligent creatures exist on other planets." However, that statement is not about radio signals; it is about intelligent creatures on other planets. Suppose, to take a different example, we can get evidence that a child has brain damage by noticing that he scores poorly on test Y. Even if this were the only way to test for brain damage, it would still not be true that talk of brain damage would be synonymous with talk of achieving a certain low score on test Y. The brain damage and the test performance are two different things. One may be evidence for the other, but that does not show that the corresponding concepts are identical.

At this point some operationists reply that the preceding difficulties can be avoided by stipulation. An experimenter can simply stipulate that all he means by *brain damage* is "scoring below 75 on test Y." If he does this we cannot criticize his definitions. In the sense he is using the term *brain damage,* it means nothing more than what has been stipulated. It must be admitted that sometimes experimenters do stipulate in this way. As Neale & Liebert (1973) point out, a psychologist interested simply in whether or not a rat turns right in a T-maze might use the word "learning" to describe only this result. He might say, "As I use the term, learning will have taken place if and only if the rat turns right in the T-maze." Sometimes it may be useful to make such a stipulation, but that is not always true. If, for example, we want to extrapolate findings from learning theory experiments with rats to conditions facilitating human learning, we do not want to use *learning* in such a narrow sense. We do not want to make it a necessary condition of a human being's learning something that he or she turn right in a T-maze. Even our hypothetical rat psychologist, who might have no interest in human learning, might find his concept too narrow for his own purposes. Suppose, for example, that he wishes to find out if the rat can be influenced by the same variables to learn how to turn *left* in the T-maze. He cannot say that learning will have taken place if and only if the rat turns *right.* His definition, then, will be too narrow even for his purposes. The general point here is that where we do stipulate that a concept be definable in terms of its test conditions, we may render our results sterile. We foreclose the possibility of obtaining new ways of testing the applicability of the concept and we block the goal of generalizing our results to new experimental situations.

Apart from the question of the utility of stipulation, the operationist is plainly wrong if he says that psychologists always stipulate that their theoretical concepts be equivalent, in whole or in part, to tests of their applicability. If this were true, then operational definitions could never be criticized as incorrect; but this is plainly false. Suppose a psychologist defines *improvement* as "achieving such and such a result on a Rorschach test." Such a definition might well be objected to if there is little correlation between the result of the test and improvement in terms of other measures. It is an empirical question whether improvement, as this term is used by many clinical psychologists and psychiatrists, is correlated in any significant way with performance on a Rorschach test, a TAT test, and so on. If there is no such correlation, the relevant definition is likely to be criticized. More generally, terms like *brain damage, anxiety, improvement,* and so on, are often used by psychologists in a way that leaves it an open, empirical question whether certain tests of their applicability are adequate. Where they are not adequate, attempts to define these concepts operationally in terms of such tests are criticizable as being incorrect, which would not be true if the definitions were always stipulative.

At this point an operationist might retreat to a much more defensible position. He might recognize the distinction between meaning and evidence and simply insist that when a theoretical concept is used in a research report, we state what is being taken as evidence for its applicability. For example, if a psychologist uses the concept *anxiety*, he should state what he is taking as evidence of anxiety. He might even put this in a form of an operational definition (e.g., "The subjects were assumed to be anxious if and only if they exhibited behavior of kind K"). Construed in this way, operational definitions would not specify the meaning of a concept, either in whole or in part (except where explicit stipulation is made); rather, they would state an evidential relation: The behavior would be evidence of anxiety but would not be equivalent to it. Operational "definitions" would not really be definitions, if definitions specify meaning.

This final position of the operationist is much more plausible. It may well be true that in writing research reports, it is good scientific practice to give so-called operational definitions. Adhering to this practice in most cases is one way to reduce the amount of obscurity and nonsense characteristic of some psychological research. Whatever the interest of this new thesis, however, it lends no support to analytical behaviorism. If so-called operational definitions do not specify the meaning of a concept, then we cannot appeal to them in defense of behavioristic translations. If, for example, anxiety behavior is only evidence for the presence of anxiety, then we cannot appeal to that fact to show that anxiety is nothing more than a certain kind of behavior.

This final, watered-down kind of operationism might still be used in support of some substantive thesis if we add the following: Where the test conditions for a theoretical concept cannot be stated, the concept is scientifically meaningless. For example, a defender of a behavioristic learning theory might object to a rival cognitive theory if the latter employs concepts that cannot be given any kind of "operational definition," not even one that simply states test conditions without specifying the meaning. We should ask, however, why even this form of operationism should be accepted. We do want a scientific theory to be empirically testable, but why believe that the only way to guarantee testability is by specifying test conditions for each concept separately? Why is it not sufficient that a theory as a whole be testable? Although P. W. Bridgman later abandoned the thesis he originated, he initially defended it by saying that he was describing the practice of physicists, in particular that of Einstein. However, Einstein's actual position on operationism was this:

> In order to be able to consider a logical system as physical theory it is not necessary to demand that all its assertions can be independently interpreted and "tested operationally": *de facto* this has never yet been achieved by any theory and can not at all be achieved. In order to be able to consider a theory as a *physical* theory it is only necessary that it implies empirically testable assertions in general. [Albert Einstein, quoted in *Spector, 1973*, p. 112.]

It is still open to an operationist to challenge Einstein's statement and to show that physicists always give separate operational definitions for each and every concept they employ, but even if this could be done it would not be sufficient. The necessity of meeting the requirement would still have to be explained; there is no reason to think that this can be done. If this is right, then even this very weakened form of operationism is unacceptable.

Conclusion. No objection has been made to the practice of giving so-called operational definitions where this can be done; on the contrary, the practice has been endorsed. Except in certain cases, mainly where a new usage is being stipulated, these so-called definitions are really empirical statements describing what is being taken as evidence that a certain concept applies. It is often possible to give such "definitions" in doing the type of research characteristic of clinical psychology, where the relationships between a small number of variables is being explored. In other areas it is sometimes not possible (e.g., where a complex theory is being tested or where a theory has been only lately proposed and ways of testing it have yet to be discovered).

II. Analytical behaviorism without operationism

Analytical behaviorism – the thesis that all mentalistic statements are translatable into statements about behavior – once seemed plausible so long as meaning and evidence were not distinguished. If we conflate the two and normally obtain evidence about a person's mental state by observing his behavior, it is easy to conclude that talk about the mind is really talk about behavior. The two doctrines that sustained this confusion were, in psychology, operationism and, in philosophy, verificationism. Not all forms of verificationism had this effect; it was the product mainly of the less sophisticated, original version, which held that the meaning of a proposition is its method of verification (i.e., its test conditions). Because this version of verificationism is open to some of the same objections as operationism and because it has been much criticized and long ago abandoned in philosophy, it will not be discussed here but will be assumed to be indefensible (Hempel, 1965; Erwin, 1970).

Without the support of either operationism or verificationism, analytical behaviorism becomes implausible. A man's overt behavior and his thinking or imaging, for example, certainly seem to be different; if they are, statements about the one are not identical with statements about the other. In any event, there are powerful objections to the doctrine. A behavior therapist who wishes to defend analytical behaviorism should be prepared to explain how these objections are to be met.

The first objection may appear to be the most superficial, but it may prove to be the most durable. On the basis of the record so far, there is no reason to think that the program of analytical behaviorism can be carried out. Now and then a few examples have been offered of behavioristic translations, but at best these illustrate the program, and most are failures from the start. It would be tedious and uninformative to run through many such failures, but consider the following few proposals made by behavior therapists.

Responding to the comment of Locke (1971) that Wolpe's descriptions are sometimes mentalistic, Eysenck (1972) concludes that they can all be translated into behavioristic language. He purports to show how this can be done by means of two examples. He points out that statements about anxiety can be correlated with verbal reports and that statements about sexual imagery can be objectively checked by use of the penis plethysmograph. Both examples fail. Once we abandon operationism, or at least distinguish between meaning and evidence, we will not make the mistake of treating such correlations as translations. A statement about a patient's sexual imagery may be correlated with a description of a plethysmograph, but the two are not synonymous. It is plainly not self-contradictory to say that the description of the plethysmograph is false and yet that the patient does have sexual imagery, but it would be self-contradictory if the statements were equivalent. The imagery and the plethsymograph are different; to talk about a plethysmograph result is not to talk about mental imagery. A similar objection applies to Eysenck's other illustration concerning anxiety.

Waters and McCallum (1973) offer the following examples of behavioristic translations:

1 *Anxiety* can be defined as a label for a verbal response evoked by a particular pattern of physiological response and response-produced stimuli occurring in that class of stimulus situation typically labeled anxiety-provoking.
2 *Awareness* is that condition of an organism in which it is responding to stimulation.

The authors also give a complicated behavioral definition of *self-awareness* that employs (2) in part; if (2) is incorrect, then so is the more complicated definition. Definition 2 is incorrect. If it were correct, a catatonic schizophrenic could not be aware of an external stimulus without responding to it, but, in fact, that can and does happen. Ullmann and Krasner (1969) describe a case in which eight catatonic schizophrenics were led or dragged daily into a meeting room where one of the authors would address them. The patients did not respond, and after three months everyone in the room, including the therapists, would sit passively as if they were unaware of any external stimuli. It later became clear that despite the absence of overt response, at least some of the patients had been aware of the therapists' earlier comments. One such patient, prodded by one of the therapists, burst out with a verbatim restatement of what the therapist had said a month earlier. There had been awareness, but no overt behavioral response.

Definition 1 is open to the objection that the relevant pattern of physiological response is left unspecified. This is not just an incidental omission; it is not clear that there is any single pattern of physiological responses that can always be correlated with anxiety (Davison & Neale, 1974, p. 105). Furthermore, even if there were, it is doubtful that that is what is meant when a patient is described as anxious. A therapist might be wrong if he were to deny that there is any physiological sign of anxiety in an anxious patient, but he would not be contradicting himself in saying that.

It might be replied that we could simply stipulate that *anxiety* and *awareness* be used in the preceding senses, but that reply has already been responded to in the discussion of operationism. If statements about awareness or anxiety, as these terms are ordinarily used, are not translatable into talk about behavior, then analytical behaviorism is false. The fact that these terms can also be used in a different sense, a behavioristic sense, is trivially true, but irrelevant. Analogously, an operationist who claimed to be able to translate all talk about electrons into talk about white tracks in a Wilson cloud chamber would not advance his case any by pointing out the obvious – that he is free to stipulate that he will use *electron* to mean "white track." If it is objected that the standard scientific use of the term *electron* or *anxiety* is unacceptable, then this would need to be demonstrated. It cannot be demonstrated merely by pointing out that the concepts have "surplus meaning" (Waters & McCallum, 1973, p. 163). To assume that surplus, unoperational meaning is necessarily objectionable is to fall back on the now discredited thesis of operationism.

As a final example, consider the statement *s*: "I am hungry." Skinner (1945) suggests that *s* is synonymous with each of the following:

1 I have not eaten for a long time.
2 That food makes my mouth water.
3 I am ravenous.

There is nothing particularly instructive about these proposed translations; all are demonstrable failures. If I am slightly hungry even though I ate relatively recently and the food in front of me is unappetizing, then *s* might be true while all the other propositions are false. That could not happen if any of the preceding were synonymous with *s*.

What *is* interesting is the underlying theory on which Skinner relies to support the translation; it is neither operationism nor verificationism. Skinner writes; "The question 'What is length?' would appear to be satisfactorily answered by listing the circumstances under which the response 'length' is emitted (or, better, by giving some general description of such circumstances)" (Skinner, 1945, p. 587). Apparently, Skinner is suggesting that we explain meaning in terms of the circumstances in which an expression is uttered. He contends, for example, that much of the ambiguity of psychological terms arises from the possibility of alternative modes of reinforcement. Thus, *I am hungry* has different meanings, according to Skinner, because its use has been reinforced by the community in different kinds of situations (Skinner, 1945).

If Skinner is proposing a theory of meaning (which may not

have been his intention), it might support certain behavioristic translations *if* the theory is correct. For example, given the theory and the fact that the verbal response *I am hungry* is reinforced when it is true that *I have not eaten for a long time,* then the two statements are synonymous. However, the theory of meaning is not correct. The mere fact that the verbal response *I am hungry* has been reinforced in different kinds of situations does not render it ambiguous. A difference in kind of situational reinforcement for the utterance of a given sentence is not sufficient to give it different meanings. For example, suppose that on two different occasions, at times T_1 and T_2, as the result of the presence of two different types of reinforcers, I say, "Last Thanksgiving, I was very hungry." What I said on each occasion may have had exactly the same meaning even though the situational reinforcers were different. If I was not very hungry last Thanksgiving, what I said at T_1 and T_2 was false; otherwise, it was true. If you were to paraphrase or translate into a foreign language what I said at T_1, a correct paraphrase or translation would serve equally well for what I said at T_2. One might distinguish between the sentence I used and what I did. What I did, a Skinnerian might say, is different if the situational reinforcers were different; nevertheless, the meaning of the sentence I used was not different. Furthermore, sameness of situational reinforcement is not sufficient for sameness of meaning. Suppose you have been reinforced for saying "That is wonderful," when the Democrats win a national election, and I have been reinforced in the same sort of way for saying, "That is *not* wonderful," in the same situation. On Skinner's theory, if taken as theory of meaning, these incompatible statements would have the same meaning, and that is obviously not true.

A Skinnerian might object that Skinner's theory is not a theory of *meaning,* a concept that is too mentalistic and that ought to be replaced. If this is what Skinner is suggesting, then he cannot appeal to his theory to prop up faltering behavioristic translations; if the theory is not a theory of meaning, it does not specify conditions of correct translation. Showing that the verbal response *I am hungry* is functionally related to the verbal response *I have not eaten for a long time* may be interesting, but in the present interpretation of Skinner's theory, that would not even ostensibly show that the two verbal responses (or, more accurately, the two sentences) have the same meaning. The theory would not say anything at all about sameness of meaning; it would thus lose all relevance to analytical behaviorism.

The second objection to analytical behaviorism presents a difficulty in principle: In describing behavioral truth conditions for many mentalistic statements, we have to employ at least one mentalistic concept. Take the statement *I believe that the ice is dangerously thin.* It is tempting to conclude, as Ryle does in *The Concept of Mind* (1949, p. 135), that to have this belief is to be prone to do such things as to skate warily, to shudder, to warn others, and so on. Whether or not someone is disposed to do such things, however, will depend in part on his having other beliefs (e.g., that falling through the ice will have a certain undesirable effect) and certain desires (e.g., the desire to avoid injuring himself). If this is true, then the attempt to give a pure, behavioristic translation of the preceding statement is bound to fail; the correct translation will have to refer to desires and beliefs, and hence will not be purely behavioristic. It might be thought that additional translations will enable us to eliminate the reference to beliefs and desires. To say that I *desire* to avoid falling through the ice, it might be suggested, is simply to say that I have the disposition to do certain things, such as to skate warily and to warn others. Unfortunately, the same problem arises. I may well lack these dispositions, even though I have the specified desire, if I do not *believe* that the ice is dangerous. Again, we are forced to bring in a mentalistic concept, that of *belief,* and thus we will have made no progress. How strong is this objection? An analytical behaviorist might reply that neither beliefs nor desires have any effect on one's behavioral dispositions; both can be ignored when giving behavioristic translations. However, this reply will not work if, as current evidence suggests (see Chapter 3), beliefs and desires do affect how one behaves and how one is disposed to behave. There may be still another way around our second objection, but if we cannot explain how to circumvent it, then we have some reason to doubt the feasibility of the program of analytical behaviorism.

The third objection to analytical behaviorism concerns the "direct access" of certain kinds of mental states. If, for example, I have a migraine headache or a mental image of a deserted farm, I can, in most circumstances, know this to be so without observing my behavior. I simply feel the headache and see the image; I do not need to look in a mirror or to ask someone how I am behaving (Malcolm, 1964). The old behaviorist joke: "Two behaviorists meet each other and one says to the other: 'You feel fine, How do I feel?'" is only a joke. This is not what normally happens. Yet this would be hard to explain if analytical behaviorism were true, if, for example, the statement *I have a migraine headache* were really a statement about my behavior.

Conclusion. Objections 2 and 3 present theoretical difficulties for the analytical behaviorist, but they may be answerable. The strongest reason for doubt may well be the failure of all attempts so far to advance the program. No one has even begun to show how the mentalistic statements utilized by behavior therapists can be translated into behavioral statements. This fact might not discourage someone committed to one of those theories that appears to support analytical behaviorism, such as operationism or a Skinnerian type theory of meaning; but once the underlying theory is made explicit and then discredited, the thesis ceases to look very promising.

Although few philosophers have defended analytical behaviorism in recent years, there has been some support for the view called *criteriological behaviorism.* There are several versions of this doctrine. What they have in common is the idea that some kind of noncontingent or noninductive connection exists between behavior and the mind. In one version it is necessarily true that behavioral data of certain types are evidence that certain mentalistic concepts apply; in a second version it is necessarily true that in *most* cases mentalistic events are correlated with certain types of behavior. Criteriological behaviorism, which developed out of the work of Wittgenstein (1953), neither entails nor is entailed by logical or methodological behaviorism. It does not say that mentalistic statements are translatable into behavioral statements, nor does it exclude mentalistic causes. The doctrine is not suitable for ruling out cognitive hypotheses or supporting behavioristic theories of learning, nor has it been invoked in the behavior therapy literature; for these reasons criteriological behaviorism will not be evaluated here. Careful formulations of the doctrine can be found in Lycan (1971); some influential criticisms are contained in Putnam (1965).

III. Methodological behaviorism

The failure of analytical behaviorism leaves us with the view that mentalistic explanations should be rejected on methodological grounds. This thesis quickly runs into an obvious objection. "What are the causes of human behavior?" appears to be an empirical question that should be settled on empirical grounds; if the empirical evidence dictates that there are mental causes, how can that evidence be overridden by purely methodological considerations? One might as well reject quantum theory because it appears to conflict with the philosophical principle that every event has a cause. That would be absurd, and for the same reason, methodological behaviorism is absurd.

The preceding objection has some force, but it is not as strong as it might appear. There once was some warrant for believing microphysical determinism, and this provided some justification for Einstein's belief that a hidden variable, deterministic theory would eventually supplant the quantum theory supported by Bohr and Heisenberg. The appeal to the philosophic principle of determinism, then, was not absurd. If it is replied that there never was any evidential support for determinism and that Einstein was just irrational, then it needs to be shown that the quantum theory case is analogous to that of antimentalism in psychology. In the latter case, there are a number of arguments in support of methodological behaviorism, and they have been persuasive enough to convince many competent psychologists. Some writers even suggest that virtually all American psychologists accept methodological behaviorism (Bergmann, 1956, p. 270; Schultz, 1969, 1975). Although this claim may be exaggerated, there is reason to believe that the thesis is accepted by many psychologists, and by behavior therapists in particular (Mahoney, Kazdin, & Lesswing, 1974, p. 15). It is one of those foundational assumptions that is deeply entrenched and that profoundly influences research and the assessment of rival theories. Is the assumption true? What follows is a review of virtually all the main arguments supporting methodological behaviorism. Some of these arguments are obviously weak and would be rejected by most sophisticated methodological behaviorists, but these arguments have been used and are included for the sake of completeness.

Twelve arguments in support of methodological behaviorism

The first five arguments are advanced by Skinner, even though he is dubious about rejecting mentalistic explanations on purely methodological grounds (1963).

1. A disturbance in behavior, Skinner says, is not explained by relating it to anxiety until the anxiety in turn has been explained. Perhaps that could be done, but the postulation of mental causes has discouraged the tracing of the causal sequence; investigators simply stop with the anxiety and fail to ask what caused it. For this

reason the postulation of mental causes is objectionable (Skinner, 1964).

Reply. The first assumption is dubious, and Skinner gives no argument to support it. It is not generally true that where *A* causes *B,* citing *A* will explain *B* only if *A,* in turn, is explained. If that were true and if we also had to explain the cause of *A*'s cause, the cause of that cause, and so on, we would have to traverse an infinite regress in order to explain anything; nothing, then, would be explainable. It might be suggested that we can terminate the regress at some point, perhaps when we get to an environmental cause; but this will not do unless we can justify the termination. It is not clear how we are to do this if we insist on starting the regress. It is also not clear that we are more likely to halt causal inquiry by postulating mental rather than environmental or physiological causes. Even if that were true, the proper antidote would be better science. We should take steps to ensure the continuance of causal inquiry where that is warranted; we should not simply ignore a cause, assuming that we want to understand its effect, merely because we are afraid of terminating inquiry.

2. "A second objection," writes Skinner, "is that a preoccupation with mental way stations burdens a science of behavior with all the problems raised by the limitations and inaccuracies of self-descriptive repertoires" (Skinner, 1964).

Reply. Skinner goes on to point out that we need not take the extreme position of ruling mediating (i.e., mental) events out of consideration, but that we should certainly welcome more satisfactory ways of treating the data. This may be true, but is compatible with a rejection of methodological behaviorism. In any event, there is no reason to believe that introspective reports are so inaccurate that they have no evidential value at all. If a patient says that his anxiety causes him to mistreat his wife, we should hardly take this unsubstantiated causal claim at face value, but if he says that his head hurts or that he now has a mental image, his saying so might provide excellent evidence that what he says is true. Even if introspective reports were found to be completely worthless, we might still have to postulate certain mental events to explain behavior. Introspective reports appear to be useful, but they are not necessary. Electrons do not issue self-reports, but postulating them still serves an explanatory function; that might also be true of certain mental events.

3. Perhaps the most serious objection, Skinner notes (1963), concerns the order of events. Instead of asserting, for example,

that either the release of a repressed wish or insight has had a therapeutic effect, we should consider the plausible alternative that a behavioral change has made it possible for the subject to recall the repressed wish or to understand his illness.

Reply. Skinner's warning should be heeded, but if the evidence shows that the seemingly more plausible behavioral explanation is wrong, then it should be rejected. In that case, the psychoanalytic explanation might be the best alternative. We need not say that this is likely – rejecting methodological behaviorism does not mean embracing psychoanalysis – but heeding Skinner's warning is no reason to reject mentalistic explanations in cases where the data warrants their acceptance.

4. "A final objection," Skinner writes, "is that way stations are so often simply invented. It is too easy to say that someone does something 'because he likes to do it,' or that he does one thing rather than another 'because he has made a choice'" (Skinner, 1963).

Reply. Skinner is right, but this point applies equally to other kinds of explanations. It is too easy to say that he did it because he found it reinforcing or because of his genes. We should be careful scientists and not accept the easy explanation unless the evidence warrants it, but this is no reason to rule out a mentalistic explanation if it best fits the evidence.

5. Mentalistic explanations are empty. Suppose we say, for example, that he is drinking because he is thirsty. If to be thirsty means nothing more than to have a tendency to drink, Skinner (1953, p. 33) contends, then this is "mere redundancy." In other words, we are simply redescribing the behavior and not explaining it.

Reply. Skinner is wrong about his own example. A subject might have a tendency to drink and yet be drinking on a particular occasion for some other reason; for example, someone might be coercing him. It is not tautological, then, to say that he is drinking in a given situation because he has a tendency to drink. What would be "mere redundancy," if the preceding translation were correct, would be to say that he has a tendency to drink because he is thirsty. However, the more important point is this: Skinner's translation is not correct. Someone can be thirsty and yet have no tendency to drink; this can happen if the person is extremely paranoid or is fasting for political or religious reasons.

Nothing weighty rests on this one example, but to assume that mentalistic hypotheses are generally translatable into talk about overt behavior is to assume the truth of analytical behaviorism; for reasons given earlier that is not a plausible assumption.

6. Mental events are not publicly observable; therefore, they cannot serve to explain anything.

Reply. The preceding argument has been widely used. Kendler and Spence (1971), for example, write, "A person's behavior cannot be explained by his state of mind, certainly, because his private experience is unavailable to the inspection of other observers." What the argument assumes, and what is quite implausible, is that if something cannot be directly or publicly observed, it cannot explain anything. If this were true, many explanations that refer to nonobservable quantum events could be ruled out a priori, but there is no reason to think that that is so. It might be replied that mental events are different from quantum events, but this would not help if it is merely the lack of direct, public observability that is being objected to. On this score, mentalistic explanations fare no worse than many explanations of physics.

7. Hypotheses about the mind are not empirically testable. Therefore, they have no place in a scientific psychology (Schultz, 1969, p. 218).

Reply. Why assume the first (and only) premise? It cannot be simply that mentalistic concepts refer to unobservables; that is also true of theoretical concepts of physics; yet some of the latter appear in testable hypotheses. In both types of cases, the unobservable event or entity is postulated to explain certain phenomena; if the postulation provides a better explanation than any known alternative, then, subject to certain restrictions, this *is* evidence for the hypothesis. It might be that the postulation of mental causes never provides the most satisfactory explanation of behavior, but this is an empirical issue that cannot be decided a priori. In any event, there is no need to rest the case for testability on abstract, philosophic considerations about what constitutes evidence; sophisticated experiments have already been carried out in which mentalistic hypotheses have been tested. See, for example, Haber and Haber's (1964) paper on eidetic imagery and the papers of Paivio and his associates on the facilitative effects of mental imagery on verbal learning (Paivio, 1973, 1976).

8. Mentalistic explanations are to be avoided on grounds of simplicity. It is more parsimonious to explain behavior in terms of variables that are environmental or at least physical.

Reply. Although the meaning and epistemic relevance of

"simplicity" remains a difficult issue in the philosophy of science, let us assume that, other things being equal, of two competing explanations the simpler is preferable. However, we cannot just take for granted, as some behaviorists apparently do (e. g., Waters & McCallum, 1973), that behavioristic explanations of human behavior will always be simpler than their mentalistic rivals. Whether or not that is generally true is an empirical question; it cannot be settled a priori. The preceding argument, then, fails so long as it cannot be demonstrated that mentalistic explanations are always less simple than their rivals. It is difficult to see how this could be demonstrated now given that so much human behavior remains to be explained.

9. An elegant formulation of the "skipping-a-link" argument is given by Skinner (1974, p. 13): "The mentalistic problem can be avoided by going directly to the prior physical causes while bypassing intermediate feelings or states of mind. . . . If all linkages are lawful, nothing is lost by neglecting a supposed nonphysical link."

Reply. This argument is analogous to the first argument we considered, but is more subtle and more interesting, For one thing, it does not assume that one has not explained an event by citing its cause unless the cause is also explained. It also raises an interesting philosophic question: If all linkages are lawful, what would be lost, once the links were known, if we were to bypass all the intermediate links? If we could overcome both the practical difficulties and quantum indeterminacies, what would be lost if we bypassed psychology and biology and predicted human behavior by appealing directly to physics? Given enough background information, we could predict, for example, that Jones will marry his neighbor or commit suicide once we had observed the movements of certain configurations of elementary particles. One thing that would be lost, however, is explanatory power. If we want not merely to predict a certain event, but to understand why it occurred, then we want to know *its* cause – not merely some initial cause lying at the end of some long causal chain. There may be lawful linkages relating Brutus' stabbing of Caesar to the big bang or to whatever event caused the origin of the universe, but to speak of the big bang is not to explain Caesar's assassination. It does not explain this particular event, as opposed to any other event that necessarily occurred once the big bang took place. What we lose, then, if we neglect a link that is the cause of some behavior is the ability to explain that behavior. It does not matter whether the link is physical or mental; what matters is whether it causes the behavior we want to understand.

10. We should not use an explanation of an observed fact that appeals to events taking place somewhere else, at some other level of observation, described in different terms, and measured, if at all, in different dimensions. Mentalistic explanations are of this type and, therefore, should be rejected (Skinner, 1950, p. 193).

Reply. The first premise of this argument might appear plausible if supported either by argument 6 (which objects to appeals to the nonobservable) or by argument 10 (the skipping-a-link argument). Once these two arguments are rejected, the premise ceases to be plausible. First, it rules out genetic, neurological, and physiological explanations of human behavior. Second, it would disqualify microphysical explanations of macrophysical phenomena. Third, and most important, it just might be true that the cause of some overt human behavior is an event that occurs, in Skinner's terminology, at some "other level." If it is true, then a refusal to countenance such "other level" causal explanations is a refusal to accept the correct explanation of the behavior.

11. If we use mentalistic explanations, we commit ourselves to a mind-body dualism and that will resurrect the traditional mind-body problem (Skinner, 1954).

Reply. Several comments are required:

First, the traditional mind-body problem, simply put, is the problem of explaining how the mental and physical can affect each other given that each is so fundamentally different. Some behaviorists assume that the problem is solved by adopting epiphenomenalism: Allow that the physical affects the mental, but deny that the mental ever affects the physical. If we accept this view, however, something like the traditional mind-body problem remains; we still have to explain how the physical can affect the mental.

Second, it is not obvious that accepting mentalistic explanations commits one to dualism. In recent years the identity theory of the mind-body relation, as first stated by a psychologist (Place, 1956) and later developed by Smart (1959) and other philosophers (Lewis, 1966; Armstrong, 1968), has received a good deal of attention. On this view, mental states do exist but are identical with physical states, most likely states of the central nervous system, just as genes exist but are identical with DNA molecules. This view has had to face certain difficulties (Kim, 1966; Kripke, 1972) but is still a possible alternative to both dualism and behaviorism.

Third, it is doubtful that philosophic considerations about mind-body relations should, under present conditions, dictate how psychologists handle their data. On the contrary. If psychologists discover empirical evidence that mental events sometimes influence physical events, then philosophers should adjust their views about the mind if necessary. There is nothing in principle objectionable about appealing to a philosophic view, such as materialism, to override low-level empirical evidence; that might be sound if the evidence for the philosophic view were very strong. In the present case this condition is not met: There are a variety of philosophic theories on the mind-body problem, including different varieties of dualism and materialism; it is doubtful that the evidence is sufficiently strong to rule out every theory but one. Given this state of affairs, the low-level empirical evidence should decide whether or not mentalistic explanations are acceptable.

12. We can explain all human behavior by appeal to modern learning theory that makes no use of mental causes. Therefore, there is no need to give mentalistic explanations.

Reply. The preceding argument offers no defense of methodological behaviorism. If the first premise is true, we should reject mentalistic explanations, not for methodological reasons but because such explanations are all incorrect. The opponent of methodological behaviorism can agree to this point; he is not advocating the acceptance of incorrect explanations. His point, rather, is that we cannot decide beforehand, by appeal to methodological considerations, that all mentalistic explanations are to be rejected; we should let the empirical evidence decide the issue. If the methodological behaviorist now agrees, he is abandoning his position.

Conclusion. Once the arguments in support of methodological behaviorism are undermined, the initial objection to it becomes persuasive. It certainly seems that the question "What causes human behavior?" is an empirical question that cannot be settled in advance by appeal to methodological dicta. No reason has been found to think otherwise.

Is there a weaker form of methodological behaviorism that is more defensible? Biglan and Kass (1977) have recently recommended that behavior therapists accept a position they describe (p. 9) as the "methodological position of behaviorism." They make clear that their position does not imply an endorsement of (1) the editorial decision of *The Journal of Applied Behavior Analysis* to publish only research concerning what is publicly observable, or (2) the recommendation that all mentalistic concepts be operationally defined, or (3) any specific learning principles. Furthermore, their version of behaviorism, they point out (p. 5), does not exclude the study of *any* occurrent event. What their view does require is this: If a behavior therapist refers to a cognitive or behavioral event to explain behavior, then evidence must be provided that the event occurred. Biglan and Kass give illustrations from the recent behavior therapy literature in which, they argue, their requirement is not met by certain theorists who employ cognitive concepts.

The first thing to notice about the preceding requirement is that it is not behavioristic; it does not exclude the postulation of mentalistic causes. The second thing to notice is that the requirement is almost wholly trivial; it would be unacceptable only to someone who believed that it is reasonable to explain behavior, *B*, in terms of event, *E*, without having evidence that *E* occurred. If there is no more to behaviorism than this requirement, then all behavior therapists should be behaviorists in this sense. What is not trivial, of course, is the empirical claim that cognitive psychologists have generally failed to provide evidence for the occurrence of any of the cognitive events cited to explain human behavior. This claim will be evaluated in the next chapter, but it is not a claim about scientifically acceptable methodology.

IV. The behavioristic basis of behavior therapy

The objections given so far undermine the most powerful arguments supporting analytical and methodological behaviorism; they also provide some reason for concluding that both doctrines are false. How does this outcome affect the questions with which we began? Most of the current disputes about the behavioristic basis of behavior therapy (Locke, 1971; Eysenck, 1972; Waters & McCallum, 1973) have concerned the question "Is the practice of behavior therapy consistent with either analytical or methodological behaviorism?" This dispute can now be resolved. It is probably true that behavior therapy is not behavioristic, if we are referring to the *practice*. Mentalistic terms, such as *image, sadistic fantasy, irrational belief, expectancy,* are used by behavior therapists to refer to independent variables. A client's sexual fantasies are assumed to contribute to the maintenance of masturbatory behavior; his images of certain phobic scenes are said to play a causal role in systematic desensitization; his irrational beliefs are assumed to help maintain some maladaptive behavior patterns; his expectations of being helped are controlled for because they are thought to account for some therapeutic change; and so on. There is no reason to think that all such mentalistic statements can be given behavioristic translations. However, there is no need to pursue any further the issue of whether or not the practice of behavior therapy is behavioristic. The question was thought to matter, presumably, because if behaviorism were true, then having a behavioristic basis would count in favor of behavior therapy as opposed to its nonbehavioristic rivals such as psychoanalysis; and if behavior therapy were inconsistent with behaviorism, that would count against it. If behaviorism is false, however, then the issue hardly matters. Being compatible with behaviorism is not an advantage; being incompatible with it is not a disadvantage.

The second question we raised – "Is the paradigm accepted by many behavior therapists behavioristic?" – has already been answered. There is some evidence that the answer is affirmative. If that is right, what effect does this have? As suggested earlier, a commitment to deeply rooted philosophic and methodological principles can have a profound effect on a scientist's research in ways detailed by Kuhn (1962). Spelling out the precise effects of the acceptance of behaviorism, in particular, is difficult, but there is some indirect and inconclusive evidence for the following general conjectures.

Watson and the early behaviorists probably performed a valuable service by promoting experimental techniques and by criticizing the overreliance on introspection. It is also likely, however, that research into certain areas, such as cognition, memory, and mental imagery, suffered because of behavioristic strictures. For example, Haber and Haber (1964) found approximately 200 studies of eidetic imagery done early in this century, but point out that by 1937 such research diminished severely; only twelve such papers are listed in *Psychological Abstracts* for the years 1937–62. They conjecture that a partial explanation for this decline in research was the behavioristic climate that prevailed in the United States during this latter period.

It may also be that a commitment to behaviorism by early behavior therapists was useful in encouraging clarity and rigor in clinical psychology and in rooting out a rampant, empirically unsupported mentalism. It is also likely, however, that behaviorism has had an inhibiting effect on subsequent behavior therapy research. Ullmann and Krasner (1969, p. 186), for example, point out that they "eschew" concepts such as needs and cognitions, presumably for behavioristic reasons. Wiest (1967, p. 223) is willing to consider the cognitive hypotheses of Breger and McGaugh (1965), but only if the terms *figuring out, wanting,* and *deciding* are operationally defined; and if they are, Wiest points out, the cumbersome translations will not contribute toward clarifying the empirical issues and may well impede an effective experimental analysis. Despite these disclaimers, behavior therapists do countenance mentalistic concepts, but often it is insisted that such concepts conform to behavioristic strictures or be abandoned. (See, for example, the conclusion reached by Waters and McCallum [1973, p. 163], and Kanfer and Karoly's [1972] behavioristic treatment of self-control.) It is difficult to believe that none of this makes any difference to the way reviewers judge journal articles, to the kinds of research problems deemed important by many behavior therapists, and to the treatment accorded mentalistic hypotheses.

V. A viable philosophical foundation

Some behavior therapists describe themselves as behaviorists because they accept an empirical theory, such as Skinnerian or Pavlovian learning theory, which employs no mentalistic concepts. It will be argued in the next chapter that no such theory can serve as an adequate foundation for behavior therapy. If analytical and methodological behaviorism are also unacceptable, then in any traditional sense of the term, behaviorism should not form part of the behavior therapy paradigm. There are, however, more defensible philosophical principles that most behavior therapists accept and that are relevant to the study and practice of behavior therapy. These include empiricism, macrodeterminism, and pragmatic behaviorism.

Empiricism

The term *empiricism* has been used to refer to a wide variety of doctrines, some of which have been tied together in recent psychological and philosophical writings. Some clarification is necessary, therefore, before saying what sort of empiricism is relevant to behavior therapy.

First, the term *empiricism* is sometimes used to refer to the doctrine that all ideas are acquired through experience. This doctrine is not particularly relevant to behavior therapy; behavior therapists need not take any particular stand on it, and there is no evidence that they do. Second, there is the brand of empiricism associated with the logical empiricists. Their most distinctive doctrine, that the cognitive meaningfulness of any nonanalytic theory is dependent on the possibility of empirical verification or falsification, is also not particularly relevant to behavior therapy. As noted earlier, this doctrine has gone through a series of transformations and has had to face difficulties similar to that of operationism (Hempel, 1965; Erwin, 1970). A third view, which is what many contemporary philosophers mean by *empiricism,* is that there are no synthetic a priori truths. Given the unclarity in the concepts of an "a priori truth" and a "synthetic truth," it is difficult to evaluate this doctrine; and there is no need to do so here. Suppose, for example, that the proposition *Nothing can be simultaneously red and green all over* is both synthetic and knowable a priori. Empiricism (in this third sense) would then be false, but this would have no direct implications for either the practice or study of behavior therapy. A fourth view is that observational evidence is required for choosing between most or all nontautological competing hypotheses. It is this kind of empiricism that is a cornerstone of the paradigm accepted by most behavior therapists, but it is often linked, unjustifiably, with some form of behaviorism or operationism. For example, Quine (1969) recommends that all criteria be couched in observation terms, a view he describes as behaviorism. This might be interpreted as requiring that there be a *definitional* link between all so-called theoretical terms and observation terms; that is, in any acceptable scientific theory, necessary and sufficient conditions must be provided for every theoretical term and these conditions must be stated partly in observational language. Interpreted in this way, the view is simply a variant of operationism or, if the observation terms are required to characterize behavior, it is equivalent to or entails analytical behaviorism. The view is then objectionable for reasons given earlier. A more innocuous interpretation of Quine's view, which may well fit his intentions, is that observational evidence is required to justify the acceptance of nontautological hypotheses; that is, it is equivalent to the last mentioned type of empiricism. There is little historical warrant for describing this latter view as behaviorism: It is not antimentalistic; it is compatible with a rejection of all behavioristic theories of learning; and it is acceptable to many critics of behaviorism, such as Chomsky (1976). *Empiricism,* as Quine himself suggests (1969), is thus a more apt label for this view. This fourth type of empiricism is not peculiar to the behavior therapy paradigm; it would presumably be accepted by most scientists. Indeed, the doctrine is relatively trivial, but not entirely so. It would not be acceptable to some existentialists and phenomenologists who regard intuition or insight as acceptable evidence. Nor is the doctrine tautological. The universe we live in might have been constructed so that intuition or insight would suffice as evidence for most hypotheses. In such a universe we might have discovered by empirical observation that reflective intuition was a wholly reliable guide in choosing between competing hypotheses. If a clinician simply thought that the use of a certain therapy would be followed by a certain result, his belief would invariably be correct. At some point there would be no need to test hypotheses by appeal to empirical observation (Erwin, 1971, 1973). We know that our universe is not like this, but our knowledge of this fact is based not on a priori reflection but on sense experience. Empiricism, as we are now using the term, is best regarded as a high-level empirical hypothesis (and the same is probably true of all acceptable philosophical doctrines) that is not directly tested by scientists but is indirectly supported by a wide range of empirical data. The view is relatively trivial, but not entirely so; and at least it is defensible.

Most behavior therapists would also assent to a slightly less trivial version of empiricism: the conjunction of the preceding doctrine with the claim that in evaluating the effectiveness of any therapy, a certain type of observational evidence is generally required (i.e., experimental evidence). This view is hardly self-evident; indeed, it has been widely rejected by clinical psychologists not working in a behavior therapy framework. Not untypical is the suggestion of Strupp (1967, p. 76) that clinical experience (i.e., the observations of psychotherapists and their patients) is sufficient evidence that beneficial effects do result from psychotherapy in an appreciable percentage of cases. A similar claim is made by Fromm (1970, p. 15). Behavior therapists, in contrast, assume that controlled experiments are ultimately required before beneficial effects can be confidently and reasonably attributed to any therapy. It is true that some behavior therapists (e.g., Yates, 1970) prefer to appeal to single case studies rather than large-scale group studies, but unlike most traditional psychotherapists, they insist that the single case be treated with stringent experimental controls.

The assumption that experimentation is crucial in clinical psychology is central to the behavior therapy paradigm; some writers cite it as a defining feature of behavior therapy (Davison &

Neale, 1974, p. 485). The assumption is not treated as an empirical hypothesis that needs to be tested; it is probably widely accepted by behavior therapists at least partly because of their training and partly because of the fact that behavior therapy developed out of an experimental tradition. Nevertheless, the assumption can be defended by appeal to indirect empirical evidence. Part of this evidence concerns the poor track record of those relying on uncontrolled clinical experience in testing therapeutic claims, and part of it concerns such things as spontaneous remission rates and placebo effects, which are an important source of plausible alternative explanations of therapeutic success. If a client improves, the therapy might have caused the result, but it might equally well have been caused by the expectation of the client, by maturational factors, or by a number of other factors not specific to the therapy. The only reliable way to choose between the competing hypotheses is by controlled experiment. Thus, the assumption that in most cases clinical hypotheses need to be supported by experimental evidence operates within the behavior therapy paradigm as a philosophic principle that guides research (it is not subjected to direct experimental test and is usually taken for granted), but it can ultimately be vindicated by appeal to a wide range of empirical evidence.

Macrodeterminism

It may be that many behavior therapists are determinists; that is, they subscribe to the view that every event has a cause (but see Eysenck, 1972, for an explicit rejection of this view). If current quantum theory is correct, then determinism is probably false, but this has no direct implications for behavior therapy. It would be sufficient for the purposes of behavior therapists that every macroevent, or at least every behavioral event, be caused. There is no need, then, for a behavior therapist to take a stand on the truth or falsity of determinism in general.

Macrodeterminism, the view that every macroevent has a cause, would probably be accepted by most behavior therapists; at the very least, they act as if they believed that changes in human behavior are susceptible to causal explanation. This view is not necessarily true; in fact, if the view entails that all human behavior falls under relatively simple causal laws, then it is doubtful that it is supported by current empirical evidence. It is doubtful that there are very many (if any) known laws of human behavior. The so-called laws sometimes cited by some behavior therapists, such as the law of effect or various principles of conditioning, generally turn out to be tautological, false, or too restrictive in scope to qualify as laws. (The evidence for this claim is discussed in Chapter 3.) If macrodeterminism has not yet been empirically confirmed, however, it has also not been disconfirmed. It is probably best viewed as a high-level working hypothesis that is accepted partly because it is useful to act as if the assumption were true; it would be hard to justify much current behavior therapy research if we did not assume that behavioral changes are causally explainable, although that need not be true of every such change.

Pragmatic behaviorism

A third philosophic assumption shared by most behavior therapists is that clinical problems should generally be analyzed in behavioral terms. We might label this view *pragmatic behaviorism.* The view could be taken to mean that clinical concepts, such as *depressed, fearful, paranoid, schizophrenic,* and so on, be *defined* in behavioral terms, but then it would be indefensible for the reasons that analytical behaviorism is indefensible. A less provocative but more adequate version is that in treating a client, behavioral counterparts should generally be sought that correlate with (but are not equivalent to) any relevant problematic mental state. The treatment should focus primarily on behavior, not because the mind is behavior, but for practical reasons. For example, it is often easy to establish a base rate and to assess therapeutic change in comparison to that rate if behavior is the focus of study and treatment. It may be of some use to learn, for example, that an obese patient has a *craving for food,* but it is even more useful to learn how many eating responses are engaged in each day and under exactly what conditions. As suggested in Chapter 1, focusing on behavior also gives a behavior therapist a surprising flexibility. Consider a patient who claims to be suffering from existential despair. Some critics have contended that behavior therapy, by its very nature, cannot be applied in such a case. This is not so. A behavior therapist can begin by determining how the despair expresses itself in behavior. The therapist can then break this behavior down into smaller components and try to replace each component by behavior patterns that are not conducive to the maintenance of a despairing attitude. For example, suppose the patient has begun reading Kierkegaard, Sartre, and other existentialists; broken his engagement with his fiancee; stopped communicating with family and friends; quit his job; spent most of his time alone, sulking in a dark room. Suppose further that these behaviors were initiated either subsequent to or just preceding the onset of his despair. It is likely that at least some of these behaviors would play some causal role in maintaining (not necessarily in originating) the despair; by changing them the despair may well be diminished. This is not to suggest that a patient cannot justifiably feel despair (perhaps his situation is truly hopeless), nor is it to suggest that just any deeply rooted feeling of despair can be so easily diminished or eliminated. The point, rather, is that by getting the patient to discuss his problem in behavioral terms, the therapist can often deal with a situation that might otherwise prove intractable.

There is a pragmatic sense, then, in which behavior therapy is behavioristic: The focus of research and treatment is characteristically on behavior. This is an advantage, and one that may have developed out of behaviorism, but it can be kept while behaviorism is rejected. In particular, a behavior therapist might allow that, in some cases, changing a patient's cognitions or imagery may also be important; he may also allow that in explaining behavioral change, mentalistic concepts might have to be employed.

VI. Conclusion

Does behavior therapy have or need a philosophical foundation? If we are referring to the therapy, the answer is negative. Not only can the therapy be used by clinicians not sharing any distinctive set of philosophic assumptions, but the techniques cannot be derived from, nor their workings explained by, any philosophical theory. If we want a foundation for the therapy, we should seek not a philosophical but an empirical theory, such as Skinnerian or Pavlovian learning theory (see Chapter 3). If our question is about the paradigm accepted by most behavior therapists, then the answer is yes – and no. Certainly, some form of empiricism, and possibly pragmatic behaviorism and macrodeterminism, are integral parts of the paradigm and are rationally defensible. The most distinctive part of the framework, however, has been behaviorism, that is, either analytical or methodological behaviorism (Eysenck, 1972); this part can and should be rejected. The practice of behavior therapy does have historical connections to behaviorism, but no logical ties of any kind. We were able to say (in Chapter 1) what a behavior therapy technique is without invoking behaviorism, and in recent years behavior therapy practice has become more and more cognitively oriented (Franks & Wilson, 1975, p. 73). Behaviorism persists within the behavior therapy framework only as an unjustifiable, a priori restriction on what is to count as acceptable scientific research. It once served a useful purpose insofar as it encouraged experimental rigor and discouraged an unbridled mentalism, but it is no longer needed for that purpose. Behaviorism is false and for that reason should be rejected; it is time to get behaviorism out of behavior therapy.

3. Learning theory foundations

Some basic issues

Is behavior therapy based on theories or principles of learning? Which learning theories or principles are at issue? Pavlov's? Skinner's? The law of effect? Other principles of conditioning? What is the evidential status of these theories and principles? Is there an alternative scientific foundation for behavior therapy?

In the previous chapter we looked at behaviorism as a possible philosophic foundation for behavior therapy; we will now consider learning theory as a possible scientific foundation. Some writers include a reference to learning theories or principles in the very definition of *behavior therapy*. For example, Franks (1969, p. 2) writes, "If behavior is defined in terms of response, then behavior therapy becomes a matter of response modification involving the application of some SR [stimulus-response] type of learning theory." We have already objected to such definitions (in Chapter 1), partly on the grounds that it is a substantive question as to what exactly is the relation between behavior therapy and learning theory; we should not attempt to answer the question a priori.

Whether true by definition or not, it has been widely held that behavior therapy is based on learning theory, or at least on some laws or principles of learning. The following illustrates this view: "Virtually all forms of behavior therapy have been derived more or less from the foundations of conditioned reflex (Pavlovian) studies and operant conditioning (Skinnerian) research on learning" (*Task Reports*, American Psychiatric Association, 1973, p. 2). Similar views have been expressed by Eysenck (1972), Wolpe (1976), and Meyer (1970).

A more moderate, and probably more widely held, view is that learning theories or principles form only part of the foundation of behavior therapy. As O'Leary and Wilson (1975, p. 16) express the point, "Behavior modification emphasizes the principles of classical and operant conditioning; but is not restricted to them . . ." A similar view is expressed by Rimm and Masters (1974, p. 11).

Even this more moderate view has been rejected by some critics of behavior therapy (e.g., Breger & McGaugh, 1965), and even by some proponents (Mahoney, Kazdin & Lesswing, 1974). Despite this minority dissent, and allowing that positions are constantly changing, it is a reasonable guess that the majority view is that behavior therapy is based at least in part on theories, principles, or laws of learning. There can be little doubt, in any event, that this position has been influential and is deserving of serious consideration.

Although one can accept behavior therapy techniques without concern for their theoretical foundation, the issue is important for several reasons:

First, if one is interested not in behavior therapy but in a certain learning theory, then one might try to test the latter by looking at the use of behavior therapy techniques. If the techniques can be derived from certain conditioning principles, then the success or failure of the techniques might constitute important evidence for or against the principles.

Related to this issue is the assumption that there is an important continuity between the learning of animals and men, so that the same principles and concepts used to explain animal learning will suffice for humans. Even if one is not committed to any particular learning theory, one might try to provide some evidence for this continuity assumption, as Estes (1971, p. 22) suggests, by looking at the results of behavior therapy.

Second, a point of more interest to the behavior therapist is that techniques derived from empirically validated principles of learning will have a greater probability of success than those lacking any antecedent support. The probability will not be so great as to render further testing superfluous, but it may nonetheless be important. The set of possible therapeutic techniques is indefinitely large; consequently, it would be extremely useful to have a criterion for judging beforehand those worthy of investigation. A sufficient condition might be that the technique be based on some validated principle of learning.

Third, a behavior therapist with theoretical interests will want to learn why certain behavior therapy techniques work. If the techniques are based on a certain learning theory, then it might be plausible to explain the success of the techniques in terms of that theory; at least, that is the expectation of some behavior therapists.

Fourth, behavior therapists are also interested in explaining the origin and maintenance of maladaptive behaviors. The hope of many is that modern learning theory will serve this purpose for many neuroses and perhaps some psychoses.

Fifth, many behavior therapists see learning theories or principles as providing the unifying element in behavior therapy. Although we argued in Chapter 1 that this is not the only way to justify grouping behavior therapy techniques together, the case for doing so would undoubtedly be strengthened by finding a common theoretical foundation.

If one says that behavior therapy is based, at least in part, on modern learning theories or principles, what exactly does this mean? One thesis is this: (1) Essential descriptions of some or all behavior therapy techniques are *derivable* from the postulates of some modern learning theory or from learning principles, presumably with the aid of some auxiliary assumptions. The relationship, then, would be similar to that which exists between certain engineering principles and modern physical theory. (2) Another thesis is that modern learning theories or principles explain how behavior therapy techniques work (when they work). These two theses are, of course, related if explanation is essentially deductive; if it is not, thesis 2 might be true even if thesis 1 is false. A theory of learning might explain how a technique works, but the technique might not be derivable from the theory. To avoid taking a stand on the nature of explanation, we can allow for the latter possibility and treat theses 1 and 2 as logically separate. (For opposing views on the deductive model of explanation, see Hempel & Oppenheim, 1948; and Scriven, 1962.)

Most writers who say that behavior therapy is based on learning theory probably have one of the preceding theses in mind. Weaker theses will be considered later, but are less interesting in that they promise less of the benefits previously mentioned. If we are talking about thesis 1 or 2, we need to raise the following questions: Which theories, laws, or principles of learning are we talking about? Are they supported by the available evidence?

We will begin by assuming that we are talking about *theories* of learning; later, we will consider the suggestion that it is laws or principles that are at issue. No theoretical weight will be placed on the distinctions (if any) between theories, laws, and principles;

hence, there is no need for conceptual clarification here. We will simply follow the practice of many behavior therapists and refer to a certain set of theoretical assumptions of Skinner or Hull, for example, as a "theory." A single assumption, such as the law of effect, will be referred to as a law or principle.

I. Theories of learning

It is not enough to say simply that behavior therapy is based on modern learning theory. Which learning theory is being talked about? Some behavior therapists accept a social learning type theory that employs cognitive concepts; an example to be considered later is Bandura's self-efficacy theory (Bandura, 1977). However, most writers who have claimed that behavior therapy is based partly or wholly on "modern learning theory" have meant a behavioristic type of theory, such as those of Pavlov, Hull, or Skinner, one that does not postulate any mentalistic causes. We will refer to someone who accepts such a theory as a "behaviorist"; this contrasts with philosophical uses of this term that occurred in Chapter 2. A behaviorist, in the present sense, can, but need not, accept analytical or methodological behaviorism.

If we are talking about a behavioristic theory, then it might be useful to begin with Skinner's version. Few behaviorists would hold that the theory of Hull or Pavlov is sufficient. The former theory has been subjected to much criticism (e.g., Thistlethwaite's [1951] review of the latent learning literature) and is not widely accepted now. The latter theory, Pavlov's, is thought to be too narrow to serve as a foundation for all of behavior therapy, although it might explain the workings of some techniques. Both of these theories may have important historical connections with the development of behavior therapy (Franks, 1969; Yates, 1970), but many behavior therapists would consider the position that either is a sufficient theoretical foundation a straw man. The point is forcefully stated by Wiest (1967, p. 218): "The news that Hull's rp does not get us very far and that the dog on the classical conditioning stand is doing more than salivating is rather well known and passe in the 1960's." The most logical place to begin, then, is with Skinner's theory, but this does not imply that all, or even most, behavior therapists accept his theory or that no support can be found for any of the other theories.

Some philosophers and linguists will not immediately see the need to assess Skinner's theory. It is sometimes suggested, for example, that the theory has been refuted by Chomsky and that this settles the issue (Fodor & Katz, 1964, p. 546). Furthermore, many cognitive psychologists have decided that, apart from Chomsky's work, there is decisive experimental evidence against all behavioristic theories of learning. Despite the prevalence of these attitudes, there is reason to doubt that the relevant issues have been resolved. First, some behavior therapists still contend that current learning theory is suitable at least as a partial foundation for behavior therapy. Skinner's theory is one leading candidate for this role. Second, criticisms of Skinner's theory by Chomsky and others have been vigorously contested (Wiest, 1967; MacCorquodale, 1970; Rachlin & Lacey, 1978). Third, as we shall see later, there are independent reasons for doubting that anyone has refuted Skinner's theory. Chomsky's criticisms are important and there is a wide body of *apparently* disconfirming experimental evidence, but the defender of Skinner's theory has a number of avenues by which to escape these difficulties; unless it can be shown how all these escape routes can be closed, the objections are not decisive.

We will begin with Chomsky's objections. A behavior therapist might complain that the disagreement between Skinner and Chomsky concerns language and verbal behavior, but is not directly related to the use of behavior therapy techniques. This is correct, but the dispute does bear on the soundness of one plausible theoretical underpinning for behavior therapy; for that reason the issues are important for a study of foundations.

II. The Chomsky–Skinner dispute

Skinner's learning theory purports to explain behavior in terms of the organism's current state of deprivation and stimulus circumstances, its genetic constitution, and its history of reinforcements; the main explanatory burden falling on past and present reinforcements (Skinner, 1953). Behavior is *not* explained in terms of beliefs, intentions, thoughts, images, or other mentalistic states or in terms of neurological or physiological states. The theory does not imply that these states are nonexistent, but it does forego appeal to them in explaining behavior. Consequently, it qualifies as a behavioristic theory of learning. Unlike some behavioristic theories, however, it is not an S-R theory; it does not assume that all responses are controlled by stimuli in the organism's current environment; environmental stimuli that figured in the organism's history of reinforcement are also important in explaining its present responses. The theory is not refuted, then, by the finding that human behavior is often free from contemporaneous local environmental control. (For a discussion of this point, see Fodor, 1975, and the reply by Rachlin and Lacey, 1978.)

Despite important successes in dealing with animal behavior, there has been some skepticism about extending Skinner's theory to cover all, or even very much, human behavior. Verbal behavior, in particular, presents a *prima facie* problem. It is not that verbal responses are not items of behavior, but that they appear to require mentalistic concepts for their description and explanation. For example, if you and I say that a response has been reinforced, we may be saying different things if we *mean* something different by that term. You may mean that the response has been rewarded and I may mean that the probability of its reoccurrence has been increased. In some cases, then, what a speaker is saying appears to depend in part on what he *means*. To take another example, if I say, "Berkeley is fascinating," I might be referring to the city in California or to the eighteenth-century philosopher, depending in part on my *intentions*. There is a *prima facie* difficulty, then, in trying to explain the phenomena without using any mentalistic notions. A Skinnerian can, of course, use such notions if they can be given behavioral translations, but the objections to analytical behaviorism (Chapter 2) should warn us not to place much confidence in that option. There is, furthermore, an apparent novelty in speech behavior that makes verbal responses in one important respect quite unlike the stereotyped responses of, for example, a rat in a bar-pressing experiment. New responses of the rat may be explainable in terms of generalization of existing responses, and the generalization mechanism can be explained in terms of the physical resemblance between old and new responses; it is not clear how that is to be done for verbal responses. A speaker who understands English, for example, is capable of producing any one of an indefinitely large number of new linguistic responses. Unless we can specify the respects in which the new responses resemble those already existing in the speaker's repertoire, it seems empty to speak of generalization in this context. How exactly is this generalization supposed to work? If we cannot answer this question, we will be unable to explain, provided that we are restricted to Skinner's theory, one of the most important facets of verbal behavior: the production of new responses.

Are the preceding difficulties decisive? Perhaps not. To meet the first problem, a behaviorist might permit the use of the concept of intention in describing verbal behavior but object to treating intentions as causes. He might try to handle the second difficulty by explaining how the generalization mechanism works for verbal responses, even if he cannot predict the direction of generalization in a particular case. Nevertheless, the preceding difficulties, especially the second, do present important *prima facie* problems for the behaviorist. It is not enough to say that the generalization of verbal behavior is like the very complex instances of the pecking behavior of pigeons that can be reproduced in the laboratory (Rachlin & Lacey, 1978). Perhaps it is, but demonstrating this is difficult because of the apparent differences in the two sorts of cases; even with complex generalization of pecking responses, it is not antecedently implausible that physical resemblances can be found between old and novel responses; it is implausible, although it cannot be ruled out a priori, in many cases of verbal behavior.

Because of the apparent difficulties posed by the use of speech, the (1957) publication of *Verbal Behavior* was an important event. In this work Skinner tries to show how his basic theory of animal learning can be applied to verbal behavior without serious modification. The work has stimulated some research (see, for example, Salzinger and Feldman, 1973) but has also been severely criticized by Chomsky (1959) in a long and influential review.

No new experimental evidence is cited in *Verbal Behavior;* instead, Skinner attempts to use his basic notions of *stimulus, response, reinforcement,* and so on, and his newer notions of *mand, tact,* and so on, to explain a wide variety of examples. In his reply Chomsky examines each of the basic concepts and tries to demonstrate that Skinner fails to show that they can be fruitfully applied to Skinner's own illustrations. Chomsky's (1959) conclusion, stated in his own words, is this:

> My purpose in discussing the concepts one by one was to show that in each case, if we take his terms in their literal meaning, the description covers almost no aspect of verbal behavior, and if we take them metaphorically, the description offers no improvement over various traditional formulations.

Notice that Chomsky's criticism is not that Skinner's account is metaphorical. The criticism is not answered, then, by pointing out that metaphors are not always objectionable in science or by saying that Skinner's account was intended to be read literally. There should be no need to belabor this point, but Chomsky's conclusion has often been misunderstood. For example, Dinsmoor (1973) interprets it as follows:

> What bothered Chomsky was that in a natural setting the relationship between behavior and its controlling stimuli are extremely complex (not "lawful"). . . . But the problem lies in the difficulty of the material, not in the limitation of the concepts. To rule out conceptual terms based on experimental manipulation because the material to be analyzed is difficult is like ruling out biochemistry when one turns to the study of medicine.

This interpretation is wrong. As Chomsky's words show, he does not rule out the use of Skinner's concepts because the material to be analyzed is difficult or complex. The point, rather, can be expressed in the form of a dilemma: If Skinner's account is read nonliterally, it offers no improvement over traditional accounts, and if it is read literally, then, as far as is known, it covers very little verbal behavior. On either option the account is objectionable.

Another misunderstanding is evidenced in Wiest's (1967) paper, which is only partially concerned with Chomsky's review. Wiest's key criticism is this: "But since the *internalization* of grammar is a theory about verbal behavior rather than a fact, Skinner cannot properly be accused of ignoring that concept. At worst, he can be accused of ignoring the theoretical constructs of traditional interpretations of verbal behavior" (Wiest, 1967, p. 220). This criticism is irrelevant to Chomsky's review. Chomsky's conclusion, as quoted earlier, says nothing about the internalization of grammar and none of the supporting arguments in the review contains the premise that this internalization occurs. Chomsky does not accuse Skinner of ignoring such internalization; he does not even discuss the issue until the final two pages of his review, after completing his criticisms of Skinner's account. Someone might try to strengthen Chomsky's original criticisms by adding to them the theory that a native speaker internalizes the transformational grammar of his language, but showing that this theory is false or unsubstantiated would not refute the original criticisms.

Skinner has never replied to Chomsky's criticisms, not because he believes them unanswerable but because he believes them irrelevant (Skinner, 1971b). However, a detailed reply that Skinner endorses has been published (MacCorquodale, 1970) and is now being cited as satisfactorily answering Chomsky's arguments. For example, Salzinger and Feldman (1973) contend that Chomsky's criticisms apply only to earlier behaviorisms and refer the reader to MacCorquodale (1970) for documentation; Carrol (1971, p.

340), without explicitly endorsing MacCorquodale's reply, describes the paper as brilliant.

MacCorquodale's paper consists of a careful, extensive commentary on Chomsky's review. Whether it is convincing or not, it is useful in clarifying the basic issues, and it represents the most important challenge so far to Chomsky's arguments; for these reasons the paper deserves a serious examination. What I shall try to demonstrate is, first, that MacCorquodale's reply should offer no solace to the theorist who hopes to found behavior therapy on current learning theory and, second, that it does not answer Chomsky's criticism.

According to MacCorquodale, Chomsky's criticisms reduce to three:

1 "Verbal Behavior is an untested hypothesis which has, therefore, no claim upon our credibility."
2 "Skinner's technical terms are mere paraphrases for more traditional treatments of verbal behavior."
3 "Speech is complex behavior whose understanding and explanation require a complex, mediational neurological-genetic theory."

MacCorquodale (1970, p. 84) admits that none of the preceding criticisms is explicitly stated by Chomsky but contends that his review "adumbrates" them. However, he provides no evidence for this claim, and it is not plausible. Neither Chomsky's conclusion nor his supporting arguments rest on any of the preceding criticisms. This by no means vitiates all of what MacCorquodale says, but it should be made clear that refuting the preceding three criticisms would not in itself answer any of Chomsky's arguments.

MacCorquodale makes a number of additional points, some of which relate to basic issues about the learning foundations of behavior therapy.

MacCorquodale makes much of the fact that Skinner was putting forth a *hypothesis:* that the principles and concepts of his system are applicable to verbal behavior. MacCorquodale (1970, p. 86) concedes that this hypothesis is not known to be true: "The fact is simply that we do not yet know if verbal behavior is within the domain of Skinner's system and whether the technical terms *stimulus, response, reinforcement* are literally applicable to verbal behavior and correctly parse it into its functional parts of speech." This need not be especially damaging for the learning theorist who is not trying to firm up behavior therapy. Skinner's hypothesis could be important even if not yet known to be true. However, this possibility offers little comfort to the behavior therapist. If we are looking for a foundation for behavior therapy in order to provide antecedent support for the techniques or to explain why they work, we want a theory that has been empirically confirmed, not merely one that could be true. Skinner's theory might have a good deal of empirical support without the evidence being quite sufficient for knowledge; but, then, that there is such evidence is what the Skinnerian behavior therapist must demonstrate. It is not enough for his purposes to say that Skinner is simply putting forth a hypothesis. Furthermore, even from the vantage point of the Skinner–Chomsky dispute, not much is gained by stressing the hypothetical character of Skinner's claims. Chomsky tried to show (assuming that Skinner is read literally) that Skinner failed to support his hypothesis; he did not deny that the hypothesis was a hypothesis.

MacCorquodale also stresses that Skinner's account has not yet been shown to be false. This too does not help the behavior therapist very much, any more than the analogous point would help a psychoanalyst; in each case the underlying theory is not acceptable merely because it has not yet been shown to be false. To be fair to MacCorquodale, he stresses the point because he takes Chomsky to be claiming to have *refuted* Skinner's theory. There are passages that support this interpretation, as when Chomsky says that Skinner's description, taken literally, "covers almost no aspect of verbal behavior." There are also passages supporting a weaker interpretation, as when Chomsky says that the notions of *stimulus* and *response* "have not been shown to figure very widely in ordinary human behavior." We need not decide which interpretation is correct, that is, whether Chomsky is saying (1) that in *Verbal Behavior* Skinner fails to provide adequate evidence for his hypothesis or (2) that the available evidence falsifies the hypothesis. It is sufficient for our purposes that (1) be true; it alone would disqualify Skinner's theory from serving as an adequate foundation for behavior therapy, assuming that there is not adequate evidence to be found elsewhere. It should be noted, however, that there is a position intermediate between (1) and (2) that probably better reflects Chomsky's views. Some low-level empirical generalizations, such as "All swans are white," may easily be falsified by finding a counterinstance, such as a black swan. In contrast, a highly abstract theory such as Skinner's can rarely be falsified in such a simple manner: Because of the distance between the theory and the data, apparent counterexamples can (up to a point) be handled by appeal to additional hypotheses. For example, if a stimulus controls the responses of one organism and not another, we can always hypothesize a difference in their reinforcement histories; if the same organism responds differently to the same stimulus on different occasions, we can refer to multiple causation; and so on. It is rare, then, that a theory of this kind can be shown to be false by appeal to a counterexample. What we can sometimes reasonably conclude is that, given the available evidence, the theory is implausible or unpromising. This is stronger than saying that the theory lacks support, but weaker than charging that it has been falsified.

If we take (1) as Chomsky's conclusion (even though he would probably opt for something stronger), then MacCorquodale does nothing to meet it. The closest he gets to it is where he discusses Skinner's hypothesis that *Mozart!* and *Dutch!* are responses (lawfully) related, respectively, to a certain piece of music and to a certain painting. MacCorquodale points out that the hypothesis is not refuted by showing that the responses often do not occur when the hypothesized stimuli are present; in such cases, the responses are said to be under the control of different stimuli. The reverse is also true: If the response occurs when the hypothesized stimulus is absent, that does not show, MacCorquodale contends, the absence of a lawful relationship; it merely shows that in that situation, a different stimulus has taken control. This defense is odd. One would think that if the response *Eisenhower,* to take another of Skinner's examples, is often made when Eisenhower is absent and is often not made when Eisenhower is present, that this would be *some* evidence, even if it is not conclusive, that the man, Eisenhower, is not (lawfully) related to the response *Eisenhower.* One cannot just assume, without evidence or argument, that the explanation for these facts is that in the anomalous situations some other portion of the environment (as opposed to something in the speaker) is what is causally responsible for bringing about the response; this is just to assume, without evidence, that the Skinnerian account of these matters is correct. However, we can waive this objection: The fact remains that MacCorquodale merely attempts to show, in each case he discusses, that Chomsky does not refute Skinner's causal claims; he provides no evidence that any of these claims is true. Hence, if Chomsky's key contention is (1), then MacCorquodale, no matter what else he does, fails to meet the key criticism.

MacCorquodale (1970, p. 84) claims that there are "no directly relevant facts" bearing on the Skinner–Chomsky dispute, which is primarily "epistemological." Skinner accepts the constraints of natural science in setting up his analytical apparatus; Chomsky does not. Chomsky does not even discuss the methodological arguments Skinner gives for these constraints; he simply ignores them, according to MacCorquodale.

What are these constraints of natural science? The terms of Skinner's theory, according to MacCorquodale, are all empirically definable; and Skinner tries to explain only the objective dimensions of verbal behavior, invoking nonhypothetical entities (MacCorquodale, 1970, p. 83). In other words, Skinner's theory meets the constraints set by behaviorism and operationism. In a review of a later book by Skinner, Chomsky (1971) makes it clear that he regards the imposition of these constraints as an unjustified, a priori attempt to specify in advance what postulates and hypotheses are legitimate. It might be objected that Chomsky does not argue for this conclusion and, therefore, begs the question against those who argue for methodological behaviorism and for the need to define empirically all theoretical terms; but that objection would be of no avail here. These arguments were examined in detail in the previous chapter and were found to be unsound. The constraints referred to by MacCorquodale are not "constraints of natural science," and there is no good reason to accept them. If the Chomsky–Skinner dispute were essentially epistemological, as MacCorquodale says, then the weight of reason would clearly support Chomsky's position.

Chomsky contends that to predict the behavior of a complex organism, one would expect that knowledge of its internal structure would be required in addition to information about external stimulation. MacCorquodale replies that this need not be so. The neurological events within the human organism are obviously lawful, and they generate and maintain lawful, functional covariations between the controlling variables talked about by Skinner's theory and the behavior they control. If that is so, then we can predict human behavior by directly discovering the functional covariations; we need not obtain information about the neurological laws that underlie them.

MacCorquodale is quite right that a psychologist might safely ignore neurological variables *if* the covariations between response and environment are lawful, but to assume that they are is to assume what is at issue: that the causes of human behavior do not lie even partly within the organism. This is what Skinner should be proving if he wants to explain human behavior in terms of his system; he cannot, without evidence, reasonably assume from the outset that his key assumption is true. Suppose, for example, that we are trying to explain the behavior of a certain type of machine. We notice that the occurrence of a certain kind of environmental event, E (the insertion of a dime in the slot and the pressing of a certain button) is sometimes followed by a certain response, R (a coffee cup slides down and is filled with coffee); but we notice that sometimes R does not follow E. Sometimes when a dime is inserted, no cup comes down; at other times the cup is filled with water instead of coffee. To account for this variability, we might look to the origin of a given machine, just as with humans we might look to their genes. If that fails, we might look to the history of responses of a machine, just as we might look to the history of reinforcement of a human organism. We might also hypothesize that multiple causation produces a given response. We notice, for example, that when E occurs and the customer is a psychology major, then R follows. If that correlation subsequently breaks down, we might make our correlations more complex. We might conjecture, for example, that R occurs when and only when E occurs *and* the customer is a psychology major and wears a white shirt or blue tie, or is not a psychology major but is born in Brooklyn and bangs the machine. If we are ingenious and persistent enough, we can always discover some kind of correlation between environmental events and R, no matter what occurs, provided that we are willing to make our correlations sufficiently complex. It just might be, however, that the correlations will not be lawful and will be too complex to be of much use in making accurate predictions except in relatively trivial circumstances. In short, the operation of the machine's inner mechanism may be an important part of the cause of R. If we were to insist for methodological reasons that our explanations not mention the inner mechanism of the machine, we might obtain many complex correlations but never explain the machine's behavior. It would be begging the question to assume without evidence that the responses of humans are analogous in relevant respects to those of our hypothetical coffee machine, but the same would be true if we assumed that they were not, as some Skinnerians do: "The real issue must still be addressed – what are the effective events in the environment (and on the organism's receptors) that enable the organism to respond appropriately to the relevant features of the environment" (Wiest,

1967, p. 221). The real issue, once the strictures of methodological behaviorism are removed, is quite simply: What causes human behavior? To assume that it must be something in the environment is to assume what needs to be proved.

MacCorquodale's comment about neurological variables, then, depends on an unconfirmed and controversial empirical premise: that there are lawful covariations between responses and environmental events (plus the other variables Skinner speaks of – genetic structure, motivation, etc.) and that they exist in sufficient number to explain verbal behavior. Without support for this crucial premise, the argument lacks cogency.

The final point to be taken up here is probably the most important, except for the methodological considerations discussed earlier. MacCorquodale contends that Skinner's hypothesis receives strong antecedent support from the discovery and empirical confirmation of certain laws of nonverbal human behavior. What are these laws? MacCorquodale mentions only one, the law of effect. He writes:

> The (functional) law of reinforcement is an enormously powerful predictive (specifying?) device. At least it is for nonverbal behavior: and no one can say that it is not powerful for verbal behavior too. . . . The functional law of reinforcement, in addition to being powerful, is an established empirical fact. It is not a theory awaiting neurological validation. [MacCorquodale, 1970, p. 92.]

If what MacCorquodale says here is true, it might help to show that Skinner's hypothesis is worth pursuing, even if Skinner fails to provide any new evidence for it in *Verbal Behavior*. Whether one agrees or not will depend, in part, on one's estimate of the counterevidence, including some of the factors cited earlier, such as the ability of a speaker to produce any one of an indefinitely large set of novel responses. What MacCorquodale says, however, is not true: It is not true that the law of effect is either powerful or empirically established. The evidence for this claim will be presented in the next section.

Conclusion. If the use of language provides important *prima facie* problems for a Skinnerian account, does *Verbal Behavior* show how they can be solved? Skinner does not present any new experimental evidence in this work, but he does attempt to show how his theory can be applied to a wide range of examples of linguistic behavior. Chomsky has tried to show, at the very least, that this attempt has failed. Neither Wiest (1967) nor MacCorquodale (1970) has met Chomsky's criticism. If MacCorquodale is trying to show only that Chomsky's review fails to prove that

Skinner's theory is false, then we do not disagree on this point; but the point should provide little comfort to those who wish to base behavior therapy on Skinner's theory of learning. If the theory is not known to be false and if it is empirically confirmed at some time in the future, then at that time it might be useful to try to derive behavior therapy techniques from the theory. Without supporting evidence, the theory will not suffice as a foundation now.

How has Skinner's theory fared since the publication of Chomsky's (1959) criticisms? Because the theory purports to explain human behavior without recourse to mentalistic explanations, evidence that this cannot be done would be evidence against the theory. Much evidence of this kind has been accumulated in recent years; some of it will be discussed in the next section and in subsequent sections.

III. The law of effect

Some behavior therapists who cite modern learning theory as the foundation for behavior therapy may be thinking not of a single, all-encompassing theory, such as Hull's or Skinner's, but of specific conditioning principles. We need to look into this possibility.

The prime candidate for such a principle is that cited by Mac-Corquodale: the law of effect. It is described as a basic principle in the American Psychiatric Association's *Task Force Report, 5: Behavior Therapy in Psychiatry* (1973, p. 57) and has been cited by a number of writers on behavior therapy (e.g., Mahoney & Thoresen, 1974, p. 6). It is likely, then, that some writers who speak of a learning foundation of behavior therapy are referring, at least in part, to the law of effect. We need to know, however, which version is being talked about. There are several possibilities.

One of the first formal statements of the principle is Thorndike's (1911, p. 3): "The Law of Effect is that: of several responses made to the same situation, those which are accompanied or closely followed by satisfaction to the animal will, other things being equal, be more firmly connected with the situation, so that, when it recurs, they will be more likely to occur. . . ." He also adds that a "satisfying state of affairs" is one that the animal does nothing to avoid, often doing such things as will attain and preserve it. A reference to discomforting states of affairs was also included in the original statement, but was later deleted.

Some of the original objections to Thorndike's principle were conceptual. Hull (1935) complained that it was too subjective, despite Thorndike's behavioral definition of *satisfaction*. Some complained that the inclusion of this behavioral definition rendered the principle circular; others objected that it implied the existence of backward causation. Because these criticisms have been answered (see Hilgard & Bower, 1966; Boring, 1950), they will not be considered here.

We might ask, however, how informative the principle is. Consider a case where someone believes that one of his responses once produced a satisfying state of affairs but that it will not do so again. For example, a psychologist may earn tenure at the university at which he wants to remain by writing a book, but he knows that he cannot earn tenure twice. Consequently, there might be, let us suppose, no increase in the likelihood that the same response, or same kind of response, will be repeated. Consider a second type of case where the subject does not believe that his response was causally connected to a satisfying state of affairs that immediately followed. For example, a mathematician familiar with the laws of chance may bet on no. 32 in a game of roulette and win $10,000 but believe that this was due to chance and will probably not happen again. The increase in strength, then, may be zero. Is either case a counterexample to Thorndike's principle? The answer is negative; the phrase *other things being equal* can, in the absence of instructions to the contrary, be interpreted to rule out these and all other potential counterexamples. We can simply conclude that not all things are equal in such cases. But, then, the principle is too trivial to qualify as a law of human behavior. Apart from the question of whether or not the term *law* should be applied, Thorndike's statement is not likely to serve as an adequate foundation for behavior therapy. It is too vague to entail any precise description of a behavior therapy technique, to provide antecedent support for such techniques, or to explain why they work.

To be fair to Thorndike, he does say something about what he means by *everything being equal,* but his explanation involves reference to his law of exercise, which he later rejects, and to cognitive factors (paying attention), which are supposed to be avoided by accepting his principle (see Wilcoxon, 1969). The general point here is that statistical versions of the law of effect (e.g., those that say "sometimes" or "other things being equal," a reward increases strength) are too vague to qualify as laws or to serve as part of the foundation of behavior therapy. Estes (1969, p. 26) expresses the point as follows: "However, the frequency with which animals and men in nonlaboratory situations repeat punished actions and fail to repeat rewarded ones is so great that, as a statistical generalization, an empirical law of effect is all but vacuous." Such versions as the following are also "all but vacuous": "While it focuses a powerful and ubiquitous class of behavior-influence conditions, the extrinsic-reinforcement conception (that subsumes the empirical law of effect) implies only that there exist stimuli which, when placed in a specified contingency with responses, will increase the rate of some of them" (Gerwirtz, 1971, p. 282). The author points out that, under this conception, reinforcers need not exist under all conditions for every response; also, the contingency described as a "reinforcer" need not be the only mechanism associated with changes in instrumental-response strength; and the fact that a stimulus functions as a reinforcer in one context does not preclude its functioning in other stimulus roles in other contexts (p. 282). He rightly concludes, "As a simple descriptive statement, therefore, the empirical law of effect would be untouched by experimental demonstrations of high-rate responses with no obvious extrinsic (reinforcing) consequences . . ." (p. 282). It is not clear that the law of effect, so interpreted, would be touched by anything. Even if we never found a single stimulus of the specified kind, that would be compatible with saying that there exists somewhere some stimuli that, when placed in a specified contingency with responses, will increase at least some of them. However, we need not contend that this so-called law is totally vacuous. It is sufficient to point out that the principle is compatible with the need to introduce mentalistic variables to explain a good deal of human behavior; it is not a law; and it is unsuitable for a foundational role.

Let us turn away from statistical versions and look to other influential accounts, such as the following:

> To paraphrase Skinner (1938), reinforcement refers to the occurrence of one of a certain class of events called reinforcers, in the proper relation to the to-be-learned response; the proper relation being that which tends to increase the probability that the response reinforced will recur with representation of the situation. . . . The statement that such events, placed appropriately with respect to some response, lead to an increase in the probability that the response will recur in the situation is a statement of the empirical law of reinforcement (effect), sometimes called the "weak" law of effect. [Hilgard & Marquis, 1961, pp. 5–6.]

The empirical law of effect, as stated previously, is a mere tautology. If we define *reinforcer* as "that which increases the probability of a response," then what we are saying is that events that increase the probability of a response will increase the probability of the response. If, for example, we give a retarded child M and Ms for pressing a lever and the probability of the response does not increase, the "law" is not falsified; rather, for that child, the candy does not qualify as a reinforcer. Nothing could happen to falsify the principle, and no empirical evidence is needed to know that it is true. In short, the principle is not a law and it is not empirical; it is true as all tautologies are, but vacuously so. There should be no need to point this out after Meehl's excellent (1950) discussion, but there is reason to believe that the implications of his comments are either not fully appreciated or not universally accepted. For example, some Skinnerians reply that it is not circular to define *reinforcement* in the preceding way and then decide empirically which events are reinforcing (see Wilcoxon's discussion, 1969). This point is correct but not germane to the preceding criticism, which says not that the procedure or the empirical law of effect is circular but that the "law" is tautologous. A second example is Rachlin's (1971) contention that Herrnstein's so-called matching law of effect, the content of which need not concern us here, is a tautology but is nevertheless useful. If the matching and empirical laws of effect are tautologies, then they are not empirical, they are not laws, and, given their vacuousness, it is difficult to see what they would be useful for. Perhaps the point is that the definition of one of the key terms in the "law" is useful. For example, it may be useful to define *reinforcer* as an "event that increases the frequency of a response." Once the definition is accepted, however, it is trivial and uninformative to add the principle: "If a response is followed by a reinforcer, its frequency will be increased." The principle reflects no discovery but is instead a trivial consequence of the stipulated definition.

In any event we need not insist that tautologies never have any use at all. The relevant point is that the empirical law of effect, because it is a tautology, cannot possibly serve as an adequate foundation for behavior therapy. The statement "Events that increase the probability of a response will increase the probability of the response" does not entail any statement describing a behavior therapy technique, nor can it be used to explain the origin and maintenance of maladaptive behavior or to explain why any behavior therapy technique works. It is not clear, then, what is intended by the authors of *Task Report 5, Behavior Therapy in Psychiatry* (1973) when they define *appetitive or positive reinforcer*

as "stimuli that increase the probability that the response they followed will recur in the future." Given this definition, the "basic"
operant principle they cite (p. 57) is simply a variant of the
tautologous empirical law of effect. Despite this fact, the authors
suggest, first, that the principle is supported by a broad range of
animal laboratory and human experimental studies (p. 57). Second, this is one of the principles they are presumably referring to
when they suggest (p. 2) that behavior therapy techniques have
been derived from Pavlovian and Skinnerian learning principles.
Because the principle is tautologous and, consequently, compatible with all possible empirical data and entails nothing about behavior therapy, both suggestions are clearly false.

Meehl's version of the law of effect

Although some nonstatistical statements of the law of effect are
empty tautologies, that is not true of all. Paul Meehl (1950) has
suggested two versions that do have empirical content:
1 The weak law of effect: All reinforcers are transsituational.
2 The strong law of effect: Every increment in strength in-
     volves a transsituational reinforcer.
In explaining (1), Meehl uses the notion of a "learnable response" to characterize those responses that can be increased in
strength by exposure to a situation rather than by surgical, drug, or
maturational changes. A *reinforcer* is a stimulus that will strengthen
at least one response; a *transsituational reinforcer* is a stimulus that
will strengthen all learnable responses. Furthermore, a response is
strengthened when the probability of its reoccurrence has been increased. Given these definitions, we can paraphrase (1) as Hilgard
and Bower (1966) do:
3 A reinforcer can be used to increase the probability of any
     learnable response.
The following comments concern (3) (i.e., the weak law of effect): The weak law of effect is too weak to serve by itself as a
foundation for behavior therapy; it might be true and yet very
little human behavior might result from reinforcement. Principle
3 might still be of some interest to the behavior therapist; once he
discovers that a certain stimulus can be used to strengthen one
behavior of a schizophrenic, he can know, by appeal to (3), that
the same stimulus can be used to strengthen other responses.
Nevertheless, by appeal to (3) alone, he will not be able to explain
why schizophrenics behave in the manner they do or why current

behavior techniques work; nor will he be able to derive behavior therapy techniques from this principle.

Although (3) is in one way too weak, it is also too strong. It implies something quite extreme about reinforcement; something that does not appear especially plausible. Suppose, for example, that we can strengthen the saluting response of a captured enemy soldier by offering him a glass of wine. For some soldiers it would be quite useless to use the same reinforcer to increase the probability, say, of their informing on their comrades. We could try altering relevant conditions of deprivation. For example, we might withhold all food and drink for forty-eight hours and then offer a glass of wine. However, we know from experience gained in World War II that some soldiers would prefer to suffer and even die under such conditions rather than inform on their comrades.

Consider a different kind of case, where a boy enjoys four different types of activities, but not to the same extent. Suppose his preference ranking, in ascending order of preference, is as follows: (a) reading children's books; (b) walking with his grandfather; (c) playing with his friends; and (d) eating ice cream. Given this fondness for eating ice cream relative to reading, we may well find that providing ice cream can be used to reinforce the reading of books but not conversely, despite the fact that allowing the child to read can reinforce other less desired responses. This kind of phenomenon has been widely studied by Premack (1959, 1965, 1971) and his results strongly support a relativity view of reinforcement. (For a more detailed discussion of a relativity view of reinforcement, see Hilgard & Bower, 1966, 1975.) If reinforcment is relative in the previously described way, then the weak law of reinforcement is false. Some reinforcers ranking low in a subject's preference scheme cannot be used to reinforce highly preferred reinforcing behaviors.

The failure of the weak law of effect might not be of too much concern to the reinforcement theorist so long as the strong law of effect stands up. If we are looking for a theoretical principle to explain the origin and maintenance of maladaptive behavior, why not be content with this principle? There are several reasons:

Principle 2 presumably entails that every increment in strength of *human* behavior is caused by the presentation of a transsituational reinforcer. If it does, there is little or no evidence that it is true. As Estes (1971, p. 27) points out, most of the data usually cited in support of the strong law of effect have been gleaned from an extremely limited range of experimental situations, involving mazes, operant-conditioning chambers, and the like, and involving, for the most part, rats, mice, pigeons, or other nonhuman organisms. This type of evidence is simply too weak to support the extension of (2) to all human behavior.

Meehl does not claim that (2) has been empirically confirmed; he admits that the empirical status of both the weak and strong laws of effect is in doubt (Meehl, 1950, p. 74). His goal is not to provide empirical support for either principle but to state non-tautological versions of what experimental psychologists have generally had in mind when speaking of the law of effect. This is not enough for our purposes, however; we are looking for an empirically confirmed principle of human learning, not merely a principle that has empirical content and that could be true. Thus, the absence of adequate evidence for (2) is sufficient to disqualify it, given our purposes, though the principle might still be of interest to a reinforcement theorist who is not trying to find a foundation for behavior therapy.

If principle 3 (the weak law of effect) is false, then it is likely that principle 2, the strong law of effect, is false as well. We cannot, then, simply reject (3) and accept (2). Suppose, for example, that (3) is rendered dubious by evidence that at least some increments in strength are due to reinforcers that are not transsituational (Premack, 1965, 1971). This same evidence would also tell against (2), because (2) says that *every* increment in strength is due to a transsituational reinforcer.

Apart from the evidence against (3), there has been independent evidence accumulating over the past twenty-five years that the strong law of effect is false (Buchwald, 1967, 1969; Humphreys, Allen, & Estes, 1968; Keller et al. 1965; Stillings, Allen, & Estes, 1968; Estes, 1969, 1971). Additional evidence will be cited later, but enough has been said so far to cast doubt on MacCorquodale's (1970, p. 92) contention that the functional law of reinforcement is an "established empirical fact." The tautological version of the law is empty, is not supported (or negated) by any empirical evidence, and has no explanatory or predictive power. The version that does have empirical content, Meehl's version, remains unconfirmed; in fact, the weight of the current evidence is against it.

IV. Additional learning principles

Perhaps we are expecting too much in trying to find either a single learning theory or a single law that can explain all or most human behavior. When some behavior therapists speak of behavior therapy being based on modern learning theory, they may have something more modest in mind. For example, Rachman and Eysenck (1966, pp. 165–6) concede that there is disagreement concerning theories of learning but contend that no learning theorist of any persuasion would deny statements of the following kind:

i "Reinforced pairings of CS and UCS under appropriate conditions produce conditioning."
ii "Intermittent reinforcement slows down extinction."
iii "Nonreinforcement produces extinction."
iv "Different schedules of reinforcement produce predictably different response rates."

They contend, further, that it is laws of this type that form the scientific basis of behavior therapy (Rachman & Eysenck, 1966, p. 166). That this is not true can be shown by the following:

Not all learning theorists would agree with principle (i) unless the phrase *under appropriate conditions* is interpreted so as to exclude most human behavior (see, for example, Wiest, 1967). The principle applies mainly, but not solely, to autonomic responses. If the principle is interpreted in this way, however, it is too narrow in scope to explain much deviant behavior.

Even if the principle is interpreted so as to apply only to autonomic responses, there is now strong evidence that it is false, although to be fair to Eysenck and Rachman, much of this evidence was gathered after the publication of their statement. (Eysenck's more recent views on foundations, as expressed in Eysenck, 1975, will be discussed later.)

There is little doubt that sometimes when an unconditioned stimulus (UCS) is repeatedly paired with a previously neutral stimulus (CS), an autonomic response that had previously followed the UCS will follow the CS. Some investigators have hypothesized, however, that in normal adult humans, the awareness of the relation between the UCS and CS, rather than the pairing, is, in many cases, what causes such responses. To test this hypothesis, investigators have used a "masking procedure," usually a task designed to prevent the subjects from becoming aware of the CS-UCS relation. In one such experiment (Dawson & Grings, 1968), students in one group were given a paper and pencil "mental" test and were told that the purpose of the experiment was to determine the effects of distracting stimuli on their performance. During the test, tones (the CSs) produced by an audio-oscillator were paired with a shock (the UCS) from a Grass Model 5 Stimulator. A written postconditioning interview was later used to determine if the taking of the test had prevented the subject from learning the CS-UCS relation. A comparison was made of galvanic skin responses of students who had not learned of the relation and students in a second group who were told of an impending CS-UCS relation but who were presented with only one such pairing. The results were that the masked CS-UCS pairing failed to establish autonomic discrimination, whereas the giving of information concerning the relation was sufficient to establish conditioned-like GSRs in the second group. Similar experiments have replicated these results (Dawson, 1970; Grings et al., 1973), providing evidence that awareness helps determine autonomic responses (Grings, 1973).

The evidence against Eysenck and Rachman's first principle tells against the remaining principles as well. If awareness often plays a crucial causal role in the conditioning of adult humans, and the evidence strongly suggests that it does (Dawson & Grings, 1968; Grings & Sukoneck, 1971; Fuhrer & Baer, 1969; Colgan, 1970; Grings, 1973), then response rates and rapidity of extinction will, in many cases, not be determined solely by the variables mentioned in principles ii, iii, and iv. To take one kind of counterexample, it has been found in many learning experiments that the effects of reinforcement on acquisition and extinction will vary, depending on whether or not the subject believes that the reinforcements are beyond his control. In an early experiment, James and Rotter (1958) compared the performance of two groups on a card guessing task controlled by the experimenter. The first group was told that their success was dependent on skill; the second, that it was due to chance. For the second group, extinction took place as predicted by Eysenck and Rachman's principle ii: extinction was significantly quicker for those who received 100 percent reinforcement compared to those who received 50 percent reinforcement. The results were different, however, for those in the first group. In fact, the 100 percent reinforcement schedule led to less (though not significantly less) rapid extinction than the 50 percent reinforcement schedule. When the 50 percent reinforcement schedule was compared between groups, it was found that extinction was significantly more rapid for those who believed that reinforcement was due to skill. Other experiments of this kind are reviewed in Lefcourt (1966).

So far, we have examined the most plausible candidates for a learning foundation of behavior therapy. Some of these have turned out to be inadequate because they are either too narrow in scope or tautological. An example of the latter is the tautological version of the law of effect. Those that do not fail in either of these respects, such as Skinner's learning theory or Meehl's strong law of effect, have not been confirmed by the available empirical evidence. This alone would disqualify them given our purposes, but the case against them is stronger than lack of proof. There is now much positive evidence against them. It has been found necessary to postulate the causal efficacy of certain mentalistic states and events in order to explain the results of a great many recent learning experiments. That this has proved necessary is evidence against Skinnerian and Pavlovian learning theory and against the strong law of effect; it is also evidence against the position taken by some methodological behaviorists that we can explain all human behavior without the use of mentalistic concepts. Some of the evidence has already been cited (Buchwald, 1969; Estes, 1969, 1971; Humphreys, Allen, & Estes, 1968; Dawson & Grings, 1968; Grings & Sukoneck, 1971; Fuhrer & Baer, 1969; Colgan, 1970; Grings 1973; James & Rotter, 1958; Lefcourt, 1966). Additional evidence concerns the causal role of such mentalistic variables as awareness, imagery, belief, and expectancy.

V. Counterevidence

Awareness

In both classical and operant paradigms, conditioning is assumed to occur directly and mechanically, without the mediation of cognitive variables. The subject may, of course, be conscious of his surroundings, but it is assumed that this plays no causal role in the conditioning process. As already indicated, there is now much evidence that this assumption is false insofar as it concerns classical conditioning (Grings, 1973). The same is true of operant conditioning. Early operant conditioning studies of verbal learning (Krasner, 1958; Greenspoon, 1962) were used to support the claim that learning can take place without awareness, but subsequent studies (Dulaney, 1961; DeNike, 1964) disputed this view. In these latter studies, more sensitive methods were used to detect awareness, and it was found (e.g., in DeNike, 1964) that the only subjects who showed performance gains were those who had become aware of the response-reinforcement contingency.

These studies do not prove that learning can never take place without awareness; there is evidence, in fact, that it can (Bandura, 1969, pp. 576–7). Nevertheless, these and other studies have provided abundant evidence that awareness does facilitate learning. For example, if the subject is made aware of the response-reinforcement contingency, this will often affect the rate at which learning occurs and in some cases will determine whether it occurs at all (Spielberger & DeNike, 1966; DeNike, 1964; Dawson & Furedy, 1974; Grings, 1973; Bandura, 1974, 1977).

The conclusion that awareness can play an important causal role in determining human behavior is relevant to the practice of behavior therapy as well as to its theoretical foundations. Many behavior therapists have become skeptical about so-called insight therapies that make insight into the origin of one's problems an essential goal of treatment. For example, Bandura (1969, pp. 93–8) points out that many of the so-called insights of patients treated by Jungian, Alderian, or Freudian therapists are not genuine; the client simply learns to use the theoretical concepts of his therapist to talk about his problems. For this reason, and because there is evidence that awareness of the origin of one's problems is neither necessary nor sufficient for therapeutic change (Paul, 1966), many behavior therapists have been led to downgrade the clinical importance of insight. Although this reaction may have been warranted, given the excessive and unsubstantiated claims made by many insight-oriented therapists, it would be a mistake to repudiate insight altogether. The fact that the pseudo-insight is of little value is hardly evidence that genuine insight is worthless. It can also be readily conceded that even genuine insight may have little therapeutic value in many cases, (e.g., where the original causes of a problem behavior have disappeared and no longer explain why the behavior is still maintained or where motivation for change is lacking). Still, there are some cases where insight can be important. For example, in studies of self-control, it has been found that making the client aware of what his behavior is and what the current controlling causes are can make an important difference to therapeutic outcome (Kazdin, 1974b; Goldfried & Merbaum, 1973; Mahoney & Thoresen, 1974).

Imagery

Another mentalistic variable widely studied in the past decade is mental imagery. A number of investigators of this phenomenon have been able to construct quite sophisticated experimental designs. They have been able to provide reliable operational tests for the presence of imagery and have effectively ruled out alternative explanations of their findings (Paivio, 1971, 1976; Bower, 1970; Kosslyn & Pomerantz, 1977; Shepard, 1978; Shepard & Metzler, 1971; Cooper & Shepard, 1973). The evidence from these studies strongly suggests that nonverbal imagery is a major factor affecting memory, thought, and verbal behavior (Paivio, 1973).

As with awareness, the finding that imagery is an important causal variable has practical as well as theoretical implications. Given this finding, one would predict that manipulation of a client's mental imagery should, under certain conditions, be therapeutically useful. That prediction has been confirmed by studies of desensitization (Paul, 1969). Additional suggestive but inconclusive evidence comes from studies of covert modeling and covert sensitization (Cautela, 1973; Kazdin, 1975).

Belief and expectancy

In some of the learning experiments alluded to earlier (James & Rotter, 1958; Lefcourt, 1966), it was found that learning was affected by the subject's belief that rewards were under his control instead of being contingent on external conditions. An analogous finding is reported in an interesting study by Davison and Valins (1969) that suggests that a subject's belief can enhance his ability to tolerate shock. The experimenters measured the subjects' tolerance of shock and then administered a placebo. The subjects were then administered shock a second time but at a reduced level. Half the subjects were then told that the drug was a placebo but were not told that the level of shock had been reduced. They were then led to believe that they could now tolerate more pain. These subjects were then able to tolerate shock significantly more than the subjects who believed that it had been the drug that had been responsible for their enhanced ability to tolerate shock. The effects of false feedback of this sort are unclear (Wilson & Thomas, 1973), but the idea of convincing the client that certain rewards and punishments are under his control has obvious clinical applications. One way to induce this belief in phobic patients, for example, is through the use of self-directed exercises with the phobic object. Bandura, Jeffery, and Gajdos (1975) treated people who were afraid of snakes by use of participant modeling alone or by participant modeling followed by self-directed contacts with a snake. Those who received the latter treatment showed less apprehension of encounters with snakes and less fear of threats not specifically treated.

The client's belief about the effects of the therapy can also be important. If a client expects that he will be helped, this will often bring about some improvement (Lick & Bootzin, 1975; Borkovec, 1972). There has long been evidence available for this facilitative effect of belief; it is for this reason that the so-called placebo effect must be controlled for if we are to determine the effects of a specific type of therapy.

Another clinical area where belief has been important is in cases where a client's emotional reactions and overt behavior are maintained, in part, by the holding of irrational beliefs. There is some suggestive evidence that in such cases cognitive restructuring (described in Chapter 1) can be therapeutically beneficial (Lazarus, 1971; Ellis, 1971; Rimm & Litvak, 1969; Goldfried & Sobicinski, 1975; Goldfried, Decenteceo, & Weinberg, 1974).

Conditioning experiments

We have been discussing some of the counterevidence to certain behavioristic theories and principles. What of the supporting evidence? Some behaviorists point to conditioning experiments with pigeons and rats to support their claim that behavioristic principles will eventually prove adequate for explaining human behavior, but this evidence is simply too weak when taken by itself. It is gleaned from a very narrow range of experimental situations and concerns organisms with behavioral repertoires and neural structures that in many respects are markedly different from those present in nonimpaired adult humans. What of the conditioning experiments conducted with adult humans, such as the verbal conditioning experiments (reviewed in Krasner, 1958)? The design of many of these experiments is too weak to rule out cognitive interpretations of the results. For example, suppose we reward someone after he emits a response and we find that he tends to increase the frequency of the response. If this is all we know, it is not firm evidence that conditioning has taken place, unless *conditioning* is simply a name for whatever causes an increase in the frequency of response; nor is it evidence for any behavioristic theory or principle. The subject might well have come to believe that a cause-and-effect relationship exists between his response and the obtaining of the reward; if he is motivated to obtain the reward and believes that there is no weighty disutility in repeating the response, he may increase its frequency. If we do not rule out the possibility that the subject's cognitive states affected his behavior, then we have failed to provide evidence that conditioning has occurred. There is a wide body of experiments, however, that are designed to permit a choice between a conditioning and cognitive explanation. Brewer (1974) has distinguished eleven different such designs. In these so-called disassociative designs, the experimenter attempts to separate awareness from the "conditioning" process and to determine which of these is causally responsible for the responses. One example is the masking design discussed earlier in connection with experiments in so-called autonomic conditioning. A second example is the informed unpairing design. In the classical conditioning version, the subject is run through one of the standard conditioning paradigms and is then told that the USC will no longer follow the CS. In the operant conditioning version he is told that reinforcement will no longer follow the operant response. The cognitive theory described by Brewer predicts that each procedure will produce extinction in both autonomic and motor responses, and that the degree of extinction should be directly related to the degree of confidence the subject has in the experiment's statement. A third type, the awareness of contingency design, involves putting Ss through a conditioning procedure in which the CS-USC relationship or reinforcement contingency is moderately difficult to grasp. After so-called conditioning, Ss are separated into those who become aware of the contingencies and those who do not. Cognitive theory predicts that only the aware subjects will show "conditioning." Brewer (1974) has carried out an extensive review of those experiments utilizing these eleven designs. His more modest interpretation is that the bulk of the so-called conditioning in these experiments is due to the operation of higher mental processes, as assumed by cognitive theory, but that there is some minimal evidence for automatic, unconscious processes. His more radical (and what he takes to be a more plausible) interpretation is that all of the results support a cognitive hypothesis and that no evidence at all is provided for unconscious, automatic mechanisms in the "conditioning" of adult human beings.

Do the studies reviewed by Brewer falsify any behavioristic theory of learning purporting to explain all human behavior without appeal to cognitive variables? There is reason to doubt that they do. The behaviorist has a number of options open, one of which is to appeal to some auxiliary assumptions to explain away the apparently disconfirming data. In his ingenious reply to Brewer, Dulany (1974) lists eight such assumptions:

1 Verbal utterances, instructions from E or covert self-instructions from S, may serve as conditioned stimuli for autonomically mediated responses.
2 Verbal utterances may serve as discriminative stimuli or cues for verbal responses and other motor behavior.
3 Verbal reports of awareness may behave as operants are said to behave within behavior theory; that is, to come under the functional control of reinforcers.
4 Fear is a response with stimulus properties.
5 Activity of the sympathetic system mediating fear and flight reactions and activity of the parasympathetic system are reciprocally innervated and respond antagonistically.
6 In order for conditioning to occur, potential reinforcers, conditioned stimuli, or unconditioned stimuli must be attended to; but the term *attention* refers not to a cognition but to an orienting response.
7 Conditioning has parameters whose values vary over properties of reinforcers, UCSs, responses, and persons; whether or not conditioning occurs, and in what direction and degree, depends on the values those parameters take.
8 Awareness is merely an epiphenomenon of some kind of neural process and not causally active in response selection in any way independent of that neural process.

One might complain that the preceding assumptions are ad hoc – brought in after the falsifying experiments are completed simply to protect a behavioristic theory from falsification. This complaint can be met. There is reason to believe that some behaviorists accepted these assumptions even before the relevant experiments were run, but whether or not this is true, let us hereby stipulate that a certain theory, T, will consist of these assumptions plus the conjunction of standard principles of classical and operant conditioning. If T can plausibly explain the data we are discussing and do so just as well as its cognitive rival, then the data do not refute T. Perhaps we have formulated T to save a behavioristic learning theory, but from an evidential point of view why should that matter? It is sufficient that the data fail to refute T; it is not necessary that our purposes be pure.

It might also be complained that T is simply too vague even if we specify the principles of conditioning to be assumed; by adding the preceding auxiliary assumptions, we give behaviorism so many escape holes that it loses all content. T may be vague and it may be extremely difficult to falsify, but it might still be true, and if the conditioning principles are adequate to explain all human behavior, it is certainly not trivial.

Because the behaviorist can invoke at least some of the preceding assumptions and because there are still other escape routes open that we will consider later, it is doubtful that the evidence cited by Brewer is sufficient to falsify all behavioristic theories of learning. It is doubtful that anyone has ever provided such evidence.

Even if the disassociative design experiments do not falsify behaviorism, they are relevant in assessing the claim that we have reason to be confident that some behavioristic theory will eventually prove to be adequate. The auxiliary assumptions cited earlier might be invoked to show that conditioning principles explain the relevant data just as well as a cognitive hypothesis; they do not show that the conditioning explanation is superior. (Dulany, 1974, p. 44, makes the same point; his purpose was not to support behaviorism but to show how difficult it is to refute.) In the absence of other ways of proving the superiority of the conditioning explanation, and assuming that other types of conditioning experiments are inadequate, then the conditioning literature fails to provide any firm support for the idea that a behavioristic theory of learning will eventually prove to be adequate.

Do the dissociative design experiments provide any evidence at all against behaviorism, or are they simply neutral? We do not have to settle this issue here, because our purpose is not to refute behavioristic theories of learning but to show that they are not supported by the overall current evidence. Nevertheless, it might be useful to indicate why such experiments are probably not neutral. The eight assumptions invoked earlier to neutralize the cognitive interpretation of the data encounter at least two serious difficulties. First, some of these are compatible with behaviorism only if certain dubious reductive theses are adopted. For example, assumption 1 concedes the causal relevance of covert self-instructions of the subject. But what is a "covert self-instruction" if it is not a cognitive state or event? Unless we can rely on operationism or analytical behaviorism, which is dubious for reasons given in Chapter 2, or on some other reductive thesis compatible with behaviorism, treating covert self-instructions as a cause may be simply a covert way of adopting a cognitive hypothesis. The same sort of problem arises for assumption 6. It is doubtful that the term *attention* refers to an orienting response. The mute catatonics discussed in Chapter 2 paid attention to the therapist's instructions without exhibiting such a response. We might just stipulate that the term *attention* be used so that it does not apply in the absence of an orienting response, but then the same case of the catatonics is evidence that so-called conditioning can occur even if the subject fails to pay attention (in this stipulated sense) to the relevant environmental stimuli. The second difficulty is that some of the eight assumptions are not antecedently plausible without independent evidence for current behavioristic theories. For example, assumption 3 says that verbal reports are under the functional control of reinforcers as specified by operant theory. However, Chomsky's review plus the *prima facie* difficulties cited earlier concerning the novelty of verbal responses renders this assumption implausible. It might be replied that no current cognitivist theory explains verbal behavior either, but this does not make assumption 3 plausible. Even if no current theory is adequate, some hypotheses can still be shown to be implausible.

VI. An expansion of the argument

How likely is it that the argument given so far will convince someone who believes that behavior therapy is based on learning theory? The answer, of course, is that it is not likely. Other writers have criticized the learning foundations of behavior therapy, (Breger & McGaugh, 1965); with few exceptions such criticisms have generally been looked on unfavorably (Rachman & Eysenck, 1966; Wiest, 1967; Yates, 1970, Chap. 19). Part of the reason for the disagreement is that what is at issue is not merely the state of the empirical evidence. As MacCorquodale (1970) points out, the disagreement is partly epistemological and methodological; it resembles a "paradigm clash" of the sort described by Kuhn (1962) and Katahn and Koplin (1968). As we saw in the previous chapter, the behavioristic paradigm is a network of interlocking strands, including principles of modern learning theory, methodological and logical behaviorism, operationism, and various other themes. Each strand by itself is vulnerable, but when all are laced together the resulting network constitutes a powerful intellectual edifice. A behaviorist confronted with recalcitrant data need not abandon the paradigm; he can simply employ one of many powerful fall-back options. Unless we can eliminate these options, simply citing empirical evidence will not be enough. To see what can be done here, let us review some of the standard replies available to behaviorists – without suggesting, which is unfair and patently false, that all would endorse each and every reply.

Possible replies

1. A behaviorist might appeal to the thesis that all talk about the mental is translatable into talk about behavior and argue, on the basis of this thesis, that the variables studied in cognitive experiments are really behavioral. For example, when experimenters talk about mental imagery, they are really talking about verbal reports; when they talk about beliefs, they are talking about dispositions to behave in certain ways; and so forth.

2. A second line of defense would be to appeal to the thesis that, for methodological reasons, we should not use mentalistic concepts to refer to independent variables. We can explain and describe thoughts and beliefs and the like, but we should not cite them as *causes* of behavior.

3. A third tactic, which might be used in conjuction with the first, is to appeal to the requirement that all theoretical concepts be operationally defined. Whenever translations of mentalistic concepts into behavioral concepts cannot be given, it can be argued that the requirements of operationism have been violated.

Reply. All the preceding claims have been dealt with in the preceding chapter. If the arguments presented there are sound, then the preceding options are no longer available; they have all been ruled out by the arguments against operationism and analytical and metholdological behaviorism.

4. One might treat the utterances of cognitive psychologists as instances of verbal behavior and then try to explain the behavior in terms of reinforcement theory. Thus, behaviorists sometimes treat their own utterances, including statements of their evidence and arguments, in this way. This may be what Skinner has in mind when he speaks of the laws of science as "descriptions of contingencies of reinforcement" (Skinner, 1971a, p. 189). The idea might be to treat scientific laws as verbal reports about the contingencies that reinforce them.

Reply. There are several glaring defects in the preceding defense, and it might be that neither Skinner nor any other behaviorist would resort to it. First, for reasons given in the previous chapter, the theory of meaning that treats verbal reports as being about the contingencies that reinforce them is defective. Second, it begs the question in the present context to assume that Skinnerian learning theory can explain verbal behavior; it is Skinnerian learning theory (along with other behaviorist learning theories) that is at issue. Third, the defense reflects a deep confusion concerning the evidence for a hypothesis and the causal explanation of why someone accepts the hypothesis. Suppose, for example, that the data from a series of verbal learning experiments makes it likely that (H): mental imagery facilitates a certain type of verbal learning. Suppose, further, that because of this data, the experimenter finds it reinforcing to accept H. Pointing this out may explain why he accepts H, but it does nothing to discredit the data. In the case described, the data make it likely that H is true, and that does not cease to be so merely because a certain type of causal explanation can be given of the experimenter's behavior.

5. One might concede that the hypothesis that all human behavior can be explained in terms of behavioristic learning theory has not yet been confirmed and even agree that there is evidence against it but take the line that the counterevidence is not yet conclusive. It is still possible that investigators working within this paradigm may develop a much more complicated learning theory than those now available, one that is able to handle what, for the present, appears to be disconfirming data.

Reply. Because the preceding defense concedes the conclusion for which I have been arguing, there is no need to argue against it here. Someone might argue that the evidence that has accumulated since the publication of Chomsky's review (1959) makes it unlikely that any behavioristic learning theory will prove adequate, and I share this pessimism; but even this is not quite as strong as saying that the behaviorist's hypothesis has been falsified. Finally, even if no such theory is likely to account for all human behavior, it may still be an open question whether it will prove fruitful in certain areas (e.g., see Rachlin & Green, 1972; and the early chapters of Brown & Herrnstein, 1975).

6. Some behavior therapists might defend behavioristic learning theories not because they are true or well confirmed but because they have been useful in suggesting testable clinical hypotheses. Kanfer and Phillips (1970) and Yates (1970) apparently endorse this suggestion. Yates (1970, p. 396) goes so far as to suggest that *no*

theory is true, that theories are merely intended as props from which to derive specific hypotheses, and that a behavior therapist is free to utilize any learning theory he fancies.

Reply. This is not a defense of the truth of any behavioristic learning theory; it is merely a defense of using the theory even if it is false. However, if a given theory is false, it cannot serve as an adequate foundation for behavior therapy in the sense discussed here. It cannot offer a correct explanation of the origin of maladaptive behavior or the workings of behavior therapy techniques. If the theory is not supported by the available empirical evidence, the derivation of a clinical hypothesis from it will not lend any antecedent probability to the hypothesis. Nevertheless, the theory might have heuristic value. By reflecting on it, even if it is false or unconfirmed, we might be led to think of a useful clinical hypothesis that we can then test. If this is what Yates means, we can agree; for heuristic purposes, an investigator might use any theory, whether it be Skinnerian, psychoanalytic, Rogerian, or whatever.

7. Even if there are problems with modern learning theory, it has no serious rival. Until a rival is proposed, we are better off trying to improve existing theory, instead of rejecting it altogether.

Reply. This expresses a widely shared viewpoint. As Kuhn (1962, p. 77) states, "once it has achieved the status of a paradigm, a scientific theory is declared invalid only if an alternate candidate is available to take its place." It might be objected that even if Kuhn's view is correct, the first premise of the preceding argument is false. There may be no single, all-encompassing non-behavioristic theory, but for certain kinds of human behavior, a number of cognitive theories have been proposed. For example, in the area of language acquisition, Chomsky's theory (1965, 1976) provides a serious alternative to Skinner's account. Other cognitive theories are discussed in Neisser (1967), Posner, (1973), and Brown & Herrnstein (1975, Chapter 9). However, we can avoid discussing the merits of these rival theories if it can be shown that Kuhn's view is mistaken. Is it mistaken?

At least one important case from the history of science, that of Newtonian mechanics, appears to lend support to Kuhn's view. For many years the theory was unable to explain certain recalcitrant data, such as the discrepancy between its predictions and the motion of mercury; yet the theory was not rejected until Einstein proposed a rival theory. On the other hand, the case of psychoanalysis appears to be different. Psychoanalysts have often contended that despite its problems, it has had no serious rival in clinical psychology. However, many experimental psychologists rejected psychoanalysis even when they were unwilling to embrace any rival theory. What, then, is the difference between the two cases? The difference is this. Newton's theory was not antecedently implausible, given the extant empirical evidence, and it did explain satisfactorily a wide body of data previously unexplained. This constituted impressive evidence for the theory; for this reason a physicist would have been unreasonable had he rejected Newton's theory in the absence of an equally good explanation of the same data. Whether or not this remained true after the Michelson-Morley experiment may be unclear, but it was probably true until at least the middle of the nineteenth century. In the case of psychoanalysis the theory was never antecedently plausible, and it has not provided a *satisfactory* explanation of a wide range of data in the way that Newton's theory did. We can, then, rationally refuse to accept the theory *if* there is no firm evidence in its favor and some evidence against it. Whether scientists, in fact, adopt this attitude is not crucial; what matters is what they should do, if they are rational, given the available evidence.

Is so-called modern learning theory more like Newton's theory or psychoanalysis? It would be gratuitous to repeat the earlier arguments, but if they are sound, then behavioristic theories of learning are not antecedently plausible as theories of human behavior. There is little or no evidence to support them and much against them, and they fail to provide a satisfactory account of a wide range of human behavior. On these grounds they can be ruled unacceptable now even without an appeal to rival theories.

8. Eysenck (1975) has recently made several points in defense of the theory underlying behavior therapy. First, he concedes that current theory is in a chaotic state, but contends that the same is true of most scientific theories, including those employed in subatomic physics. Second, he argues that the learning theories we do have, though imperfect, have shown considerable usefulness. For example, the bell and blanket method for treating *enuresis nocturna* owes much to well-known conditioning principles. Third, the theories accepted by behavior therapists denote a policy: to rely on laboratory experiments and general laws deriving from them; to deal with facts rather than speculation; and to pay particular attention to the outcome problem. It is the acceptance of this policy that sets behavior therapists off from their predecessors and

guarantees that their underlying theory will never become a dogmatic creed.

Reply. I agree with Eysenck that some behavior therapy techniques have proved useful and have developed out of reflection on conditioning principles. If Eysenck is saying that current learning theories or principles underlie behavior therapy only in this weak sense (i.e., they serve a heuristic purpose in the manner suggested by Yates), then again I agree and I also agree that some behavior therapists do mean nothing more than this. Once more, however, this is compatible with saying that all currently accepted behavioristic theories or principles of learning of sufficient scope to serve as a foundation for behavior therapy are tautologous, false, or unconfirmed by current evidence.

As to the comparison with theories in subatomic physics, there is an important disanalogy to be noticed. Although there have been competing theories in physics, including various "hidden variable" accounts, there is one account, the standard quantum theory, that has a good deal of empirical support. (If that were not true, then the following complaint would apply in physics as well.) The complaint being made here concerning proposed foundations for behavior therapy is not that there are competing formulations but that the nontrivial behavioristic theories and principles lack empirical support.

Finally, it is not clear what is meant by saying that the policy stated by Eysenck is "denoted" by the underlying theories accepted by behavior therapists. Eysenck presumably does not mean that Skinner or Hull's theory, or any similar theory or conditioning principle, *entails* the policy. Someone might consistently accept such theories but reject the policy, or accept the policy but reject the theories. It may be that Eysenck simply means that it is the acceptance of this policy that (partly) guarantees that the study of behavior therapy is and will remain nondogmatic and scientifically respectable; if so, one can agree and yet reject the theories and principles of learning.

Conclusion

Many behavior therapists have contended that at least some behavior therapy techniques are based on modern learning theory or on one or more laws of learning (Wolpe, 1976; Eysenck, 1972; *Task Report 5,* American Psychiatric Association, 1973). Some theorists build this contention into the very definition of *behavior therapy technique* (Franks, 1969; Wolpe, 1976). This widely accepted contention is important for several reasons. First, if it is true and if the respective learning theory or law has been empirically confirmed, then behavior therapy techniques will have a significantly greater than zero initial probability of success. Thus, we will have a criterion for selecting from a potentially infinite set of possible techniques those that are worthy of study: Select those based on the relevant theory or law of learning. Second, if the learning theory or law can explain all or most human behavior, we should be able to use it to explain the origin of maladaptive behavior. Third, we should be able to explain why certain behavior therapy techniques work. It is important to know, for example, that desensitization works for certain types of problems, but it is also important to know why.

The usual candidates for the learning theory best suited to serve as a foundation for behavior therapy are the theories of Skinner and Pavlov. The "laws" of learning most often cited are the law of effect, the law of classical conditioning, and the more modest principles cited by Rachman and Eysenck (1966). What I have argued is that all these theories and "laws" are either unconfirmed by the available empirical evidence, tautologous, or too narrow in scope to play the role envisaged for them by the behavior therapists who appeal to them. It has also been argued, although this is unnecessary insofar as the goal is to demonstrate present inadequacies, that there is a wide body of evidence against these theories and "laws," unless they are rendered tautologous or given narrow scope restrictions, either alternative making them unsuitable for a foundational role. This evidence also runs counter to the hypothesis (Waters & McCallum, 1973) that we can adequately explain human behavior in the most parsimonious fashion by not introducing mentalistic concepts to refer to independent variables. In brief, the widely accepted contention that at least some behavior therapy techniques are based on empirically confirmed behavioristic laws or theories of learning is not supported by the current evidence.

VII. The question of derivation

It is widely held that behavior therapy principles have been derived from learning theory research (Eysenck & Rachman, 1966, p. 167; *Task Report 5*, 1973, p. 2). The question of whether this is so or not loses much of its interest once it is agreed that there is no learning theory or principle that is both suitable to serve a foundational role and possessed of adequate empirical support. Nevertheless, we might take a moment to express some additional skepticism. Is it being claimed that there is some theory or principle of learning from which someone derived one or more statements describing a behavior therapy technique? Who did this? Where in the entire behavior therapy literature does anyone show how even *one* such statement can be derived? Perhaps a weaker claim is intended: that the derivation could be carried out, not that anyone has ever done so. This claim is more plausible (assuming the learning theory or principle is conjoined with one or more auxiliary assumptions), but not if it is intended to apply to all behavior therapy techniques. One of the most widely studied techniques, systematic desensitization, involves the manipulation of a client's imagery. An adequate description of this technique will thus contain an expression referring to mental imagery, but no behavioristic learning theory or principle will contain such an expression, even when supplemented with auxiliary assumptions. If that is so, then the derivation cannot even in principle be carried out. It is a rule of deductive logic that, except for special cases of truth-functional logic that are not relevant here, if a term appears in the conclusion of a valid derivation, it must appear in at least one of the premises. It might be possible to circumvent this objection if, as claimed by Eysenck (1972), talk about mental imagery could be translated into talk about behavior. However, as argued in the last chapter, there is good reason to think that such translations are not possible.

What might be true is that those who developed the behavior therapies did so as a result of reflecting on principles or theories of learning; they thought they saw an analogy between certain conditioning principles and certain clinical principles. The learning principles served a heuristic not a logical function. They did not serve as premises from which therapeutic principles were logically derived; with desensitization, at least, that would have been quite impossible.

VIII. Rejecting the old paradigm

Some behavior therapists are likely to fault the conclusions reached so far, not because they are false but because they are already accepted. In recent years behavior therapists have been quite willing to use mentalistic concepts. Is it not true, then, that the old paradigm, which includes a commitment to some form of behaviorism and theories or principles of learning, has already been rejected? The answer is yes and no.

Some behavior therapists are undoubtedly skeptical of the paradigm we have been discussing. Davison and Neale (1974), for example, argue for a mediational view (p. 510) and suggest (p. 501) that "self-control places a strain on the behavioristic paradigm." Nevertheless, there is evidence that the learning theory paradigm is still accepted by many leading behavior therapists, although many temper their acceptance with reservations of some sort. It is true that behavior therapy has become more cognitive oriented, but that is perceived as being compatible with the existing paradigm. A typical view is the following:

> As we said last year, it is a fallacy to assume that modern behavior therapy is monolithically "behavioristic." The common element is *not* some nebulous and questionable entity called "behaviorism," but an adherence to the principles of operationally defined learning theory and conformity to well established experimental paradigms. . . . One can study inferred events or processes and remain a behaviorist as long as these events or processes have measurable and operational referents; the alternative to "strict behaviorism" (in which *only* observable behavior is studied) does not have to be mentalism. [Franks & Wilson, 1974, p. 7.]

The same point of view is endorsed by Eysensk (1972) and Waters and McCallum (1973). In brief, these writers do not reject the learning theory paradigm; they simply try to fit mentalistic variables into it, usually by appeal to analytical or methodological behaviorism. The same is true of many other behavior therapists. It is common, for example, to say that symbolic activities are assumed to obey the same psychological laws as do overt behaviors (Meichenbaum, 1971b, p. 416) or that mental processes can be explained by a Skinnerian account (Kanfer & Karoly, 1972, p. 412). Others confidently assert that psychological research has overwhelmingly supported behavioral determinism and that it is now reasonably safe to say that behavior is a function of the environment (Mahoney & Thoresen 1974, p. 3).

It is likely that the continued acceptence of a learning theory paradigm has had a pervasive effect on behavior therapy research. O'Leary and Wilson (1975, p. 360), for example, claim that electrical aversion conditioning has continued to be recommended as the optimal method of behavioral treatment of alcoholism, not because of any supporting empirical evidence but because the use of chemically produced aversion has been thought to violate crucial parameters of traditional S-R learning theory. Another example is

Feldman and MacCulloch's (1971) use of an avoidance learning technique and an intermittent schedule in treating homosexual behavior; the justifying assumption, taken from traditional learning theory, is that the use of these methods will minimize extinction of therapeutic gains. O'Leary and Wilson (1975, p. 315) rightly comment that the connection between these methods and resistance to extinction in animal studies appears to be that the animal is unable to discriminate between the reinforcement contingencies operating during acquisition and extinction. In contrast, the patients of Feldman and MacCulloch were aware that they would not be shocked for homosexual behavior after they left the therapist's office. Sometimes the commitment to traditional learning theory promotes rather bizarre suggestions. Fordyce et al. (1973) quote with approval Sternback's (1968) suggestion that pain be conceived of as a set of responses. The authors then report the use of operant conditioning techniques to alter what they call the pain behavior of thirty-six patients suffering from chronic pain. The behavior included taking medication, moaning, gasping, verbalizing the presence of pain, and communicating its presence by gesture or facial expression. A significant reduction in pain behavior did take place, although the authors do not claim to have proved that the changes could be accounted for only by reference to the operant techniques. What is bizarre is the suggestion that appears to have motivated the research: that pain might be nothing more than pain behavior. The authors raise the question whether the change in pain behavior constituted a change in the amount of pain experienced and conclude that the question hinges on whether pain is conceived of as a neurophysiological phenomenon and a set of responses or as the responses themselves (p. 708).

None of the preceding attempts to salvage the existing paradigm is likely to work. There is no reason to think that the mentalistic concepts used by behavior therapists can be given behavioral definitions. Pain, for example, is clearly not pain behavior. In the study by Fordyce et al. (1973), the patients reported experiencing considerable pain even after the modification of their pain behavior. There is no reason to think that the pain would have ceased even if all the pain behavior had been extinguished. Once the appeal to behavioral translations is blocked, it should be clear that the postulation of mental causes is incompatible with behavioristic theories or principles of learning. Calling thoughts and images "internal behaviors" does nothing to change this fact; it simply blurs the distinction behaviorists tried to draw between behavior and mental events. It might be true that the same set of principles will suffice to explain human behavior and thinking and imaging, but as far as we know, these principles do not include the law of effect or other principles of operant and classical conditioning. There is no firm evidence, furthermore, that very much human behavior is controlled by the environment or that it is under stimulus control, unless this is simply a way of saying that it is caused by something or other.

The arguments for the preceding claims have already been given (in the present and previous chapter) and will not be repeated, but if they are cogent, then the continuing appeal to modern learning theory or principles is no longer defensible.

Our results so far have been largely negative, even if sweeping the foundations clean can serve a useful purpose. It is now time to see if something more positive can be said. One thing that needs to be explained is this: If there is no important connection between learning theory and behavior therapy, how could so many behavior therapists make the mistake of thinking otherwise? A second important question is this: If learning theory is not the scientific basis of behavior therapy, then what is?

IX. The relation between learning theory and behavior therapy

We have argued that learning theory cannot now serve as an adequate foundation of behavior therapy. It is doubtful that some of the techniques such as modeling and systematic desensitization, can be logically derived from any learning theory or principle that makes no reference to mentalistic variables. Even if the derivation were possible, none of these theories or principles have been empirically confirmed, and all run counter to much of the current evidence. To say this, however, is not to imply that there is no important connection between learning theory and behavior therapy. There are, in fact, several; it is likely that some behavior therapists are thinking of one or more of the following connections when they speak of a learning theory foundation.

Historical connections

As many writers have emphasized (e.g., Rachman & Teasdale, 1969), there are important historical connections between the development of behavior therapy and developments in learning theory research. Most of the original behavior therapists were heavily influenced by the work of Watson, Pavlov, Thorndike, Hull, and Skinner. Even if their learning theories are inadequate, it seems unlikely that behavior therapy techniques would have been developed and studied as they were in the past twenty-five years if no such learning theory had been available. Furthermore, concrete experimental findings of learning theorists were utilized in behavior therapy research. One example is the work on the effects of different types of schedules of reinforcement (Ferster & Skinner, 1957); a second is Solomon's work (1964) on avoidance conditioning; a third is experimental work on the effects of punishment (Azrin & Holz, 1966).

Methodological and Philosophical Connections

As Eysenck (1972) and Krasner (1971a) note, many behavior therapists have been influenced by analytical or methodological behaviorism, both of which developed out of the learning theory tradition. There are also more concrete methodological contributions made by learning theorists; for example, many behavior therapists who emphasize single-subject designs do so because of the influence of that type of design in operant research. Other methodological features of behavior therapy research, such as the emphasis on base rates, the use of controlled observation, and so on, were also emphasized in learning theory research, although they were prominent as well in other areas of experimental psychology.

Conceptual connections

A third important connection is conceptual. Many of the key concepts used in behavior therapy research, such as *shaping, reinforcement, operant,* and *reinforcement schedule,* were borrowed from learning theory research, although in some cases the terms are the same but the concepts different. For example, it is doubtful that in the phrase *operants of the mind* (Homme, 1965), *operants* means what it does in operant conditioning studies. In any event, there is a danger in uncritically extending the use of such terminology. For example, speaking of cognitions as "behaviors" (Ullmann, 1970, p. 202) helps to foster the illusion that we are "incorporating" cognitive phenomena into the behavioristic model (Kanfer, 1970). This is only an illusion: If *behavior* is used in the sense behaviorists have traditionally used it (i.e., to draw a contrast between behavior and the mind), then talk about cognitions is not translatable into talk about behavior. If the term is being used in a new sense to cover mental phenomena, then this signals the abandonment of the behavioristic model. Another example is the use of the phrase *internal sentence* in cognitive restructuring studies to refer to a client's irrational beliefs (Goldfried & Goldfried, 1975, p. 99). The practice may be harmless, but it can encourage the idea that we have made some progress in analyzing or avoiding the concept of a belief. Neither is true. A client may have many beliefs that he has never expressed in the form of a sentence. For example, he may believe that he should be loved by virtually everyone he encounters, yet he may never have said that to anyone, not even himself. In fact, on one plausible view of belief, most of us have an infinite number of beliefs we have never articulated. For example, most of us believe that $10<33,000$, that $10<33,001$, that $10<33,002$, and so on. It might be suggested that the idea of an internal sentence is intended not as an analysis of but as a replacement for the idea of a belief. It is difficult, however, to see any gain in clarity in attributing to a client internal sentences that he has never articulated, not even internally. Perhaps he has done so unconsciously, but the idea of an unconscious internal sentence is at least as puzzling as that of belief.

We need not suggest that behavior therapy research be purged of all learning theory and behavioristic terminology, but the preceding examples clearly suggest a need for at least some modest linguistic reforms.

Heuristic connections

There are important heuristic connections between behavior therapy and learning theory (or, more broadly, learning theory research); and these are of more than historical interest. By reflecting on learning principles and experiments, behavior therapists are often led to new avenues of research and to new therapeutic techniques. Sometimes these new ideas prove fruitful, sometimes they do not. Eysenck and Beech (1971, p. 597) cite the following as an apparent success. The occurrence of spontaneous recovery of extinguished responses suggested to Rachman (1966) that extinguished anxiety responses should build up again; his demonstration that this did in fact happen is thought to be an important new contribution to the practice and theory of behavior therapy. We earlier cited some apparent failures, such as the persistent use of electrical aversive conditioning in the treatment of alcoholism, even after that practice was not justified by the available evidence. Whether or not the successes outnumber the failures is hard to tell, especially because reports of the latter are rarely published.

In allowing that there has been an important heuristic connection between learning theory and behavior therapy, we are not backsliding on our earlier insistence that the former is not an adequate foundation for the latter. Bohr's theory of the atom may well have been suggested to him by reflection on the movements of the planets, but the theory cannot be deduced from a statement describing planetary motion, nor can the latter serve to explain atomic phenomena. A theory or principle, furthermore, need not be true or well confirmed to serve a heuristic function. There need not even be any relevant theoretical analogy involved; it is sufficient that the scientist thinks he perceives such an analogy. Almost any theory, then, can serve a heuristic purpose. Psychoanalytic theory or principles of gestalt psychology could have served this function for behavior therapists; the fact that learning theory was selected for this role is partially explainable in terms of the background and theoretical allegiances of most leading behavior therapists. It is unlikely, however, that this tells the whole story. Even if the heuristic hunches have often failed, they have been right enough times to require an additional explanation. If the theories and principles of learning are inadequate in the ways we have charged, how is it that at least some of them have proved to be useful heuristically, as, for example, in suggesting the development of systematic desensitization and token economy programs? Behavior therapists could have looked to psychoanalytic theory for inspiration, but is it likely that they would have had the same success? Probably not. How do we explain this fact? Unfortunately, answering that question in any detailed way is likely to involve us in explaining why behavior therapy techniques work, when they work; that kind of commitment is best avoided, given the present state of the subject. What follows is only a conjecture, and a sketchy one at that.

Consider a principle cited by Rachman and Teasdale (1969, p. 6): "Response contingent aversive stimulation will produce suppression of deviant behavior, but non-contingent stimulation will fail to do so." This principle is false. Quite often, response-contingent aversive stimulation fails to suppress deviant behavior, or does so only for a brief period, as has proved to be the case in aversive treatments of smoking (Hunt & Matarazzo, 1973). Non-contingent aversive stimulation, on the other hand, can be quite effective. For example, an adult may never repeat a certain response if it is followed by a delayed but severe punishment *and* a credible warning that a repetition will cause a similar punishment. Despite the falsity of the principle cited by Rachman and Teasdale, a behavior therapy technique suggested by it might be effective where the operation of cognitive variables is at a minimum, as, for example, in the case of the autistic children treated by Lovaas and his associates (Bucher & Lovaas, 1969). Consider another example. The contingent presentation of a reward will often fail to increase the frequency of a response in a normal adult human who, for example, believes that the reward will not be forthcoming again or who values indolence more than the reward. Nevertheless, a systematic and contingent reward system, of the kind used in token economy systems, might work well with brain-damaged children or with adult schizophrenics (although in both cases, biological variables may set important constraints). Even with relatively normal adults, cognitive, motivational, and biological variables may not be very important in certain areas. A client with a snake phobia may be acquainted with evidence that many snakes are relatively harmless and yet be unmoved. In such a case, the association of the phobic object with a neutral or pleasant state may, under typical conditions of systematic desensitization, be therapeutically useful. This is not to suggest that association is, in fact, the key mechanism in desensitization; what the mechanism is, is still an open question (Davison & Wilson, 1973). The point, rather, is that there is no incompatibility between the following claims: (1) The extension of learning principles to all human behavior is not justified by the current empirical evidence; and (2) techniques suggested by reflection on these principles may well be effective where motivational, cognitive, and biological variables are not important. In brief, where maladaptive behavior in humans is maintained by variables analogous to those that explain the behavior of rats and pigeons, it is not surprising that techniques suggested by principles of animal learning are often effective, even though the principles are not generally true of human behavior.

X. The scientific basis of behavior therapy

If learning theories and principles do not constitute an adequate foundation for behavior therapy, then what does? The position taken here is that there is no known theory or law of any kind that is of sufficient scope to serve as a foundation and that has also been empirically confirmed. We cannot even be certain that such a theory or law will ever be developed. Some philosophers and psychologists are likely to resist such skepticism: Human behavior, it is thought, must have a cause; if it does, we should in principle be able to formulate causal laws and, eventually, a general theory that unifies these laws. How could it conceivably be otherwise? Well, it just might happen that, try as we may, we will never be able to formulate relatively simple general laws of human behavior. Human behavior might just prove to be too complex. Whether we are able, even in principle, to succeed in the quest for an adequate theoretical foundation for behavior therapy is an open empirical question; it cannot be answered solely by philosophic reflection.

If behavior therapy has no adequate underlying theory, should it be viewed simply as a technology, as London (1972) suggests, or does it have a scientific foundation of a different sort? Behavior therapy is not merely a technology; its claim to scientific respectability is supported by several factors:

First, there is the empirical evidence that has been gathered in support of specific therapeutic claims. Much of this evidence is still rudimentary, but, as outlined in Chapter 1, there is some fairly firm evidence supporting the effectiveness of certain techniques, such as modeling and systematic desensitization, when used to treat certain kinds of problems.

Second, insofar as behavior therapists confirm the efficacy of certain techniques, they are confirming causal claims and thereby offering explanations of behavioral change. If we have evidence, for example, that the use of systematic desensitization has helped to eliminate certain phobic responses, then we can explain these behavioral changes by talking about the therapy. It is not true, then, that behavior therapy is simply a technology; behavior therapists have tried, with some success, to explain behavioral changes. Furthermore, efforts are being made to find out exactly which ingredients in specific therapeutic packages, such as desensitization, explain their therapeutic effectiveness and why (Lick & Bootzin, 1975; Davison & Wilson, 1972, 1973; Emmelkamp & Walta, 1978). Efforts are also being made to explain why maladaptive behavior patterns persist; why performance gains often fail to generalize; and why behavior therapy works better with some clients than others (Stunkard & Mahoney, 1976; Jones & Kazdin, 1975; Bandura, 1977).

Third, behavior therapy practice and research is guided partly by specific experimental findings; some examples cited earlier were the findings on punishment (Azrin & Holz, 1966) and on avoidance conditioning (Solomon, 1964). These findings serve more than a heuristic function; they sometimes make it antecedently plausible to think that certain strategies will succeed and others fail. For example, the work of Bandura and others (Bandura, 1965; Bandura & Walters, 1963) on observational learning served such an evidential function for modeling.

A fourth significant factor is the methodology of behavior therapy: Sophisticated experimental and statistical techniques are employed both in the practice and study of behavior therapy. The use of such techniques is not unique to behavior therapy; they have sometimes been used, for example, by psychoanalysts (Kline, 1972). Behavior therapists, however, have tended to place greater emphasis on such techniques than therapists of other persuasions; this lends support to the idea that behavior therapy is, in at least one important respect, scientifically respectable.

Fifth, although a good part of the commonly accepted theoretical underpinnings has been borrowed from the learning theory literature, some behavior therapists are developing and testing their own theories that are specifically designed to explain clinical phenomena. An interesting example is the cognitive theory recently proposed by Bandura (1977). The theory distinguishes between two types of expectancy: *outcome* and *self-efficacy* expectancies. The former refers to the belief that a given behavior will lead to certain outcomes; the latter, to the conviction that one can successfully execute the behavior required to produce the outcomes. Sometimes a client lacks either the required skill or the necessary incentives for behaving in a certain sort of way, but given the appropriate skills and incentives, Bandura's theory hypothesizes that psychological treatment procedures work through altering the client's self-efficacy expectations. These expectations are derived primarily from four sources of information: performance accomplishments, vicarious experience, verbal persuasion, and physiological states. The more dependable the sources, the greater are the changes in perceived self-efficacy. An increase in perceived self-efficacy will affect both initiation and persistence of coping behavior. At the initial level, perceived self-efficacy helps determine whether people become involved in situations that would otherwise be intimidating. Once the coping efforts are initiated, efficacy expectations determine how much effort people will expend and how long they will persist in the face of aversive experiences. Those who persist in activities thought to be threatening, but which are relatively safe, will gain corrective experiences that reinforce their sense of efficacy, thereby eventually eliminating their defensive behavior.

Although the theory needs to be rigorously tested, Bandura has tried to show how it can account for a wide range of experimental findings. In particular, it purports to explain the mechanisms of modeling and systematic desensitization; it accounts for behavioral variations in people receiving the same kind of treatment; and it predicts performance successes at the level of individual tasks during and after treatment. How well the theory will stand up under further testing cannot be judged now, but preliminary reports are encouraging (Bandura & Adams, 1977; Bandura, Adams, & Beyer, 1977).

4. Competing models of behavior disorder

Some basic issues

Is homosexuality an illness? Alcoholism? Schizophrenia? How do we tell? Is anything a mental illness or is the idea of a *mental illness* a conceptual absurdity?

We concluded in the last chapter that behavior therapy presently has no adequate underlying theory but argued that we should look for one employing at least some cognitive concepts; a purely behavioristic foundation is not likely to suffice. Someone who accepts our cognitivist viewpoint, however, encounters at least two problems not facing the behaviorists.

The first is to explain the nature of behavior therapy without appealing to behavioristic theories or principles of learning. How can we do that if no current cognitivist theory is adequate? The solution we proposed in Chapter 1 was to give a relatively theory-neutral account: Behavior therapy is a psychological, non-medical treatment that developed largely out of learning theory research and that is normally applied directly, incrementally, and experimentally in the treatment of specific maladaptive behavior patterns. The acceptance of this account leads to a second problem. If behavior therapy is a psychological rather than a medical procedure, and assuming its usefulness in treating a wide range of behavior disorders, then it seems plausible to question the utility of the traditional medical model. On this model, behavior disorders are conceptualized as *mental illnesses*. It is appropriate, then, to classify clients as *patients* who display *symptoms* caused by an underlying *illness*. The illness needs to be *diagnosed, treated,* and *cured*; and the appropriate remedy is a *medical* treatment. In short, if behavior disorders are mental illnesses that are analogous in relevant respects to physical illnesses, then it seems appropriate to conceptualize clinical phenomena by using concepts borrowed from physical medicine.

Almost all behavior therapists who have discussed the subject have expressed reservations about the medical model and the con-

131

ceptual scheme associated with it (Bandura, 1969; O'Leary & Wilson, 1975; Rimm & Masters, 1974; Ullmann & Krasner, 1969, 1975). (The medical model is also rejected by some psychiatrists, including some who are not behavior therapists, [e.g., Szasz, 1961].)

The belief that this model is inadequate has become a foundational assumption for many behavior therapists, which is not surprising given the nature of their techniques, and is sometimes even cited as a defining characteristic of behavior therapy (e.g., Brown & Herrnstein, 1975, p. 602). The second problem, then, confronting the cognitivist is to justify this assumption without appeal to philosophical behaviorism or any behavioristic learning principle (or, failing this, to show how to reconcile behavior therapy and the medical model). The behaviorist does not have this problem; he is free to use analytical or methodological behaviorism or principles of classical or operant conditioning to justify his rejection of the medical model. The most developed version of this behavioristic approach is due to Ullmann and Krasner (1969, 1975). First, they provide trenchant criticisms of current definitions of the concept *mental illness* and then argue (p. 22) that no behavior is sick or abnormal in itself, that all behavior is learned and maintained in accordance with general laws of learning. As a replacement for the concept *mental illness,* they recommend a behavioristic substitute, the idea of *deviant behavior.* Finally, they take specific diagnostic categories and reformulate them in behavioral terms. A good example is their treatment of schizophrenic behavior. They view it as learned behavior that is maintained by environmental stimuli. On their theory, the schizophrenic is labeled "sick" because he exhibits behavior patterns that others consider "bizarre." The explanation of these "bizarre" behavior patterns is that the schizophrenic fails to pay attention to learning cues attended to by nonschizophrenics. On the surface this formulation seems nonbehavioristic because it employs the concept *paying attention*; it is contended, however, that the concept can be defined in behavioral terms (Ullmann & Krasner, 1969, p. 382).

A cognitivist cannot rely on the preceding sort of strategy or on any arguments presupposing behaviorist doctrines. Some of the standard arguments he can consistently employ have an a priori character; they are designed to show that the very idea of a "mental illness" is logically incoherent and, consequently, that the concept applies to nothing. Other arguments appeal to empirical data and purport to prove that most behavior disorders, but not necessarily all, are not illnesses. To keep these two different sorts of arguments separate, it is useful to distinguish between a weak and strong version of the medical model. In Secion I we will use the term *minimum medical model* to mean that at least *some* behavior disorders are mental illnesses; in Section II the term *robust medical model* will denote the assumption that *most* are. In Section III we will consider some related issures. Two further terminological stipulations will be adhered to. First, we will follow the practice of those writers who use the terms *mental disease* and *mental illness* interchangeably, even though in ordinary speech these terms might not be synonymous (on this point, see Boorse, 1975). Second, we need some neutral term to denote conditions treated by psychiatrists, behavior therapists, and other mental health workers. We will use the terms *behavior disorder* and *psychiatric problem* for this purpose without implying that such conditions are medical or that they are psychological.

I. A minimum medical model

The routing slip theory

Should anyone at all be labeled *mentally ill*? Ellis (1967) has argued, with some reservations, for an affirmative answer; Sarbin (1967) has replied that the term *mental illness* should be deleted from our vocabulary. How do we decide this issue? One view is that labeling or classifying is a social act that ought to be judged by its social consequences. Brown & Herrnstein (1975) develop this view in some detail and apply it specifically to the use of the label *mental illness*. On their account, classification is not a way of discovering the way things really are, but is a "human social process" that ought to be carried out with some purpose in mind and judged accordingly (Brown & Herrnstein, 1975, p. 683). The main purpose of categorizing types of deviant behavior is to provide a "routing slip" that directs society to treat a person in a certain sort of way. The only criterion in deciding whether use of the routing tag *mental illness* is justified is this: Do the signs, symptoms, and evidence that lead to that classification route the person into institutions that are optimally effective for restoring him to full citizenship? Using this criterion, it is right to label schizophrenia a *mental illness* and not, for example, a *crime* if persons showing the symptoms of schizophrenia respond well to therapy and not to imprisonment; the use of the category *criminal* is justified, in contrast, if imprisonment and punishment modfy or deter criminal behavior (except that society might protect itself by detaining some deviants even if they cannot be helped). On the basis of the preceding considerations, Brown & Herrnstein conclude that it is probably reasonable to classify schizophrenics as *mentally ill* rather than to use some other category of deviant behavior, such as *criminal*; but they concede that the issue is not entirely closed.

There is something illuminating in the preceding account, but it is not satisfactory as it stands. It is not generally true that labeling is *merely* a social process if this entails that no question of truth or falsity can arise. On the contrary, it is generally either true or false that a concept applies to a certain item (borderline cases might be an exception to the rule). Someone either has cancer or does not, is schizophrenic or not. There are, of course, cases in which it is extremely difficult to tell whether a concept applies, either because of lack of empirical information or lack of conceptual clarity. Both kinds of difficulties are prominent in cases of alleged mental illness, the second problem being the more troublesome. It is difficult to tell whether or not the analogies between mental and physical illnesses are sufficiently important to call both kinds of disorders *illnesses*. Nevertheless, we should not decide prematurely that there is no way to resolve the issue. There are also important analogies and disanalogies between different kinds of physical illnesses, such as pneumonia and hypertension, but we might still be able to decide rationally that they are illnesses; that might also be true of some so-called mental illnesses. We need, then, to distinguish two questions that tend to be collapsed together when we talk of labeling people as being *mentally ill:* (1) Is anyone mentally ill? (2) Is it useful to employ the concept *mental illness?* The answer to question 1 might be yes and to question 2 no, or conversely.

The routing tag theory is designed to answer question 2 only; when used for that purpose, it is instructive but incomplete. If by tagging some people as *mentally ill* we can help route them to the proper institution for treatment, then there is some utility in using the concept. However, we also have to weigh the disutilities. These include the fact that someone so classified may: (1) suffer from unjust discrimination when seeking a job; (2) be unjustly incarcerated against his will; (3) incorrectly excuse himself from taking responsibility for his actions; and (4) incorrectly conclude that his condition is beyond treatment. Counterbalanced against these disutilities are certain additional utilities. For example, the concept *mental illness* does have at least a minimal amount of explanatory value *if* some people are mentally ill. For example, if someone is acting in an extremely hostile or irrational manner, we might be able to explain why by noting that the person is mentally ill. If he is not criminally liable for what appears to be criminal behavior, that too might be partially explained in the same way. Furthermore, sometimes people who are classified as *mentally ill* receive certain benefits that would otherwise be denied them – their bizarre behavior is looked on with sympathy and compassion instead of being castigated as "evil" or "eccentric"; they are protected from doing harm to themselves or others; and they can learn to be more tolerant of their own problems. No doubt these results are not always beneficial, but sometimes they are. On balance, do the long-run utilities outweigh the disutilities? It is exceedingly difficult to answer this question, especially because some of the alleged utilities and disutilities might well remain regardless of whether or not we use the concept *mental illness*. For example, if some political dissidents are now incorrectly classified as *mentally ill* and then placed in mental hospitals, the incarceration might well continue even if the concept were not used; the political authorities might simply substitute some other term such as *emotionally disordered* or *inherently dangerous* to justify their practice. Given these uncertainties, it is difficult to establish that a net gain in utility would result from eliminating talk of mental illness; writers who confidently assert that this result would ensue provide no firm evidence for their view. It is doubtful that anyone has such evidence. For the present at least, the weighing of long-run utilities and disutilites is bound to be based on empirical conjecture. If the preceding comments are correct, there will probably be justification for at least a limited use of the concept *mental illness* if (but not only if) three conditions are met: (1) the person so labeled *is* mentally ill; (2) there is some obvious and immediate net gain in utility in saying so; and (3) the long-run utilities and disutilities appear to cancel each other out. We turn now to our other question: *Is* anyone mentally ill?

The myth of mental illness

Some of the key arguments against even a minimum medical model are due to Thomas Szasz (1961, 1974), a psychiatrist who contends that mental illness is a myth, and whose work has been influential in the behavior therapy movement. Whether or not Szasz's basic contention is correct, he deserves credit for raising fundamental questions about the concept of *mental illness* and about related issues, such as the forced incarceration of the mentally ill and the relations between psychiatry and the law. Additional arguments against the existence of mental illness can be found in Albee (1969), Sarbin (1967), Laing (1971), and Scheff (1963). The arguments for the nonexistence of mental illness are a heterogeneous lot. Some contain blatant logical flaws, but others raise important issues and are not so easily disposed of. The following arguments against the existence of mental illness are probably the most important, judged either by their cogency or their repetition in the literature.

One fallacious argument is the following: "Let us launch our inquiry by asking, somewhat rhetorically, whether there is such a thing as mental illness. My reply is that there is not. Of course, mental illness is not a thing or physical object. It can exist only in the same sort of way as do other theoretical concepts" (Szasz, 1961, p. 11). The mistake here is to confuse what is denoted by a name or concept with the name or concept itself. It would be an obvious mistake, for example, to confuse the concept of an electron with an electron; the concept is used to talk about electrons and is not itself an electron. It would be a more subtle mistake to identify a nonphysical thing with its corresponding concept, but a mistake nonetheless. The concepts *the largest natural number* and *the smallest prime greater than 5* both fail to denote anything physical, but neither concept can be identified with its denotation. The former denotes nothing. There is no largest natural number; the latter denotes the number 7. To infer, then, from the assumption that mental illness is not a physical object, that it can exist only in the way that other theoretical concepts exist, is to assume that *it*–that is mental illness–is a concept. The concept *mental illness* is used to talk about mental illness, which is not itself a concept, any more than physical illness is.

It does seem odd to say that mental illness exists, but the oddity remains if we say that physical illness exists. In each case what is usually meant is that at least one person is physically ill or is mentally ill.

A second argument against mental illness can be put in the form of a dilemma: If so-called mental illness is a disease of the brain with a physical cause and physical symptoms, then it is simply a physical disease; and if it is characterized by mental symptoms, such as a belief in communism or a belief that one's organs are rotting, then it cannot be explained by a defect or disease of the central nervous system (Szasz, 1961, p. 12). Szasz does not use the preceding dilemma to show that mental illness does not exist, but rather to demonstrate the conditional: If mental illness is taken to be a sign of brain disease, then it does not exist. Even given this more limited purpose, the argument lacks cogency. Not all psychoses involve deviant beliefs as symptoms, but for those that do, it is the irrationality of the belief, not the belief itself, that constitutes the symptom. Even if a brain lesion does not explain why someone holds any particular belief, it might explain why he generally holds irrational beliefs. At least, we cannot rule out this possibility a priori, any more than we could have ruled out a priori a neurological explanation of why the ingestion of LSD sometimes causes people to entertain irrational beliefs. The preceding dilemma fails, then, in the absence of empirical evidence for the assumption that if a symptom is mental, it cannot be caused by a defect of the central nervous system.

Some writers have pointed out that the same type of behavior may be accepted as normal in one society and diagnosed as paranoid or schizophrenic in another. This is cited as evidence that what is abnormal or pathological is relativistic (Bandura, 1969, p. 62.; Ullmann & Krasner, 1969, p. 12). If that is true, and if physical illness is not relativistic in the same way, then this would appear to be an important difference between physical and mental illness. It might then be argued that this difference is sufficiently important to disqualify so-called mental illness from being an illness.

To evaluate the preceding argument, let us define *relativistic* such that something is relativistic if and only if its existence is *logically* dependent on the beliefs or attitudes of a group of people. Suppose, then, that someone suffers from paranoia and lives in a society where paranoid behavior is common. His behavior may not be diagnosed as paranoid but by hypothesis it is; whether it is or not depends on what the behavior is (and possibly on its cause), not on what people believe about it. If someone, on the other hand, is not paranoid and is not ill at all, but is surrounded by paranoids, he may appear to them to be sick; but, by hypothesis, he is not – their belief is false. Analogously, suppose a logician is surrounded by the logically illiterate; his arguments may be considered invalid even when they are logically perfect. This hardly shows that the notion of validity is relativistic. What is illogical to the incompetent and what is pathological to the insane may, in fact, be neither. We may not be able to convince such people that their behavior and not ours is defective; but this is not surprising if they are illogical or insane. The obvious moral is that the notion of abnormal or pathological behavior is not relativistic merely because what is considered to be abnormal or pathological can vary from culture to culture.

Someone may choose to use *relativistic* in a sense different from ours, but then it has to be shown that physical and mental illness differ in this new sense. For example, suppose we stipulate that something is relativistic if the way it is *classified* can vary from culture to culture. On this definition, paranoid behavior is relativisitic if it is classified differently in different cultures. It is also true that some physical illnesses are relativisitic if they too are classified as illnesses in some cultures but not others. Malaria might be such an example; hypertension might be another.

Although none of the preceding arguments is cogent, we have yet to examine what some consider the most important argument against mental illness, to be referred to here as the *values argument*. The key idea is that *mental illness* but not *physical illness* is an evaluative or value-laden concept in that its use entails value judgments. As a rough-and-ready test of what counts as a value judgment, let us include only those that contain an evaluative term such as *good, bad, permissible, ought, just, unjust, evil, right, wrong,* or *reprehensible*. The idea, then, is that in saying that someone is mentally ill we always imply a value judgment, and we do not do that when we say that someone is physically ill.

One influential version of the values argument is due to Szasz (1961, p. 14), and can be reconstructed as follows:

1 The use of the concept *illness* implies a deviation from a clearly defined norm.
2 In the case of physical illness the norm is definable in physiological and anatomical terms.
3 In the case of mental illness the norm is definable in evaluative terms (e.g., moral or political terms).
4 If premises 1, 2, and 3 are true, then no mental disorder is an illness in the same sense that certain physical disorders are.
5 If premise 4 is true, there are no mental illnesses.
6 Consequently, there are no mental illnesses.

The term *illnesses* in both premise 5 and the conclusion is used in the sense in which, say, cancer or pneumonia, are illnesses. Szasz agrees that we can also use *illness* in a metaphorical sense and thus label some people's problems as *mental illnesses,* but we should recognize that the use of this metaphor can be harmful. For example, when we describe someone with bizarre beliefs as being mentally ill, we disguise that fact that we are making a moral instead of a medical judgment. Consequently, people are misled into seeking medical remedies for moral problems, and this causes a great deal of confusion and unhappiness. It would be better, Szasz suggests, to eliminate the mental illness metaphor from our discourse and to replace it by a more apt phrase, such as *problems in living.*

The reasoning of Szasz's argument is valid; to avoid its conclusion, we must reject at least one of the premises. Which one? Premise 3 is probably the weakest link. It is true only if any judgment that someone is mentally ill entails a value judgment. Is this true? Consider the proposition: "X is mentally ill." What value judgment does it entail? One possibility is that it entails: "X ought to be treated." It is not obvious, however, that there would be any contradiction in asserting and denying it; but if there is no contradiction there is no entailment relation. It does seem plausible to say that if someone is seriously ill, whether mentally or physically, then, other things being equal, he ought to be treated if he wants to be; but that is also true of someone who is not ill, but who has, say, a broken leg. In both cases we can explain in the same way the tendency to infer that the victim ought to be treated. We tacitly presuppose some such moral principle as: Other things being equal, we ought to treat someone if doing so will reduce suffering or mitigate future harm. It is the moral principle and the assumption that someone with a serious illness or a broken leg is suffering (or will suffer) that together license the inference that he ought to be treated. What else is explained by saying that the judgment that someone is mentally ill – or, for that matter, that he has a broken leg – by itself entails a value judgment? It might be replied that what is explained is the rationale for categorizing certain states as illnesses: We do so because we believe that the condition ought to be treated. Consider, for example, the sort of case discussed by Glover (1970). Suppose we found for a certain class of people that the ability to do higher mathematics was caused by the presence of an extra chromosome or a brain lesion, and suppose that the cause did not produce any untoward effect. Would we classify these people as *sick*? Probably not. Why? Is it not because in our society we value the ability to do higher mathematics, whereas we do not value the behavior typically associated with, for example, mental retardation?

It is not true, then, that in general we designate a behavior as pathological simply because of some underlying organic defect. In many cases of so-called sick behavior the cause is unknown; and even if the cause were known to be organic, that alone would not sustain the judgment *sick*. Is it not also required that the behavior or trait be undesirable? Does not this strongly suggest that the concept *illness* is applied partly on the basis of evaluative criteria?

The preceding argument is somewhat compelling because it is hard to explain why certain conditions count as illnesses and others do not. However, we shall later offer an explanation that does not assume that ascriptions of the term *illness* entail value judgments. If that explanation is at least as adequate as its rivals, then the case of organically caused mathematical ability is not evidence that *illness* is an evaluative concept.

The main reason for being skeptical about treating *illness* as an evaluative notion is that no matter what value judgment we cite it will not be obvious that denying it and affirming that someone is ill, be it mentally or physically, constitutes a contradiction. Suppose that two psychiatrists examine a patient who displays symptoms of schizophrenia. For example, the patient tends to hallucinate; he claims to hear voices from outer space and to see objects not in his field of vision. He also suffers from gross delusions. He reports sometimes that he is Jesus Christ and sometimes that he is Napoleon. On the basis of these symptoms the psychiatrists agree that the patient is schizophrenic. Need these doctors have relied on any evaluative criterion to justify their diagnosis? No. They might avoid all value judgments and yet determine that the patient hallucinates and suffers from delusions and that the best explanation of these facts is that he is schizophrenic. It is implausible, then, to say that the judgment that someone is schizophrenic entails or presupposes some value judgment. What about the judgment that the patient is mentally ill? Need the psychiatrists render a value judgment to reach this conclusion? It does not seem so.

Suppose one psychiatrist accepts and the other rejects the view of R. D. Laing (1971) that it is a useful experience to be schizophrenic and that schizophrenia should be allowed to "run its course." They could both agree that the patient is mentally ill (even though Laing might not say this because of his views about etiology). Yet they could disagree about any and all value judgments that might be made about the patient or his symptoms. One psychiatrist might think that the patient should not be treated, that it is useful for him to be schizophrenic, that it is good that he has these false beliefs, and so on; the second psychiatrist might disagree with all these judgments. What value judgment, then, would these two psychiatrists be making when they agree that the patient is mentally ill? There is no relevant value judgment here that both share. It might be replied that one psychiatrist is contradicting himself; if he agrees that the patient is mentally ill, then to be consistent he must agree that the patient's condition is undesirable. But this is not obviously true. A paranoid who believes, contrary to all the available evidence, that his relatives are trying to poison him may be quite lucky to be paranoid if his belief is true. A schizophrenic who, for some reason, could not possibly get out of a schizophrenic ward even if he were cured might be better able to adapt to his environment with his illness than without it. It is surely not obvious that in describing such cases one would be uttering a contradiction in saying: These patients are mentally ill, but given their living conditions that is not a bad thing.

What might also seem to support the idea that ascriptions of *mental illness* entail value judgments is that the concept is often misused. People are often said to be mentally ill when what is meant is that their behavior or beliefs are odd, eccentric, or morally or politically undesirable. For example, it has been alleged that the poet Ezra Pound was said to be mentally ill merely because of his fascist political pronouncements. If this is true, why not simply say that a mistake was made? Those who said that Pound was sick did not say what they meant. They meant he was a fascist; they said he was sick. These people were misusing the concept *mental illness*. Szasz is quite right to object to such misuses, but these cases are not evidence that the concept, when properly used, must entail or presuppose a value judgment.

If it could be shown that ascriptions of *mental illness* entail value judgments, that would probably create a difficulty for premise 2. It would raise doubts about the possibility of defining *physical illness* without using evaluative terms. Szasz does not see this difficulty because he thinks he has already found a satisfactory value-free definition of *physical illness:* Someone is physically ill if and only if his condition deviates from a norm and the norm is the structural and functional integrity of the human body (Szasz, 1961, p. 14). If this definition were satisfactory, a defender of the minimum medical model could give the same kind of definition, but simply substitute the words *structural and functional integrity of the human mind*. Neither definition is satisfactory, however, without some independent clarification of *structural and functional integrity*.

The difficulty, then, facing a defender of the values argument is that he must defend premise 3 without simultaneously undermining premise 2. That is, he must show that ascriptions of *mental illness* entail value judgments and yet not give us reason to think that ascriptions of the term *physical illness* do the same. We need not decide in the end between the following two views of ascriptions of the term *illness*. On the first view, such judgments *by themselves* entail value judgments. On the second view, that is not true; what licenses the inference to an evaluative conclusion is the judgment that someone is ill *plus* some tacit evaluative assumption. We have favored the second view, but it is difficult to find a decisive test for choosing between these two views. Fortunately, that is not necessary. In evaluating the values argument, it is sufficient to point out that on either view the argument fails. On the first view, premise 2 is false and on the second view, premise 3 is false.

We can conclude that none of the preceding arguments demonstrates that "mental illness is myth" if this means that mental illness does not exist. It is now time to see whether something more positive can be said. Is there any hard evidence that mental illness does exist? Let us begin by distinguishing two questions often conflated in the literature:

1 Does *mental* illness exist?
2 Does mental *illness* exist?

A negative answer to either question would be sufficient to show that mental illness does not exist, but the grounds in each case are likely to be different; that is some reason for treating the preceding sentences as expressing different questions when the stress is different. We shall begin with the first question.

Does mental *illness exist?*

Suppose that schizophrenia and paranoia (in its extreme form) qualify as illnesses. On that supposition, it is likely that there are *mental* illnesses, because they are characterized primarily by the occurrence of mentalistic symptoms, such as disordered cognitions, hallucinatory experiences, and irrational beliefs. To avoid misunderstanding, it may be useful to point out what is *not* presupposed here:

As Kraepelin pointed out a long time ago (1902), it is not clear that talk of "diseased minds" makes any sense, except when interpreted metaphorically; but we need not speak this way. To say that there are mental illnesses is not to imply that there are, literally, diseased minds. It is sufficient that there be illnesses characterized by mental symptoms in the sense discussed above.

To assert that there are mental illnesses is not to imply dualism. The dualist will treat the peculiar mental states of a schizophrenic as being nonphysical, but an identity theorist will take them to be identical with states of the brain or the central nervous system. The choice between these two viewpoints cannot be made merely by pointing out that there are mental illnesses.

Do *mental* illnesses *exist?*

Even if schizophrenia qualifies as a mental disorder, is it an *illness?* We might find it easy to answer that question if we could formulate an adequate definition of *illness,* but that is not easy if we require of a definition that it state necessary and sufficient conditions for applying the concept. The absence of an adequate definition, however, does not mean that our question is unanswerable. In Chapter 1 we were unable to define the term *behavior therapy,* but we were still able to say what behavior therapy is by listing important characteristics. We can use the same approach here.

Consider the following lists of illnesses: cancer, pneumonia, diabetes, Addison's disease, multiple sclerosis, hypertension, Parkinson's disease, tuberculosis, arthritis, asthma, and hepatitis. What justifies grouping them under a single classification? A plausible hypothesis is that the following characteristics are important:

First, there is a sense, although it is difficult to clarify, in which the symptoms of illnesses just "happen" to people; they are involuntary; they are outside of the individual's control. The patient may or may not try to get sick; but once he becomes sick, he does not simply choose to cough or to develop a high fever or a tumor – these things happen to him. This characteristic would be unimportant if all our behavior is outside of our control; if all behavior is causally determined *and* if this rules out free choice, then there may be no distinction between those behaviors that "happen to us" and those that do not. We will take up this issue in the final chapter, but for the present we can say this: If there is such a distinction, it is of some relevance in distinguishing between illnesses and nonillnesses. For example, even if catatonic behavior is symptomatic of a certain type of mental illness, we would still not apply the term *sick* to someone we knew to be deliberately displaying such behavior in order to avoid prosecution for a crime.

Second, most illnesses are disabling, or at least, if left unchecked, typically cause suffering or discomfort to the patient. In some sense, again difficult to clarify, the illness "directly" causes the unpleasant consquences (on this point, see Glover, 1970). Certain political beliefs, when they occur in citizens of certain states, and when left unchecked, may also produce unpleasant consequences; usually, however, the mediation of other people is required. The belief that one is free to criticize one's government can produce pain and suffering for the individual, but it does not do so directly in the way that cancer or schizophrenia do (although it may be true that *some* of the suffering associated with these latter disorders does result from the way people react to the victim).

Third, most illnesses are primarily due to or involve structural changes in body tissues. The situation is complicated by the fact that many illnesses result from an inextricable admixture of organic and environmental causes. Despite this, the discovery that a disorder was due primarily to a genetic or biochemical cause would greatly increase the plausibility of classifying it as an *illness*. This characteristic is not sufficient (high intelligence is not an illness even if it has a large genetic component), but it is important.

Fourth, most conditions classified as *illnesses* are associated with a relatively specific set of symptoms. We should not, however, make too much of this point. Some sick people do not display any symptoms, and sometimes the symptoms produced by a certain illness vary greatly. This last characteristic, then, is probably less important than the other three.

The preceding description of important characteristics is not complete; the presence of all four characteristics is not sufficient for a condition to qualify as a disease. Consider, for example, the following conditions: pregnancy, genetically caused physical abnormalities (such as the absence of a limb), mental retardation, and old age. All of these conditions are characterized by specific symptoms; the symptoms appear involuntarily; they are organically caused; and the conditions typically are the direct cause of pain or disablement. There might be some temptation to classify these conditions as illnesses, but at the very least they are not clearly and obviously illnesses. This suggests that to provide a complete explanation of why certain conditions are justifiably grouped together as illnesses, we would need to list one or more additional characteristics. Even if we could complete our list, it is likely that some of the characteristics would be superseded in importance by new ones as medical research deepens our knowledge of disease. Rather than pursue what might prove to be a fruitless search, we can adopt the following strategy. Let us use the term *inhibitor* to refer to those characteristics that explain why a condition is not an illness despite its possession of the four characteristics on our list. In the absence of evidence that a condition possesses an inhibitor, the presence of all four of our important characteristics makes it likely that the condition is an illness; the absence of one or more of these characteristics makes that less likely.

Although the preceding account is not altogether satisfactory, it might still be used in determining if there are any mental illnesses. The most obvious candidate for that designation is schizophrenia; the main impediment to its acceptance concerns doubts about its etiology. For example, R.D. Laing (1971, p. 115) suggests that those labeled *schizophrenic* invent a special strategy in order to live in what would otherwise be an unlivable situation. If this explanation were correct, it would be plausible to argue that schizophrenia is not an illness. The same comment applies to Scheff's (1963) attempt to explain schizophrenic reactions as the result of being labeled *schizophrenic* and being forced to play the role of a sick person. Scheff intends his account to explain the maintenance and not necessarily the origin of schizophrenic behavior, but if it were shown to cover both, then there would be some reason to deny that schizophrenia is an illness. A similar result might follow if certain learning theory accounts of schizophrenia were empirically confirmed. One such account mentioned earlier is Ullmann and Krasner's (1969) attempt to explain schizophrenic behavior in terms of the individual's learning to disregard cues usually attended to by those not labeled *schizophrenic*.

If any of the preceding theories were empirically confirmed, that might provide reason to doubt that schizophrenia is an illness; but as of now empirical confirmation is lacking. The current evidence makes it likely, moreover, that schizophrenia arises partly because of genetic factors. If that is true, then none of these theories by itself will be able to give a satisfactory account of the origin of schizophrenia. Such theories might be able to explain why a genetic predisposition to schizophrenic behavior is triggered in some people but not in others, but it is not clear that this weakened explanation would be sufficient to show that schizophrenia is not an illness. The admixture of genetic and environmental causative factors is not generally sufficient to make a disorder a nonillness; if it were, diabetes would not be an illness.

The new evidence for genetic causation of schizophrenia comes mainly from studies of children separated from their parents early in life. Rosenthal (1971) reports one such ongoing study in which he has been the principal investigator. The files of 10,000 Danish parents who had given up their children for nonfamilial adoption were studied and the children of those diagnosed schizophrenic or manic-depressive were placed in an index group. From the remaining pool of 5,500 adoptees, a group of controls was selected and matched on a case-by-case basis to those in the index group, on the basis of sex, age, age at transfer to the adopting family, and socioeconomic status of the adoptive parents. Neither of the biological parents of those in the control group was known to have any psychiatric history. Those in each group were then given an intensive two-day examination, without the examiner knowing to which group they belonged. Of the forty-seven adoptees in the control group, only one was diagnosed as borderline schizophrenic and none as schizophrenic. Despite the fact that the index group had fewer subjects (thirty-nine), seven were diagnosed as borderline schizophrenic and three as schizophrenic. An analogous study by Kety et al. (1968) was carried out, again in Denmark, using parents and other biological relatives of adoptees as the subjects. The files of approximately 5,500 children given up for nonfamilial adoption at an early age were examined. Those children who were admitted to a psychiatric facility and diagnosed as schizophrenics were selected as index cases; a matched control group was then selected from the remaining group of adoptees. Both the adoptive relatives and biological relatives were examined for each group to determine the incidence of schizophrenia. No significant difference was found when the adoptive relatives of index cases were compared to control cases. This is consistent with the hypothesis that schizophrenia is largely genetically determined. This same hypothesis would predict that if the controls and index cases were compared for the group of biological relatives, a significant difference would emerge. The index group should contain a significantly greater number of schizophrenic-spectrum disorders. This is exactly what was found. Similar results have been found in other studies of adoptees (Alanen, 1966; Wender et al., 1968; and Heston, 1966; Kety et al., 1975).

Rosenthal (1971, p. 84) concludes that the current evidence is sufficiently strong that the issue of whether genetic factors contribute appreciably to the development of schizophrenia must now be considered closed. Whether or not the issue is closed, the new evidence when combined with the findings from the earlier (and inconclusive) studies of monozygotic twins (reviewed in Rosenthal, 1971) is impressive. Our best bet at present is that at least one mental disorder, schizophrenia, results largely from organic factors.

Schizophrenia also possesses the other important characteristics referred to earlier. It has a relatively specific set of symptoms (Franks, 1975); it tends to be disabling; and the symptoms are involuntary. On these grounds, then, it does seem plausible to extend the notion *illness* to cover schizophrenia. If that is so, and because the main symptoms (at least for certain types of schizophrenia) are mentalistic, then the case is strong for concluding that there is at least one mental illness.

Conclusion. We can now sum up the entire argument. We began by defining the term *minimum medical model* to denote the view that some mental disorders (i.e., at least one) are illnesses in the same sense that some physical disorders are. We reviewed and rejected the main arguments for the opposing view, the view that mental illness is a myth. We then compared schizophrenia to certain paradigm cases of illnesses and concluded that they were sufficiently analogous to justify extending the term *illness* to cover this disorder. Without having a clear, formal definition of *illness* or an adequate theory of what constitutes a change in meaning, it is difficult to prove beyond all doubt that the term *illness* can be applied univocally to both physical and mental disorders. The analogies cited appear plausible, but are not beyond all challenge. Nevertheless, if the question "Are there any mental illnesses?" has any clear answer, then the weight of the evidence supports the affirmative.

II. A robust medical model

Those who object to even a minimum medical model have tended to rely on abstract, a priori arguments purporting to show that the very idea of a mental illness is objectionable. Their opponents have tended to be content with finding flaws in these arguments or in citing one or two counterexamples. The result is that little at-

tention has been paid to concrete details concerning most behavior disorders, but that is exactly what is needed if we wish to
move from a minimum to a robust medical model.

Are most behavior disorders illnesses? It is difficult to answer
this question without some specification of types of behavior disorder. To facilitate discussion, we will consider those types listed
in the *Diagnostic and Statistical Manual of the American Psychiatric
Association* (DSM II, 1968), excluding mental retardation and the
organic brain syndromes. A behavior therapist might object to this
choice on the grounds that the DSM is too medically oriented, but
if this is so, then the robust medical model will have received a
fairer test. If the model cannot be defended by appeal to the DSM
categories, then it is unlikely that the use of a different system will
help.

There are three versions of the DSM, but we will concentrate
mainly on DSM II (1968), because the latest version (DSM III,
forthcoming) is too new to have been referred to in previous discussions of the medical model and the first version has not been in
use for the last ten years.

If schizophrenia qualifies as an illness, then there is some reason
to think that one or more of the other psychoses also qualify. For
example, there is some evidence, although not as firm as that for
schizophrenia, that genetic factors are partly implicated in the development of manic-depressive psychosis (Rosenthal, 1971).
Once we leave the psychoses, however, the case for extending the
concept *illness* to other functional disorders becomes much
weaker. To show that this is so, we will begin with some of the
more controversial categories.

Homosexuality

The nomenclature committee of the American Psychiatric Association has recommended that the classification *homosexuality* be
removed from the list of mental illnesses contained in its *Diagnostic and Statistical Manual,* but this recommendation has proved to
be controversial. As O'Leary and Wilson (1975) note, some critics
have charged that the decision was made because of political pressure. Whether or not the charge is correct, the recommendation is
defensible. There are important disanalogies between homosexuality and standard sorts of illnesses.

In the first place, there is no firm evidence that homosexuality
has an organic cause. The small amount of genetic data available

indicates that homosexuality is not inherited (Davison & Neale, 1974). Some studies have found lower levels of hormones in male and female homosexuals (Loraine et al., 1971; Kolodny et al., 1971), but the studies do not demonstrate that these deficiencies cause the sexual behavior.

Second, it is far from clear that homosexuality *directly* produces pain, suffering, or disablement in the way that paradigmatic cases of untreated illnesses usually do. Homosexuals tend to suffer in societies where their behavior is not tolerated but have thrived in more hospitable climates, such as ancient Greece. Even in our society, recent studies indicate that homosexuals are not necessarily more disturbed than comparable heterosexuals and do not invariably lead unhappy lives (O'Leary & Wilson, 1975).

Third, there is no evidence that homosexual behavior, in general, is something that just happens to people like a cough or tumor, whereas heterosexual behavior is not. Assuming that there is free choice at all, some homosexuals adopt their particular lifestyle because they prefer it. That is probably true, for example, of some male prostitutes who act for material gain; of some feminists who are persuaded by ideological arguments; of some soldiers and prisoners who have no opportunity for heterosexual contacts. Some homosexuals, it is true, are incapable of engaging in heterosexual behavior, but it is also true that many heterosexuals who are revolted by homosexuality are incapable of forming homosexual relationships. There is no general distinction between homosexuality and heterosexuality on this score. Some people are homosexuals by free choice and some are not; the same is true of heterosexuals.

Alcoholism

The official position of Alcoholics Anonymous is that alcoholism is a disease like any other disease; others contend that the disease theory of alcoholism has been largely discredited (O'Leary & Wilson, 1975, p. 387). Who is right? The issues are complicated and confused. Before we answer, some distinctions need to be made.

One might adopt a disease view in order to explain why alcoholics drink excessively when it is not in their interest to do so. Why would someone ruin his or her career or marriage by constantly engaging in such destructive behavior? Answer: The person must be sick. This answer is too glib. Not everyone who engages in very self-destructive behavior is sick. Some people apparently decide on rational grounds to commit suicide; others ruin their lives because of their political or religious beliefs. We cannot just assume, then, that the alcoholic drinks because he is sick; we need evidence that this explanation is correct.

The chronic alcoholic is likely to ruin not only his career or marriage but also his health. Excessive drinking can adversely affect, for example, the heart, liver, or brain. Nevertheless, this does not show that alcoholism itself is an illness. We are not asking, "Does chronic alcoholism cause certain illnesses?" Rather, we want to know if alcoholism (roughly, the long-term disposition to drink regularly to excess) is itself a sickness. Some organizations specify what it is to drink to excess partly in terms of damage to one's physical health. For example, the American Psychiatric Association classifies people as alcoholics only when their alcoholic intake is great enough to damage their physical health, their personal or social functioning, or when alcohol has become a prerequisite to normal functioning (DSM II, 1968, p. 45). Acceptance of this definition would not affect the basic point: Alcoholism might adversely affect someone's physical or mental health without being an illness. We might also define *workaholic* so that it includes only people who have a tendency to work so much that their health is damaged; but that would not by itself show that the tendency to work too much is a sickness.

Some who think that alcoholism is a disease have a theory about its etiology: They believe that it is inherited or caused by biochemical or neurological defects. There is, however, no hard evidence to support such a view. Rosenthal (1971) reviews two of the few studies done on the genetic origins of alcoholism. In one, Kaij (1960) compared monozygotic and dizygotic twins with respect to alcohol consumption and found a difference that was statistically significant at the 0.001 level. Although this finding precludes a chance explanation of the results, the study is open to criticisms similar to those leveled at many twin studies of schizophrenia; the study did not adequately rule out an environmental explanation of the observed differences.

A second study (Roe et al., 1945) concerned children reared in foster homes. The alcoholism rates of those who had an alcoholic father were compared to those in a control group. No significant difference was found. Because this study was relatively well controlled, it provides impressive, although not conclusive, evidence that alcoholism is not caused primarily by genetic factors.

The disease view might also seem to receive support from the chain reaction theory of alcoholism. On this theory alcoholics as a class are physiologically different from nonalcoholics. Once they take their first drink, a chain reaction is set off and they subsequently cannot help but drink to excess. A modified form of this theory might be used to explain not the origin but the maintenance of alcoholism. If either version of the theory is true, then the prescription for cure is total abstinence. The theory predicts that if an alcoholic tries to modify his drinking habits so as to become a "social drinker" – one who can stop after the first or second drink – then this attempt will invariably fail. Even one or two drinks will set off the unwanted chain reaction. There is now evidence that this prediction is false; it is this evidence that O'Leary and Wilson (1975) cite when they claim that the disease model has been discredited. Part of the evidence comes from a study by Sobell and Sobell (1973) in which seventy chronic alcoholics were assigned to one of four groups: a controlled drinking control group, a nondrinking control group, a controlled drinking experimental group, and a nondrinking experimental group. Those in the two control groups received conventional treatment for alcoholics and those in the experimental groups received behavior therapy. Those in the controlled drinking experimental group improved significantly more than those in the comparable control group, and continued to reflect this advantage during a two-year follow-up period. The results not only provide evidence for the efficacy of a behavior therapy treatment of alcoholism but also indicate that at least some alcoholics can learn to drink in moderation. Other recent studies have also provided evidence against the chain reaction theory (Marlatt, 1973; Lloyd & Salzberg, 1975; Pomerleau et al., 1976).

Probably the strongest remaining reason for thinking of alcoholism as a disease has to do with its effects on the central nervous system. If an alcoholic drinks excessively for many years, he is likely to become physically addicted to alcohol; if he tries to stop drinking, he may suffer severe withdrawal symptoms. If he continues to drink because of this physical dependency, then his condition is, in one important respect, analogous to paradigm cases of illnesses. The analogy is strengthened by the fact that the condition is painful and often disabling in the same way that arthritis or polio are. Nevertheless, this is not sufficient reason for saying that alcoholism is a sickness. Not all alcoholics who drink excessively do so because of a physical dependence, and those who do did not originally do so for that reason, at least as far as we know.

Conclusion. The case, then, for saying that alcoholism per se is an illness is weak, although it is not altogether without merit if we are referring only to that advanced stage where a physical dependence has developed. Alcoholism is often disabling, but recent evidence does not support the chain reaction theory, nor the idea that all alcoholics drink excessively because of some organic cause. It is likely, rather, that some alcoholics, like some heavy smokers, indulge themselves for a variety of reasons; one of these reasons is that the habit can be immensely and immediately rewarding.

Sociopathy

There has been much disagreement as to whether or not sociopathy (or psychopathy) is an illness; some of this disagreement is reflected in disputes about criteria for an insanity defense (see, for example, *United States* v. *Brawner,* 1972). In DSM II the term *antisocial personality* is used as a substitute for both *sociopath psychopath*. The criteria are explained as follows:

> This term is reserved for individuals who are basically unsocialized and whose behavior pattern brings them repeatedly into conflict with society. They are incapable of significant loyalty to individuals, groups, or social values. They are grossly selfish, callous, irresponsible, impulsive, and unable to feel guilt or to learn from experience and punishment. Frustration tolerance is low. They tend to blame others or offer plausible rationalizations for their behavior. (DSM II, 1968, p. 43.)

If the possession of most of these characteristics is sufficient for being a sociopath (or having an antisocial personality), then someone can be a sociopath without being sick. That might be true, for example, of a grossly selfish, callous, irresponsible, and impulsive socialist who lives in a predominantly fascist society and, consequently, has repeated conflicts with his fellow citizens and is incapable of loyalty to any of these people or their values. If it is necessary to have all the characteristics, then it is likely that most people who are diagnosed as sociopaths do not qualify. For example, it is unlikely that a typical sociopath would have a *general* inability to learn from experience; if he did, he would not survive very long. It is not even likely that he would have a general inability to learn from punishment. In one experiment bearing on this issue, Schmauk (1970) compared the effects of punishment on the performance of a group of prisoners diagnosed as sociopaths and a second group of nonsociopaths. Two of the punishments – the experimenter's saying "wrong" and electric shock – were more effective with the nonsociopaths; but a third punishment, the losing of a certain sum of money, was more effective with the sociopaths.

Instead of using either most or all of the standard criteria, we might treat some as being much more important than others. Some writers (e.g., Davison & Wilson, 1974, p. 208) stress the sociopath's lack of emotional response after committing an act that generally elicits shame and guilt in most people. There is some evidence, reviewed in Hare (1970), that this lack of emotional response may be caused by physiological factors. If that is true, should sociopathy (or the possession of an antisocial personality) be viewed as an illness? In at least one important respect, it is disanalogous to paradigmatic cases of illnesses; it is not disabling, nor does it necessarily directly cause pain in the individual. Given the legal strictures of our society, some sociopaths suffer adverse consequences because of their actions; but these consequences are mediated by the actions of others. Furthermore, some sociopaths probably benefit from their lack of normal guilt feelings. McNeil (1967) refers to such an individual, who apparently succeeded as an actor and disc jockey partly because of his ability to mistreat people without feeling remorse (described in Davison & Neale, 1974, pp. 204–5).

Additional personality disorders

The DSM II (1968) lists nine kinds of personality disorders in addition to *antisocial personality*. These include (1) *obsessive compulsive personality,* characterized by excessive concern with conformity and adherence to standards of conscience; (2) *inadequate personality,* characterized by ineffectual responses to emotional, social, intellectual, and physical demands; and (3) *explosive personality,* characterized by gross outbursts of rage or of verbal or physical aggressiveness. It is not obvious that people possessing any of these three types of personalities thereby suffer from a *disorder*. It is even less clear that they, or any of those having the remaining six types of personality (paranoid, cyclothymic, passive-aggressive, schizoid, asthemic, and hysterical) are necessarily sick. If it is true (or to the degree that it is true) that we do not choose our personalities, then these so-called disorders happen to people, but the same is true of so-called normal personalities. Unlike clear cases of illnesses, none of these nine personalities need be disabling or the direct cause of suffering in the individuals who have them. Most important, there is no firm evidence that these personalities are organically caused, except insofar as physical factors help to shape all personalities. The justification, then, for describing these personalities as illnesses appears weak.

Neuroses

The DSM II lists three types of hysterical neurosis and eight other types of neurosis: anxiety, phobic, obsessive compulsive, depressive, neurasthenic, depersonalization, hypochondriacal, and "other" (this last category includes "writer's cramp" and other occupational neuroses). This is a heterogenous group. What is thought to bind the various conditions together is the presence of anxiety, conscious or unconscious. All these disorders resemble an illness in some respects. They tend to cause suffering directly and in some cases are disabling; they do just happen to people; and, with certain qualifications, they are associated with recognizable clusters of symptoms (Franks, 1975). If the concept *illness* is extended to schizophrenia, why not extend it to the neuroses? The main difference is the lack of implication of organic causes. Sound genetic studies of neurosis are relatively few, partly because of the difficulty in reliably diagnosing the disorder. Rosenthal (1971, p. 144) reviews the few studies available and concludes that there is little reason to doubt the importance of environmental factors in the development of clinical neurosis.

Apart from genetic studies, there are various theories available about the etiology of neurosis, including Freudian and learning accounts. Some of the main theories are reviewed in Davison and Neale (1974), who conclude (p. 150) that they all rest on little direct evidence. Because the etiology of most neurosis is still unknown, it is possible that some will be found to have an organic cause; but for those with causes that are primarily psychological, as appears antecedently plausible in the case of phobic and occupational neuroses, the case for regarding the disorders as "illnesses" is seriously weakened.

Sexual deviations

The category of sexual deviations includes homosexuality, which we have already discussed, and fetishisms, pedophilia, transvestism, exhibitionism, voyeurism, sadism, masochism (DSM II, p. 44). The case against treating these so-called disorders as illnesses is similar to that made earlier in connection with homosexuality and need not be discussed at length.

It is true that the behavior falling under the preceding categories is statistically deviant, but that is also true, or once was true, of other unconventional sexual practices, such as oral or anal sex, which are clearly not illnesses. There are, moreover, specific and important disanalogies between illnesses and sexual deviations. First, the latter are not generally disabling, nor do they generally cause, in a direct way, suffering or discomfort to the individual. Second, there is no firm evidence that they are caused by organic rather than psychological factors. Third, if people ever have free choice about their sexual practices, then it is likely that that is true of at least some people who engage in each of the types of sexually deviant behavior listed in DSM II.

Conclusion. We define a robust medical model as one that assumes that most of the problems treated by both psychiatrists and clinical psychologists are illnesses. A review of the major functional disorders listed in DSM II, excluding the psychoses, shows that the available evidence does not support the acceptance of this model and that there is some reason to reject it. The case for rejection is strengthened when we consider that many additional problems treated by both psychiatrists and psychologists are not listed in DSM II (or have not been mentioned here) and clearly are disanalogous in one or more important respects to illnesses. These include marital problems, smoking, stuttering, fear of public speaking, test anxiety, overeating, lack of assertiveness, toilet training, shyness, troublesome sexual fantasies, temper tantrums, and poor self-image.

At least two reservations about the preceding discussion should be stressed. First, in those cases where the lack of organic cause appears to be the sole important disanalogy between the disorder and illnesses (as may be the case with certain neuroses), then we need to be careful in rejecting the illness label too quickly. The evidence concerning etiology is usually too fragmentary and too subject to modification to support anything more than a reasoned conjecture. Second, we have relied in part on our hypothesis that certain characteristics of illnesses are important. The evidence offered for this hypotheses is that it, or one very much like it, offers a partial explanation of why certain conditions are justifiably grouped together as illnesses. Our list of important characteristics, however, may need to be revised; at the very least, it is incom-

plete. This possibility of revision weakens our argument as it
applies to specific disorders, but it does not destroy the cogency of
the overall argument unless there is a serious possibility of a radical revision of the entire hypothesis. Even then, the defender of
the robust medical model would still have the burden of proving
that most psychiatric disorders are illnesses; the prospects of that
happening do not seem great. A defender of this model might also
try substituting DSM III (forthcoming) for DSM II (1968), but
this is not likley to help his cause. Although there have been some
changes, the conceptual scheme in the new version is similar to
that of DSM II. The most important change lies not in the basic
scheme itself but in the provision of operational criteria in DSM
III to improve the reliability of diagnosis.

A proponent of a medical approach might want to go further
than defending a minimum medical model but not so far as accepting the robust model. There are many possibilities here, but it
would be tedious and uninformative to examine them all; enough
details have already been provided to discern how such theses
might fare. It is time now to ask why it is important to decide
whether or not psychiatric disorders are illnesses.

The significance of the medical model

Why does it matter whether or not the medical model is accepted?
We have already mentioned one reason: The model seems inappropriate for a behavior therapist who recommends a form of
treatment that by its very nature is nonmedical. A second reason,
given by Albee (1969), is that use of the medical model helps
determine the institutions we develop for intervention and pre-
vention, and this in turn dictates the kind of manpower we use to
deliver psychiatric care. A rejection of the medical model in favor
of what Albee calls a social–developmental model would result, he
claims, in state hospitals and public clinics being largely staffed by
people with bachelor degrees rather than medical degrees. Albee
(1970) also suggests that the medical model helps justify the drug
industry's selling hundreds of millions of dollars of drugs each year
for the relief of so-called mental diseases. This state of affairs
would change, he suggests, if the medical model were abandoned,
but for that to happen, psychiatry would have to become a social
and behavioral science rather than part of medicine.

The conclusions cited by Albee do not follow directly from a
denial of the premise that most behavior disorders are illnesses.

Indeed, it is difficult to cite any interesting conclusion that follows directly from denial of either the minimum or robust medical model, but that does not mean that disputes about mental illness are unimportant. What is primarily significant is not the logical implications of saying that most behavior disorders are illnesses; rather, it is the causal consequences that are likely to follow the rejection of that assumption and all that goes with it. The medical model is presupposed by the continued use of a whole network of concepts traditionally employed in psychiatry and clinical psychology. As noted earlier, therapists are said to work in the field of mental *health;* their clients are *patients* who are *ill* and need to be *diagnosed* and *treated* and *cured;* such clients need *medical* treatment and the natural dispenser of such treatment is a *medical* doctor. If most psychiatric disorders are not illnesses, this network of medical concepts is applicable in far fewer cases than is often assumed. The abandonment of this network of ideas is likely to constitute a fundamental conceptual change, in some ways analogous to (although far less dramatic than) that which occurred when a demon model was replaced by a sickness model (i.e., when social deviants began to be seen as being sick rather than possessed by demons). This new change of conceptual framework may well affect the way we view other issues. Besides the issues discussed by Albee, such a change might affect, for example, accepted views of the kind of expert testimony required for an insanity defense. It has been assumed by most courts of the United States that because those disorders that must be present for an insanity defense are illnesses, psychiatrists are uniquely qualified to present expert testimony concerning the condition of the accused. An exception to this generalization is the court's finding in the Brawner decision (*United States* v. *Brawner,* 1972) that expert testimony of psychologists is also admissible as evidence. Even here the court explicitly refused to disentangle the insanity defense from a medical model. In particular, it ruled that such conditions as somnambulism and drug addiction should be governed by a rule comparable to that set forth for mental diseases only if *medical* opinion is taken into account that such conditions negate free will. This deference by the courts to medical opinion in connection with the insanity defense is likely to diminish if many more behavior disorders are seen as psychological rather than medical in nature. As Leifer (1970) points out, a similar effect might well occur in connection with the decision to treat or incarcerate a client against his will. If a condition is seen as a psychological disorder rather than an illness, then the psychologist as well as the psychiatrist may be called on to decide the question of forced treatment or incarceration. The psychiatrist may still have an important role to play, but not a unique one – except in areas that are specifically medical, such as in the treatment of organic brain syndromes.

It is difficult to know in advance exactly what effects would result from an abandonment of the robust medical model, but it does not seem unduly speculative to conclude that some important changes are likely to occur. If so, there is justification for taking debates about the concept *mental illness* seriously. However, some behavior therapists (e.g., Ullmann & Krasner, 1969) define the term *medical model* more broadly to encompass a cluster of issues, only one of which concerns the concept *mental illness*. We turn now to some of these additional issues.

III. Additional issues

Symptom substitution

One of the key issues involved in disputes about the medical model in the broader sense concerns symptom substitution. Some writers who liken psychiatric disorders to diseases accept a traditional psychoanalytic account of psychiatric symptoms: A symptom represents the most economical expression of an id-ego conflict. If treatment eliminates a symptom but does not resolve the underlying conflict, another symptom, usually a less advantageous one, will result. This view is often referred to as the *symptom substitution hypothesis*. The hypothesis need not be accepted by everyone who sees psychiatric disorders as illnesses; in fact, for many physical illnesses, such as the flu or diabetes, successful symptomatic treatment does not normally result in anything analogous to symptom substitution. The hypothesis is mainly attractive to those who accept the previously mentioned psychoanalytic explanation of symptoms. Behavior therapists, in contrast, are motivated to reject the hypothesis, not merely because of the way they read the available empirical evidence or because they reject pychoanalytic theory, but also because they favor a "direct" kind of treatment. If the symptom substitution hypothesis is true, then one would predict that behavior therapy, which is not directed at resolving id-ego conflicts, will tend to be unsuccessful in that it will not eliminate the client's symptoms or will be superficial in that it will result in symptom substitution.

Although the symptom substitution hypothesis has an empirical character, evaluation of the relevant data has been somewhat hindered by conceptual disputes. As Cahoon (1968) points out, some writers appear to define *symptom* in a way that presupposes a theory that behavior therapists reject. For example, Greenson (1959) writes, "Neurotic symptoms are derivatives of the neurotic conflict. They are a compromise formation between the instinctual impulses of the id and the defending forces of the ego." Behavior therapists are reluctant to use the term *symptom* in the preceding sense (assuming that the writer is giving a definition and is not merely presenting a theory about the cause of neurotic symptoms). Even if *symptom* is defined in a more neutral sense, many behavior therapists are still reluctant to use the term if its use suggests a commitment to the medical model (Ullmann & Krasner, 1965).

Given the disagreement about the use of the term *symptom,* a behavior therapist and psychoanalyst can agree that the elimination of a patient's problem has been followed by the generation of a new problem and yet disagree about whether or not this counts as symptom substitution. Even if both therapists were to say that symptom substitution has occurred, they might disagree because they use the term *symptom* in different senses.

Cahoon (1968), in an excellent discussion of the key issues, suggests two alternative ways of dealing with this conceptual impasse: (1) formulate the symptom substitution hypothesis using concepts linked to psychoanalytic theory or (2) define the relevant concepts in a theory neutral sense. Cahoon favors the second alternative so that the issues can be decided on empirical grounds, but he admits that considerable support could be offered for accepting option 1 and then rejecting the hypothesis as meaningless. If that is so, then the impasse can easily develop again. Some psychoanalysts will insist on option 1 but will not agree that the symptom substitution hypothesis is meaningless. Those who accept a behavioristic theory may argue otherwise, as Cahoon contends, but then the dispute is in danger of dissolving into a philosophic mist. Instead of arguing about low-level empirical data, the disputants will argue about behavioristic principles. The way to avoid this result, while keeping with the spirit of Cahoon's valuable suggestions, is to allow the psychoanalyst option 1 but to ask him to specify the kinds of characteristics he counts as symptoms. Presumably, he will include some items that behavior therapists classify as maladaptive behaviors, including wetting the bed, stuttering, temper tantrums, paranoid behavior, sexually impotent behavior, and so on. He might also include confused thoughts, feelings of anxiety, hallucinations, and other non-behavioral items. We can label both types as maladaptive characteristics without presupposing any theory disputed by either psychoanalysts or behavior therapists. Next, we can ask the psychoanalyst to specify how long it will usually take for symptom substitution to occur. Referring to that time as time *t*, we can infer that the hypothesis of symptom substitution (SS) is true only if the following is true:

(S): If a treatment eliminates a maladaptive characteristic without resolving any underlying id-ego conflict, then either symptom substitution will usually occur within time *t* or the characteristic is not the most economical expression of an underlying id-ego conflict.

(S) is necessary but not sufficient for the truth of the symptom substitution hypothesis (SS). It is not sufficient because (SS) makes a causal claim not made by (S). That is, even if the elimination of a maladaptive characteristic is invariably followed by the appearance of a new maladaptive characteristic, the symptom substitution hypothesis might still be false; the new characteristic might result from some cause in the client's environment and not from the treatment. If (S) is false, however, then the symptom substitution hypothesis is false as well.

Is (S) false? The hypothesis is unclear partly because we have not specified the time or the percentage of cases in which a new maladaptive characteristic is to be expected to appear. Nevertheless, the available empirical evidence does not support (S) and runs directly counter to any version of it that specifies a relatively brief period, say six months, and that stipulates that the phenomenon occurs in most cases. In his 1963 review of the evidence, Rachman concludes that new maladaptive characteristics rarely appear after successful behavior therapy. His estimate is that it occurs at most in 5 percent of such cases. Subsequent studies have included follow-ups to discern the appearance of new maladaptive characteristics and have found that the phenomenon sometimes occurs, but not usually (Paul, 1969; Young & Turner, 1965; Lovibond, 1964; Bucher & Lovaas, 1968; Bandura, 1969; Lazarus, 1971).

Some writers sympathetic to psychoanalysis now concede that symptom substitution does not normally occur but argue that this result is compatible with psychoanalysis. For example, Rhoads and Feather (1974) distinguish between "ghost" and "nonghost" symptoms. A ghost symptom once served as an expression of an underlying psychic conflict that has now been resolved as a result of further maturation of the ego. The symptom remains as a "learned" habit no longer serving a significant need. A nonghost symptom is simply the usual kind of Freudian symptom, that which acts as a vehicle for expressing or resolving a *current* conflict. A psychoanalyst might say, then, that the current evidence shows that most symptoms are ghost symptoms, and that is why they can be directly extinguished without symptom substitution taking place. If that is true, however, then the standard Freudian explanation of the *maintenance* of most neurotic symptoms in adults would have to be abandoned, even if the explanation of their *origin* could be retained. There are other options open to psychoanalysts (see Weitzman, 1967), but they need not be discussed here. If psychoanalytic theory is formulated in such a way that it, plus other plausible assumptions, does not entail assumption (S), then the behavior therapist will become less interested in the fate of psychoanalytic theory, or at least in this version of it. At least one apparent implication of the theory that conflicts with his own theory will have been abandoned, and with it one of the main supports for the charge that behavior therapy, by its very nature, must be superficial.

As noted earlier, a defender of the medical model who is not committed to psychoanalysis can reject the symptom substitution hypothesis; he might, however, argue for a relapse hypothesis. That is, he might reason that most psychiatric problems are like physical illnesses: They consist of symptoms (in a non-Freudian sense) and an underlying cause; if we extinguish only the symptoms, the symptoms are likely to return. The common result of behavior therapy, where it is successful in extinguishing symptoms, will be not symptom substitution but symptom reappearance.

The issue of relapse is a serious one for the behavior therapist (although not for him alone), and given its complexity, it cannot be treated adequately in a short space. A few remarks, however, may suffice to place the issue in perspective insofar as it relates to debates about the medical model.

Those who liken psychiatric problems to illnesses are presumably not using the phrase *underlying cause* to refer to just anything that causally explains the maintenance of maladaptive characteristics. If they were, then few behavior therapists would disagree with the idea that such characteristics have an underlying cause; to do so would be to allow that psychiatric problems are causally inexplicable. Furthermore, that there are underlying causes in this sense does not make it probable that, in general, so-called symptomatic treatment, where successful, will be followed by relapses. Whether relapse is likely or not will depend in part on the type of underlying cause that is present. For example, if someone felt anxious because of a biochemical dysfunction and a drug were used to eliminate only the symptom, then it would not be surprising if the anxiety returned when the effects of the drug wore off. In contrast, if a child had an exteme phobic reaction to dogs because of being bitten by a dog, then a proper use of a modeling procedure to eliminate the phobic reaction might be expected to achieve long-lasting results.

Let us assume, then, that the defender of the medical model is using the term *underlying cause* to refer to a particular type of cause (i.e., an organic or psychic cause that in some sense is *within* the organism displaying the maladaptive characteristic). On that assumption, the following remarks are relevant. First, the presence of relapse is not itself evidence for the medical model, because relapse will predictably occur in some cases even if a learning theory account is correct. For example, if someone smokes excessively because of intense pressure generated by his working environment, a learning theory account would predict that the modification of his smoking behavior by aversion therapy will be short-lived, unless the environment is altered or the client learns to respond to it differently. Second, as indicated in Section II of the present chapter, the current available evidence does not support the assumption that most psychiatric problems are maintained by an underlying cause, in the sense we are now using this term. In the case of some psychoses, such as autism or schizophrenia, there is some evidence of an organic cause, but that is not true generally. However, because so little is currently known about the etiology of most psychiatric disorders, we cannot infer that most such disorders either are or are not maintained by "underlying causes," especially if the phrase is used to denote cognitive and emotional states as well as organic dysfunctions. Third, the question of whether relapse generally occurs is best settled by appealing not to theoretical considerations, such as presumed analogies between psychiatric disorders and physical illnesses, but to the available empirical evidence. Some of that evidence has already been discussed (Chapter 1, Section II) and does suggest that relapse is a continual problem for certain types of disorders when treated by certain types of behavior therapy procedures. For example, the use of aversive conditioning techniques in the treatment of alcoholism, smoking, and obesity has encountered serious relapse problems. The treatment of other types of problems, or the same types with different behavior therapy procedures, has fared much better. For example, controlled studies with follow-ups of the use of desensitization for public speaking anxiety (Paul, 1968) and of certain operant techniques for alcoholism (O'Leary & Wilson, 1975) report success without serious relapse problems.

The classification of behavior disorders

Even if the concept *mental illness* has a limited usefulness, we still need a substitute concept if the robust medical model is rejected. The substitutes most often used by behavior therapists are (1) *abnormal behavior;* (2) *deviant behavior;* (3) *maladaptive behavior;* and (4) *problems in living.* Unfortunately, each of these concepts embraces too much. Alternatives 1 and 2 are equivalent if interpreted in a statistical sense and are then objectionable for the same reason; both apply to many types of behavior not treated by therapy, including running for president of the United States, marrying a movie star, or receiving a Nobel Prize. Alternatives 1 and 2 can be interpreted in a nonstatistical sense, but then they are unclear unless explained further. If we are not speaking statistically, then exactly what is meant by calling a behavior abnormal or deviant? Ullmann and Krasner (1969) suggest the following answer: They speak of statistically deviant behavior of a certain kind, one that *sanctions* or *calls for* the intervention of a mental health practitioner. But what does this mean? It looks as if, in using the word *sanctions,* an evaluative criterion is being introduced; the concept then draws a distinction not between what is and is not treated in therapy but between what ought and ought not to be treated. Furthermore, the concept is unclear unless some independent clarification is offered for *sanctions* or *calls for.*

The third concept, *maladaptive behavior,* is also too broad; it applies to many behaviors not treated by therapists but that can be maladaptive under certain conditions, such as speaking the truth, refusing to fight in wartime, and writing political propaganda.

The fourth notion is open to a similar objection: It draws no distinction between the problems in living treated in therapy, such as anxiety or schizophrenia, and those that are not, such as the problems people have in balancing their budgets, obtaining promotions, or finding suitable housing.

Although all the options used by behavior therapists are unsatisfactory, this is also true of those used by other therapists. There is no relatively brief, illuminating phrase that can be used to draw just the right kind of distinction: between clinical and nonclinical problems. All the phrases now used by psychiatrists and psychologists cover too much, too little, or both. If the behavior therapist must choose from a bad lot, he can at least pick the least objectionable concept. On these grounds there is some reason to prefer *maladaptive behavior,* or something very much like it. Alternative 4, *problems in living,* can be seriously misleading, in addition to covering too much. People often go to behavior therapists because their behavior is causing problems for other people. For example, a child may wet the bed or an adult may expose himself in public. What is treated is not the problem in living that is caused by these behaviors but the behaviors themselves. Speaking of *problems in living* in such cases can obscure this fact.

The notions of *abnormal behavior* and *deviant behavior* can cover too little as well as too much, at least if interpreted in the statistical sense. For example, smoking is not a deviant or abnormal behavior, or at least it might not be if more people begin to smoke; yet this behavior is treated by behavior therapists. In addition, describing a client's behavior as abnormal or deviant may explain why others want it modified, not why he does. Speaking of maladaptive behavior, in contrast, does help explain this fact; the client wants such behaviors modified because he finds them ill suited for adapting to his environment. This notion can be applied, furthermore, to behaviors that are treatable even if they are not statistically deviant, and this is all to the good. The concept might be objected to on the grounds that it is too behavioristic; it does not apply to emotional states, such as anxiety, or to unwanted thoughts or imagery. The same objection, however, applies equally well to *deviant behavior* and *abnormal behavior*. One reply is to concede that *maladaptive behavior* is too narrow (besides being too broad) but to argue that it applies to most items treated by behavior therapy; after all, one distinguishing feature of this type of therapy, in contrast to insight therapies, is that it deals primarily with unwanted *behaviors*. If, however, we need a term to cover all (or almost all) items treated by behavior therapists, then the term *maladaptive characteristic* can be used. It can cover not only unwanted behaviors but also images, thoughts, feelings, and so on.

Etiology and treatment

If a behavior therapist scans recent issues of the leading psychiatry journals, he is likely to see advertisements showing sad, lonely, bewildered-looking people who are depicted as having medical problems that require a medical solution, usually a form of drug therapy. The advertised drugs are said to be useful for treating a wide variety of problems, including aggressiveness, compulsive masturbation, exhibitionism, hostility, incest, indecent exposure, suspiciousness, rape, transvestism, and voyeurism (*American Journal of Psychiatry*, 1975–6; *British Journal of Psychiatry*, 1975–6).

Not all psychiatrists would recommend drug therapy for all the preceding problems; some are quite skeptical about providing medical solutions of any kind for psychiatric problems (Coles, 1967; Werry, 1965). Nevertheless, some medically-oriented therapists do agree that most psychiatric problems require some form of medical treatment, such as drug therapy, electroconvulsive shock treatment, or, in very special cases, psychosurgery. Regardless of how many hold this view, it is one of a cluster of views that many behavior therapists mean to reject when they reject the medical model. A behavior therapist need not deny, however, that for some psychiatric problems drug treatment is preferable to any known alternative. For example, lithium might be very useful in treating manic-depressives. The view being rejected is that medical solutions are required not for some but for most psychiatric problems.

Part of the disagreement about treatment reflects disagreement about etiology. Is it true that most psychiatric problems are traceable to an organic impairment? Given our current ignorance about etiology, this question cannot be definitively answered now. Nevertheless, there is reason not to be sanguine about finding organic causes for most psychiatric problems. In particular, the current evidence does not usually indicate organic causation for such problems as aggressiveness, compulsive masturbation, exhibitionism, and so on.

Even when evidence of organic causation is found for a particular problem, that alone does not settle the issue of whether medical or psychological treatment is warranted. The connection between etiology and treatment is a complicated one; an inference from one to the other obviously must be made with care. For example, as Davison (1968) points out, it is a mistake to infer merely from the fact of successful treatment by some form of behavior therapy that a certain disorder had a nonorganic etiology. Obviously, it is a logical mistake to argue as follows: "If this behavior developed because of environmental causes, it is treatable by behavior therapy techniques. This behavior is treatable by such techniques; consequently, it developed because of environmental causes." The argument is of the form "If p then q; q; therefore, p"; it commits the fallacy of affirming the consequent. Someone may, of course, reach conclusions about causation without using this fallacious reasoning. He may simply claim that the successful use of a behavior therapy technique provides strong evidence (but does not entail) that the disorder had a nonorganic etiology. This too is quite often a mistake, although not such an obvious one. We already have evidence that despite organic impairment, brain-damaged children can have some of their behaviors modified by use of behavior therapy techniques (Watson, 1973). This is also true of schizophrenics even though the evidence points to a strong genetic component in its etiology. We cannot, then, assume without further argument that if behavior therapy techniques are useful in treating autistic children, for example, this is strong evidence that autism is caused primarily by environmental factors. The same sort of error is made if we infer that if a drug can suppress a certain type of behavior, then the behavior was probably caused by organic factors. Some disruptive children, for example, may be reacting to a stifling school envirmonment, yet their disruptive behavior may be suppressed by the use of tranquilizers. In general, to infer a conclusion about etiology from a premise about treatment is a mistake, unless there are supplementary premises that license the inference. The opposite sort of mistake is to infer a conclusion about treatment from a premise about etiology. Imagine someone reasoning as follows. "Disorder y is a medical problem. If it is a medical problem, then its etiology is due to organic factors; and if that is so, then the most effective treatment will be a medical treatment, such as the use of drugs, convulsive shock therapy, or psychosurgery." Even if we grant that a disorder has an organic etiology, we cannot infer, without additional evidence, that the most effective treatment will be a medical technique. For example, behavior therapy may be the most effective mode of treatment, at least for the present, for some cases of autism and schizophrenia even if these disorders have an organic etiology.

If Davison is correct in objecting to inferences about etiology based on assumptions about treatment, then the opposite type of inference, as noted previously, is also fallacious. If that is so, then what is the point about stressing etiology? Presumably, etiology is thought to be important mainly because it is a guide to treatment; if it is not, then it loses much of its importance. We seem to have been led to an absurd conclusion: that etiology is not very important. Behavior therapists are likely to reply that etiology *has* been overstressed. What is often of more importance is not the original cause of a maladaptive behavior, but what currently maintains it and what can be done to eliminate the maladaptive characteristics. Even where the current cause is organic, as with brain damage, there may be no known way of eliminating the organic malfunction; but it might be possible to provide special training or a special environment to mitigate the effects of the organic dysfunction. Having made this reply, the behavior therapist can still agree that etiology is of some importance. If we learn the cause of autism, for example, we may learn ways to prevent it and we may also confirm that there are certain constraints that set the boundaries of effectiveness for a purely behavioral treatment.

The preceding comments bear on a medical viewpoint about treatment in the following way. Even if a given disorder is a "medical problem" in the sense that its etiology is primarily organic, one cannot infer from this alone that medical treatment is warranted. The question "What is the most effective method of treatment for a problem of kind k?" is a fairly straightforward empirical question that usually cannot be answered without controlled empirical study of specific techniques. Which technique is the treatment of choice for each problem is, of course, still an unsettled question, but the available evidence suggests that behavior therapy techniques can be used effectively for a wide range of psychiatric problems (see Chapter 1, Section II). This provides some reason to doubt that medical solutions are required for most of these problems. Insofar as the behavior therapist is expressing this doubt when he complains about the "medical model," his complaint appears justified.

Diagnostic categories

One additional issue underlying disputes about the medical model concerns the use of traditional psychodiagnostic classifications. Although the issue is too complex to be discussed adequately in a brief space, several points deserve mention here.

As Phillips and Draguns (1971) point out, some writers appear to oppose all diagnostic labeling, on the grounds either that such activity is invariably harmful or that it is useless because each client is so different from every other. It is difficult to accept these grounds. Every client is undoubtedly different in a large number of ways (perhaps an infinite number, depending on how we count characteristics), but it is also true that many clients have many characteristics in common. It would be difficult to prove that *no* useful clinical purpose could ever be served by grouping some of the shared characteristics together. It would also be difficult to prove that the use of any possible diagnostic categorization must, on balance, be harmful. Even if one use of a certain category has bad effects, another use (e.g., for research) might provide countervailing benefits. It would be difficult to establish that, for any category, the benefits are always outweighed by harmful effects. In any event, no one has ever demonstrated that this is true. In sum, a blanket rejection of all diagnostic activity is difficult to justify.

Even if diagnostic labeling per se is not objectionable, a behavior therapist might object to the categories currently used by psychiatrists. This rejection is also too sweeping. Some of the current categories are relatively useless, but some are not. Examples of categories that might be useless include *protest psychosis* (Bromberg & Simon, 1968) and *neurosis of conscience* (Benda, 1967). The former is supposed to fit certain black militants and is characterized by mutism and rejection of white culture; the latter is defined on the basis of immaturity with a dependence on ego-foreign authority (Phillips & Draguns, 1971). It does not seem *prima facie* likely that individuals falling into either category will have common characteristics of interest to clinicians, although empirical evidence could conceivably show otherwise. The category of schizophrenia, in contrast, does appear to be useful. First, there is evidence that the category can be used by different clinicians with a fairly high rate of consistency. Sandifer et al. (1964) report a 74 percent agreement rate, although agreement drops sharply if we subdivide the category into *simple, paranoid, catatonic, hebephrenic,* and so on. Second, the utility of using the concept (but not necessarily its subclassifications) has already been demonstrated by the value of the genetic information gleaned in the adoptee studies cited earlier (Rosenthal, 1971). It is doubtful that such studies would have been carried out if the investigators had not used the concept *schizophrenia* or some analogous alternative.

Granted that some diagnostic categories are useful, a behavior therapist will be on firmer ground if he argues simply that the majority of the most widely used psychiatric categories are inadequate for his purposes.

The most systematic and widely used diagnostic schemes are the World Health Organization's International Classification of Diseases and the American Psychiatric Association's Diagnostic and Statistical Manual (DSM). Because of the similarities between the two sets, some of the following remarks, although aimed directly at the DSM, will apply to those of the World Health Organization as well.

There has been much criticism of the categories in the DSM. It has been charged, for example, that the descriptions are too imprecise; that they relfect, in some cases, controversial theories of human behavior; and that many of them cannot be used reliably (Ullmann & Krasner, 1969; Kanfer & Saslow, 1969). These criticisms have been important, but they can be answered if they apply not to the categories themselves but to the particular formulations given in DSM I and DSM II. Although it is too early to tell, the new formulations of DSM III may not be vulnerable to the earlier criticisms; in particular, the provision of operational criteria may eliminate the problem of imprecision and help to improve the reliability of diagnostic judgments.

A more telling criticism is that the DSM classifications are not sufficiently informative. Franks (1975) provides a thorough review of the evidence bearing on this issue and concludes (p. 64) that the DSM system is purely descriptive. Apart from describing a patient's immediate symptoms, it provides no useful information concerning the individual's life, the prognosis for his rehabilitation, or the best method of treatment.

If Frank's pessimistic conclusion is correct, this may be because the scheme presented in the DSM is far too ambitious relative to our current knowlege. As in traditional organic medicine, the diagnostic categories are designed to reflect a common *symptomatology, etiology,* and *indication of treatment*. For many functional disorders, we know far too little about etiology and methods of treatment to meet such an ambitious goal; but even if that were not true, for many cases treated by the behavior therapist, this is the wrong kind of grouping. For example, in cases where two behaviors have a different etiology but are maintained by a common cause, it may be more useful to classify them together. This would not be done if etiology were partly the basis of classification. In other cases a behavioral problem in two clients may be maintained by different causes (e.g., a learning deficit in one child by mild brain damage and in another by environmental deficiencies); but the same type of treatment – say a form of operant retraining – may be suitable for both problems. Furthermore, the behavior therapist is often interested in eliminating specific characteristics the client finds unacceptable; these characteristics often do not fit neatly into any of the classifications of DSM. For example, a client who eats too many fattening foods, who stays in bed most of the day, or who is troubled by sadistic sexual fantasies or by feelings of inadequacy may not fit any of the traditional categories. Finally, even where he does fit, the classification may not be helpful; the client may qualify as a "neurotic," but the behavior therapist still wants an additional classification of the particular characteristics that the client deems maladaptive. For these reasons the behavior therapist would be justified in trying to develop an alternative diagnostic scheme even if the criticisms of DSM could be met. Given his specific therapeutic goals, an alternataive system might prove useful as a supplement rather than a rival to the traditional scheme. One such system has been developed by Kanfer and Saslow (1969) who recommend a behavioral approach based on modern learning theory. Their approach includes the categorization of the clients' major complaints into classes of specific behavioral excesses and deficits. It also includes obtaining information about the biological, social, and behavioral conditions responsible for the maintenance of the problematic behaviors. Further details of behavioral approaches, as either a supplement to or a substitute for traditional psychiatric diagnosis, are discussed in Goldfried and Kent (1972) and Goldfried and Sprakfin (1974). One limitation of such approaches is their linkage to modern learning theory. If one rejects behaviorism and learning theory as a foundation for behavior therapy, as we have done in this book, then the analysis of the client's problems should be widened to include cognitive and affective elements, and the causal analysis should be similarly broadened to include, where relevant, both mentalistic and physiological factors. Apart from these limitations, the Kanfer and Saslow approach should prove useful in that it requires a more detailed description of an individual client's problems and links classification primarily to treatment rather than to etiology.

Conclusion. We have argued against a complete rejection of a medical viewpoint in clinical psychology and psychiatry. The arguments for the myth of mental illness or for a ban on the use of the concept *mental illness* are unconvincing. An acceptance of what we termed a *minimal medical model* does appear justified, given current evidence concerning the etiology of certain psychoses and the important features of illnesses. It was also argued that discussing the issues solely in terms of the existence or prevalence of mental illness can be misleading; there are other issues at stake besides the illness issue. Now that we have teased some of these issues apart and discussed them separately, we can ascend again to a higher plane of abstraction by grouping some of them together. Let us say that when behavior therapists speak of rejecting a "medical model" (in a broader sense), they sometimes are referring to some conjunction of theses such as the following:

1 Most psychiatric problems are mental or behavioral illnesses.
2 Most such problems are best treated medically.
3 Any treatment that eliminates a patient's symptoms without removing either an underlying psychic or organic cause is likely to result in symptom substitution.
4 A client's problems are best classified using the system contained in DSM.

If the arguments in the present chapter are sound, none of the preceding theses is acceptable; each is either false or at least not supported by the current evidence.

5. Moral foundations

Some basic issues

Does behavior therapy need a moral foundation? Should a therapist simply give the client what he wants? Can a behavior therapist accept determinism and still distinguish between a free and a coerced choice to accept therapy? When is the use of aversive conditioning morally acceptable? Should it be used in prisons or on nonconsenting hospital patients?

In one sense behavior therapy neither has nor needs a moral foundation. No moral theory can explain why any technique is effective, nor can it aid in the derivation of new techniques. For either of these purposes, we need a theory that explains not what ought to happen but what does happen. We might, however, speak of a *moral foundation* in referring to a set of general principles that can justify the *application* of behavior therapy techniques. Does behavior therapy require a foundation of this sort? Why not simply check to see if a particular technique is effective with a particular sort of client who has a particular sort of problem? If the empirical evidence shows that the technique is effective, use it; otherwise, do not. The proper reply, of course, is that the proposition that a given technique will work does not entail that it ought to be used. To derive the latter proposition, we need some additional premise saying what ought to be done (i.e., we need to appeal to some moral principle). Assuming that moral principles are required, what kind do we need? The basic model is designed to answer this question.

I. The basic model

Even if moral principles are needed, it might be that nothing more subtle is required than the appeal to such an obvious principle as the following: If someone needs help and asks for it, then help ought to be given (at least, giving help is permissible, even if not always obligatory). Assuming that this principle is acceptable, what

172

else is needed? Problems might arise in a special setting, such as a mental hospital where certain patients are not capable of asking for help, but in an outpatient setting, let the client decide whether or not he wants to change his behavior. For certain sorts of changes, moral issues can arise. (For example, should a homosexual adjust to his or her homosexuality, or try to become heterosexual? Should a docile wife learn to become more assertive or learn how to accommodate a domineering husband?) But these are moral problems for the client, not the therapist. Except in very rare cases, the client should be given what he wants; the therapist should not impose his own values on the client. The therapist, according to this view, may be thought of as a social engineer; his or her job is to decide which therapy is best suited to the client's problem. This raises an empirical, not a moral question. The engineer tells us how to build a bridge; it is for others to decide whether a bridge ought to be built.

The analogy to bridge building can be pressed a bit further. There are special circumstances when an engineer may be faced with a moral issue concerning a request to build a bridge. For example, the proposed project may involve extensive damage to the physical environment; it may cause the killing of wildlife; it may involve the relocation of poor people. It is too strong, then, to say that moral issues can *never* arise for the bridge builder; but that does not mean that we need a moral foundation for bridge building. Does anyone seriously suppose that we do? Analogously, the behavior therapist may be confronted with delicate moral issues in rare cases, but that hardly shows that he needs a moral foundation for his general practice any more than the engineer does.

The preceding account can be distilled into the following thesis, which I shall refer to as the basic model:

Basic model: The practice of behavior therapy needs no moral foundation except for the following: It is right (permissible or obligatory) to help people who request help.

The basic model would probably be acceptable, with some minor qualifications, to some behavior therapists; but I shall not assume that this is so. My point in elaborating the view, which is a very natural one, is to use it as a foil in explaining the importance of developing a moral foundation for behavior therapy. It might be true that in most cases behavior therapists face no special moral problems (i.e., none requiring for its solution anything more than the use of some very obvious moral principles), but whether or not this is so, there are some clear and important disanalogies between behavior therapy and bridge building. First, bridge building is almost invariably done with the free consent of someone who requests the service; that is not true of behavior therapy. What I have called the basic model is applicable (at best) to outpatient settings, but behavior therapy is often used in certain institutional settings, such as mental hospitals or prisons, where the client lacks the ability to give his free consent or where he is at least coerced to some extent by the authorities who control his behavior. Second, some critics of behavior therapy contend that it is not morally neutral in the way that bridge building normally is; they object to its use on moral grounds even if it is effective. These critics may be wrong, but to show this it is likely that we will need to discuss some abstract moral issues. At the very least, neither appeal to the basic model nor comparisons with bridge building will provide answers to the relevant criticisms. Third, there is a clear difference between bridge building and the practice of behavior therapy in that the latter, but not the former, sometimes involves the deliberate infliction of pain on people (as in aversive therapy), the deprivation of things that people are normally entitled to (as in some token economy programs), or the use of people for research purposes (which can occur in the use of any behavior therapy technique). Because behavior therapy has these special features and bridge building does not, the former raises special and difficult moral issues of a sort not raised by the latter; for that reason, an inquiry into moral foundations, though not necessary for bridge building, can be important for behavior therapy.

II. Behavior therapy and free choice

One fundamental issue that is logically prior to the relevant moral questions concerns free choice. Many behavior therapists accept some form of determinism, but also try to distinguish between a free and coerced decision to change one's behavior. The issue is whether one can consistently draw this distinction and still accept determinism. Some behavior therapists doubt that they can. A recent president of the Association for the Advancement of Behavior Therapy expresses the point as follows:

Even though behaviorists are metatheoretically committed to determinism, nonetheless I believe that most of us fall into the habit of distinguishing between situations where people are forced to change their behavior and situations in which people make free or voluntary decisions to change. It seems to me that if we are to take the basic deterministic dictum of science seriously, however, we must come to grips with the conditions surrounding even those decisions in therapy which have hitherto been termed voluntary or free. [Davison, 1976.]

Skinner (1971a) has also suggested that a belief in determinism and a belief in free choice are logically incompatible; and it is likely that many behavior therapists feel uncomfortable in assuming something (i.e., that free choice exists) that they believe runs counter to a fundamental dictum of science.

If we assume that clients in outpatient settings never freely decide to undergo therapy, then the basic model collapses altogether. That view presupposes that the behavior therapist can usually avoid difficult moral issues by letting the client decide what behavior should be modified, but the burden cannot be so easily shifted if the client has no capacity for free choice. More is at stake, however, than merely retaining the basic model. For example, consider the concern of some humanists (e.g., Matson, 1973, p. 22) that behavioral techniques will be used to take away or severely diminish our capacity for free choice. If we have no such capacity, then obviously neither the government nor any other group can take it away. In any event, any group that tries will have no free choice about the matter; that will be true of both behavioral psychologists who develop the techniques and their humanistic critics who complain about the dangers of misuse. In addition, the denial of the existence of free choice will have profound implications for moral issues about behavior therapy; many of the standard distinctions, such as the difference between the use of aversive therapy on someone who freely requests it and its use on an unwilling prisoner, will have to be rejected or redrawn.

Should a behavior therapist deny free choice if determinism is true? It depends on what is meant by *determinism*. Consider two different deterministic views:

1 All human behavior is caused.
2 All human behavior is caused by a process of classical or operant conditioning.

Thesis 1, but not thesis 2, is entailed by what philosophers usually call determinism: the proposition that every event (or at least every macroevent) has a cause. Apart from quantum indeterminacies, it might be true that every event has a cause but also true that some human behavior is caused by something other than the processes of classical and operant conditioning. Theses 1 and 2, then, require separate discussion.

Thesis 1 does not obviously entail the denial of free choice; there is no obvious contradiction in asserting that it is true and that some choices are free. *Free choice* does not obviously mean an "uncaused choice." Many philosophers, though not all, accept the opposite view, called *soft determinism:* that free choice can exist even if every event does have a cause. Widespread acceptance hardly proves that the view is true, but it is also supported by plausible arguments. Because the arguments have been expressed elsewhere (Pap, 1962; Grunbaum, 1953), there is no need to repeat them here. As long as soft determinism remains a plausible view, the claim that free choice does not exist cannot be inferred from thesis 1 alone. We need an additional assumption – that is, if all human behavior is caused, then free choice does not exist. It is not easy to prove that this additional assumption is true. We cannot, then, simply take for granted that all free choice is illusory if thesis 1 is true (i.e., if all human behavior is caused).

It may be that some behavior therapists reject free choice not simply because they assume thesis 1 but because they also accept thesis 2, "All human behavior is caused by processes of operant or classical conditioning." Is thesis 2 incompatible with free choice? To simplify the issue, let us neglect any possible causal role played by physiological variables and assume, as many operant theorists do, that if thesis 2 is true, then all human behavior results solely from the organism's current state of deprivation and stimulus circumstances, its genetic constitution, and its history of reinforcement. Given this assumption, it seems plausible to say that if thesis 2 is true, then there is no free choice. If thesis 2 is true, then our beliefs and desires have no consequences; they are mere epiphenomena. Consider, for example, a client who deliberates about the kind of therapy he needs. After reviewing all the evidence and reflecting on his problem and the cost of various therapies, he decides to seek the help of a behavior therapist. If thesis 2 is true, his reflection makes no difference and his preference for behavior therapy does not affect his behavior. Given his genetic constitution, it is only external circumstances (i.e., his past reinforcement history and his present stimulus conditions and state of deprivation) that determines his behavior. These conditions act on his behavior automatically and mechanically if thesis 2 is true. No intervening variable, such as the client's beliefs, wants, desires, preferences, and so on, makes any difference whatsoever. It seems plausible, then, to conclude that if thesis 2 is true, then there is no free choice. However, this conclusion has been challenged. In his thoughtful presidential address to the American Psychological Association, Bandura (1974) makes the following objection to Skinner's views about freedom. Although it is true that behavior is regulated by its contingencies, the contingencies are partly of a person's own making. Thus, the behavior of an organism partly creates the environment, and the environment influences the behavior in a reciprocal manner. People are at least partially free, then, insofar as they can influence future contingencies by managing their own behavior (Bandura, 1974, pp. 866–7). If Bandura is right, then thesis 2 is compatible with free choice, for it is consistent with the idea that people, by acting on the environment, influence their own behavior. Indeed, Skinner and other operant theorists stress the importance of an organism's acting on his environment, sometimes altering the very stimulus conditions that regulate behavior. What is dubious in Bandura's argument is the premise that insofar as someone can make such an alteration, he is at least partially free. Suppose we build a robot incapable of free choice; it is programmed to react automatically and mechanically to its environment. It might still be able to alter those conditions that regulate its behavior, but, by hypothesis, it would still not be free.

If the Skinnerian account is correct, we are all like the robot in at least one crucial respect: Given our genetic makeup, the environment acts mechanically and automatically to control our behavior. For reasons given earlier, if this is true, then it does seem plausible to deny the existence of free choice. The fact that we, like the robot, also affect the very environment that controls us does not undermine Skinner's rejection of free choice.

The most plausible way to reply to Skinner is to question thesis 2, which Bandura (1974) also does. We argued earlier (Chapter 3) that the best available evidence does not support the idea that all human behavior is caused by a process of operant or classical conditioning. If that is right, then we can agree that thesis 2 is incompatible with free choice but reasonably refuse to accept it.

Conclusion. Davison (1976) is probably correct in suggesting that some decisions to seek therapy that hitherto have been viewed as free and voluntary may be neither. As will be seen later, the client who seeks help for his "social deviance" may be coerced even if he is treated in an outpatient setting. Someone with a different sort of problem may also be coerced if he has been ordered by a court to undero therapy.

We should reject the idea, then, that a client is choosing freely simply because he is being treated in an outpatient setting, but we need not reject free choice altogether in order to retain determinism. So long as soft determinism is a viable option, a behavior therapist can consistently accept the view that all human behavior is caused and still allow for the existence of free choice. What might logically compel one to deny the existence of free choice is a different belief, that is, that all human behavior is caused solely by a process of classical and operant conditioning. But then one should be clear that the denial is being compelled by the acceptance of that theory of learning, not by determinism.

III. Critiques of behavior therapy

If we concede that even in outpatient settings clients can be coerced, that weakens but does not destroy the basic model; it can still be applied to those cases where coercion is minimal or nonexistent. A more fundamental challenge is presented by critics who raise moral objections to the use of behavior therapy even where there is no coercion. We turn now to some of these objections.

Some psychologists who place great value on free choice have complained about the therapeutic goals of behavior therapists. For example, Carl Rogers, in his (1956) symposium with Skinner, agrees that a therapist should control his client up to a certain point, but not beyond. The therapist should institute a set of conditions that will cause a certain change in the client, and the client will have relatively little voice in the establishment of these conditions. The therapist's control over the client should end at this point. The therapist should select those conditions that will enhance the freedom of the client. The goal is to make the client more self-directing, less rigid, more open to the evidence of his senses, better organized and integrated, more similar to the ideal that the client has chosen for himself. Rogers suggests that it is the choice of this therapeutic goal that essentially distinguishes the kind of behavioral control he advocates, the kind found in client-centered therapy, from that advocated by Skinner (Rogers, 1956, p. 1063). Although Rogers was objecting specifically to a

Skinnerian-conceived behavioral technology, and not necessarily to all types of behavior therapy, an advocate of client-centered therapy might extend the objection to behavior therapy in general. Would this extended objection be justified? Is it generally true that because of a difference in therapeutic goals, client-centered therapy is morally preferable to behavior therapy where (and if) both are equally effective, neglecting other variables, such as duration and cost of treatment? There are several reasons to doubt that this is so. First, some behavior therapies are commonly used to enhance a client's freedom of choice. For example, one goal of the use of self-control techniques in weight reduction programs is to help the client to be free not to eat certain foods and to attain whatever level of weight he or she desires. Another example is the use of assertive training to enhance the client's ability to react as he desires in social situations. A third example is the use of cognitive restructuring to free the client from the grip of false beliefs that inhibit his freedom of action. Second, even where enhancement of free choice is not specifically part of the goal of the therapy, elimination of a specific problem often has that effect. For example, if a salesman has a phobic reaction to airplanes, the elimination of his fear of flying can greatly increase the travel choices open to him. Third, the enhancement of free choice is not the only desirable or legitimate goal of therapy. If an autistic child is destroying his body, then it is desirable to eliminate the self-destruction even if this has no effect on the child's ability to choose. Where Rogers's point does have some force is in the following kind of case. Suppose a homosexual is about to undergo therapy and has a choice of undergoing aversive conditioning or client-centered therapy. It is an empirical question whether or not both types of treatment would be equally effective, but *if* they were and if everything else were equal (including the cost and duration of treatment), then it seems plausible to opt for the client-centered therapy; that is, it seems more desirable to institute conditions that enable the client to choose freely and rationally to change or not to change his sexual orientation. Even in this hypothetical situation, however, the therapist who values free choice might be unjustly imposing his goal on the client. It just might be that the client does not want to become more self-directive or less rigid; the goal he desires might be simply to change his sexual behavior. Perhaps we should not help him achieve his goal sometimes, but, as shall be argued later, sometimes we should.

Some humanists are concerned about behavior therapy because they see the development and use of such techniques as creating a potential danger. Matson (1973, p. 10) expresses this concern and warns that the behavioral technology heralded by Skinner may well be with us, if not now, then all too soon. Humanists are concerned at least partly because they are worried that a dictator may use such a technology to take away people's freedom of choice.

It might be tempting to reply to this objection by saying that science is value-free. Scientists seek knowledge; others decide what ought to be done with it. The difficulty, of course, is that we may know what others are likely to do with our knowledge. Sheer scientific curiosity might have motivated some of the rocketry experts working in Nazi Germany during World War II, but they nonetheless could have made a reasonable guess as to where the rockets were likely to land. If there were a comparable danger of misuse of behavioral technology, that would be a powerful reason not to develop it.

A more plausible response to the humanists' concern is to acknowledge responsibility, but to place the danger of misuse in some reasonable perspective. Is it true that we now have or are likely to have in the near future a behavioral technology that can be used to control the behavior of the average citizen? It is no doubt true that we can control a good deal of human behavior if we use a large enough reward or a sufficiently severe punishment (a lot of money or a gun often do nicely), but, presumably, critics of behavior therapy have something more subtle in mind, something more specifically connected with behavior therapy. For example, consider the treatment of Alex in the movie *A Clockwork Orange.* Alex volunteers to undergo the therapy, but his consent is depicted as unessential. Once he is strapped to a chair and forced to watch certain scenes on film after being drugged, he is automatically and mechanically conditioned to react peacefully even when physically attacked. As a consequence, he can no longer protect himself when his life is endangered. Can the average adult be conditioned in a similar manner? It is interesting to note that at least some behavior therapists do not think that this is possible. For example, Marks (1976, p. 255) states flatly, "Behavioral treatment can only be given to adult neurotics if they are cooperative; successful treatment cannot be forced on patients against their will." Other behavior therapists make a similar admission (Davison, 1973; Bandura, 1975). It might be replied that such behavior therapists fail to appreciate the power of their techniques, but then what evidence is there that behavior therapy can generally be used to alter peoples' behavior against their will? Some writers probably believe that this can be done (McConnell, 1970) because they accept behaviorism or some behavioristic learning theory. They believe that human behavior is mechanically controlled by the environment and genetic endowment. If we manipulate the client's environment according to our theory of learning, then we can shape his behavior whether he cooperates or not. However, a humanist who is concerned about the diminishment of free choice presumably rejects these theories; if such theories were true, there would be no free choice to be concerned about. In any event, the evidence discussed in Chapters 2 and 3 shows that there is no good reason to accept these theories. Once the behavioristic and learning theory foundations of behavior therapy are rejected, what reason is there to believe that currently used behavior therapy techniques can be generally used to significantly alter peoples' behavior against their wills? Where is the evidence that this has been done, or that it can be done? There is no such evidence. What is true is that certain behavior therapy techniques when used with clients with special cognitive deficits, such as small children or adult schizophrenics, can sometimes be used to effect behavioral change without the subject's consent. Where this is possible, special moral problems do arise in the use of behavior therapy, or any therapy that is effective. We will discuss some of these problems later, but they do not present any objection to the use of behavior therapy in general; nor do such special cases provide any evidence that behavior therapy can be similarly used with unwilling clients not having similar cognitive deficits.

Even if there is no evidence that we now have or are likely in the near future to have the kind of behavioral technology feared by Matson and other humanists, it is conceivable that this might happen. Behavior therapists should at least be sensitive to the moral concerns of those who take the possibility seriously. If, however, we now have evidence that behavior therapy techniques will help relieve a good deal of human suffering, then we cannot reasonably renounce the study or use of such techniques merely because of a bare possibility that their use will foster a powerful behavioral technology that could be used to control people's lives. There is also a possibility that research in brain chemistry or drug therapy might some day produce unwanted means of behavioral control, but the bare possibility of this occurring is not weighty enough to abandon all such research, assuming that abandonment is likely to cost us substantial benefits.

Conclusion. There are good reasons to be concerned about the misuse of behavior therapy; some of these reasons will be discussed later. It is doubtful, however, that these reasons present any sound moral objection to the use of behavior therapy in general.

Sometimes it is said that behavior therapy is morally objectionable because it is dehumanizing; it treats man as if he were a mere physical object, instead of a person. Here it is important to distinguish between behavior therapy as a paradigm and as a kind of therapy (see Chapter 1). The complaint may have some force if directed at the paradigm accepted by *some* behavior therapists. Someone who is a behaviorist may hold that we can reasonably ignore a subject's mental state and view him as if he were not a person; but a behavior therapist need not, and should not, accept this view. If the complaint is extended to the therapy, it does not seem particularly plausible. It *might* be that a case could be made that a particular use of a certain type of behavior therapy, such as the use of electric shock in modifying homosexual behavior, is dehumanizing. For example, in the procedure developed by Feldman and MacCulloch (1971), a male homosexual is typically shown slides of males he finds attractive. If he fails to press a button removing the slide he is viewing, he will receive a painful electric shock; if he presses the button, a slide of an attractive female will be substituted. Because the procedure is so mechanical and because it is directed at something so deeply personal as one's sexuality, some might charge that the procedure is dehumanizing. It is not clear that the charge would be justified even in this case; it is not true that the patient's mental states are ignored; it is not *obvious* that the client is "not treated as a person." (Perhaps it is not obvious because this idea is not very clear.) Even if the complaint is justified in this or in some other case, it is not likely that it will apply to behavior therapy in general but not apply to other sorts of therapy. It may be that in some sense it is "dehumanizing" to have to undergo any sort of therapy for certain types of very private problems; but in exactly what respect is it true that systematic desensitization, modeling, assertive training, cognitive restructuring, and self-control procedures are all "dehumanizing" in a way that nonbehavior therapies are not? It is not likely that there is any such respect that is also morally relevant. (We could always stipulate that a technique is "dehumanizing" if and only if it is approved of by behaviorists, but that would not be morally relevant.)

Some critics who are concerned about dehumanization may object to the sharp distinction drawn here between behavior therapy practice and paradigm. It might be argued that one influences the other, that because many behavior therapists are behaviorists they are insufficiently concerned about treating clients as persons. Even if there is some truth in this charge, the complaint, as now understood, is still limited to what some or many behavior therapists do; it is not a complaint about behavior therapy techniques.

Is the preceding complaint justified, when interpreted correctly? Cases can probably be found in which clients have not been properly treated because the therapist accepts some form of behaviorism, but what evidence is there that behavior therapists as a class tend to treat their patients in a dehumanizing manner? Some evidence bearing on this question can be gleaned from the important comparison study done by Sloane and his associates (1975) of behavior therapy and psychoanalytically oriented psychotherapy. In addition to comparing the results of the respective therapies, the Truax scales were used to measure characteristics of the therapists. Behavior therapists were judged by independent raters to be operating at the second highest stage in the therapist self-congruence scales, indicating that "they displayed genuine feeling, and meant what they said, although they did not say all they could." The psychotherapists were rated one scale lower on this variable. Behavior therapists also showed a significantly higher level of accurate empathy and interpersonal contact than did the psychotherapists. Both groups showed an equal degree of warmth or unconditional positive regard to the patient (Sloane et al., 1975a, pp. 147–9). Although this evidence is inconclusive if we are talking about behavior therapists as a class, it clearly lends no support to the charge that behavior therapists tend to act in a dehumanizing manner. Descriptions of the case studies of leading behavior therapists, for example, Lazarus (1971) and Wolpe (1973), also show evidence to the contrary. Many leading behavior therapists have also displayed in their writings a sensitivity to the moral and legal rights of behavior therapy clients (e.g., Davison, 1976; Bandura, 1975; Davison & Stuart, 1975; Krasner, 1976; Stuart, 1973). In sum, there is no firm evidence that behavior therapists as a class are significantly less sensitive to the needs of their clients than are other therapists or that they tend to treat their clients in a dehumanizing manner; there is some evidence that the opposite is true. However, unless we can specify the class of therapists being talked about, it would be unreasonable to be confident about this issue. Is a behavior therapist anyone who uses or endorses behavior therapy techniques, or is more required? In the absence of a satisfactory answer, it might be more reasonable to talk about specific therapists rather than about behavior therapists in general. As we shall see later, some therapists have misused behavior therapy techniques; the danger of this happening in the future is likely to increase as more and more people use these techniques.

It is sometimes complained that behavior therapists have no criterion for deciding which behaviors ought to be modified. They simply talk about "deviant" or "maladaptive" behavior, but this is inadequate unless we can independently specify which behaviors fall into these classes and then explain *why* they ought to be altered. For example, is the sexual behavior of a male homosexual or the verbal behavior of an aggressive woman deviant, and if it is, why is that a reason for changing the behavior? Without a moral criterion, it is argued, the behavior therapist is in danger of simply supporting society's view of what is acceptable and desirable even if that view is radically wrong.

The concern underlying the preceding complaint is important, but the complaint itself is much too broad. "Which behaviors ought to be changed?" is a question to be faced not only by behavior therapists but by all therapists; it is also a question for educators, the clergy, parents, politicians – in fact, for all of us. If we ask for a single, general criterion to aid us in answering such an abstract question, we are inviting some very general, and in this context unilluminating, response, such as, "Modify a particular type of behavior if and only if doing so will maximize human happiness." This utilitarian criterion, whether defensible or not, is not very helpful as a guide to therapeutic practices. If utilitarianism (or some competing simple, normative theory) is true, then it can be used by the behavior therapist as an abstract guide, but we still need to have more concrete criteria for deciding whether the conditions specified in the theory are met in any given case. Would it maximize human happiness, for example, if therapists commonly altered the sexual behavior of homosexuals? To develop more concrete criteria, we need to ask less abstract questions than "Which behaviors ought to be modified?" It is also necessary to ask about specific types of therapies, specific types of clients, and specific

types of therapeutic situations. We now turn to some of the more
ethically interesting types.

IV. Aversive conditioning

In addition to its other limitations, the basic model runs into special
difficulties if applied to aversive conditioning (also referred to as
aversion therapy). If the deliberate infliction of pain on another
human being is always *prima facie* wrong, then aversive conditioning, because it necessarily has this feature, always requires justification. In this respect it contrasts with some operant techniques that
make rewards contingent on the emission of certain types of behavior, for we do not generally need to justify dispensing rewards.
Other behavior therapy techniques, such as modeling or desensitization, also do not generally involve the deliberate infliction of
pain; for that reason they do not generate exactly the same issues
raised by aversive conditioning. (As will be argued later, however,
all these techniques can cause pain to the client in some circumstances.)

In many cases it may seem that the therapeutic benefits are by
themselves sufficient justification for the use of aversive conditioning, but that is because certain requirements are met that are tacitly
taken for granted. Where one or more of these requirements is
violated, even a substantial therapeutic gain may not be enough
justification. Consider the following hypothetical cases.

Case A

Someone has a mild drinking problem but believes it to be quite
serious. He believes this because he falsely conjectures that the
ruination of his marriage and the stunting of his career have resulted
from his habit of drinking at social functions to the point of being
tipsy. He asks a behavior therapist to help him solve his problem.
The therapist recommends the use of scoline (a curare-type drug)
but points out that this drug may have some unpleasant side effects.
Because the patient perceives his drinking problem to be quite
serious, he gives his consent and the therapy ensues. What the
therapist does not explain, however, is that this drug can cause the
client to have what may prove to be the most horrifying experience
of his life. Injection of scoline into the bloodstream normally
produces a total paralysis for a period of between 30 and 150

seconds. During this period the patient is unable to breathe and feels as if he is dying (Rachman & Teasdale, 1969, p. 95). When the therapy is finished, the client never drinks again; but he later suffers from the memory of his terrifying experience far more than he would have suffered had he continued drinking.

Case B

A psychiatrist in charge of a mental hospital becomes acquainted with behavior therapy techniques and decides to use them on his patients. Because he believes that too many patients remain in custody indefinitely because they cannot prove that they are fit for discharge, he decides that it is important that everyone be made to work in or around the hospital. The work itself should be therapeutic, because those who work will no longer loll around all day in their typically purposeless manner; furthermore, those who can perform their assigned tasks for an extended period will prove their suitability for discharge. Most of the patients, however, refuse to work. Consequently, he uses electric shock on all the "malingerers." The shock treatment proves effective with most of the patients, but not all. The therapist then decices that he needs to use an effective reinforcer and that food will do quite well, but only under the right conditions of deprivation. He thus starves the remaining patients for three days. At the end of this period, all the patients agree to work.

The preceding cases are hypothetical, but they resemble in important respects actual cases that have been reported in the literature. Scoline has been used in the treatment of alcoholism, and apparently patients have not always been given adequate warning concerning its harrowing effects (Rachman & Teasdale, 1969, p. 95). Another case resembling case A has been the subject of a lawsuit that reached the U.S. Court of Appeals. The plaintiff, James Mackey, was a prisoner in 1967 at Folsom state prison in California. Mackey agreed to undergo shock therapy, but charges that without his consent he was given a "breath-stopping and paralyzing 'fright drug'" (*Mackey* v. *Procunier,* 1973). Mackey also contends that as a result of this treatment, he regularly suffers nightmares in which he relives the frightening experience and awakens unable to breathe.

Case B resembles one reported by an American psychiatrist, L. H. Cotter, who was assigned to Bien Hoa Mental Hospital in 1966 and used on his patients what he describes as "operant conditioning." He was motivated to do so, he reports, after witnessing the practice of a leading behavior therapist, Ivan Lovaas, and reading the works of B. F. Skinner (Cotter, 1967). When all but 10 of his 120 male, Vietnamese patients refused to work, Cotter forced them to undergo electroconvulsive shock therapy (ECT), which is not a form of behavior therapy. The ECT treatments were then repeated three times a week. After this treatment, most of the remaining patients "volunteered" for work. The same treatment was less successful when tried with the female patients; so Cotter starved them and the remaining idle males for three days. At the end of this period, all the remaining patients volunteered for work. Cotter explains this result by appealing to the following principle: "As has been repeatedly demonstrated, when the subject is hungry food is one of the strongest and most useful of positive reinforcements" (Cotter, 1967, p. 25).

A problem arose later concerning the disposition of those cases in which the patients completed their three-month work period. The problem was solved when Cotter met in the officer's club a Special Forces commander who had been unable to recruit workers to tend crops in Viet Cong territory. An arrangement was worked out whereby the Special Forces would hire volunteer patients who were discharged from the mental hospital. Cotter notes that one benefit of this arrangement was that the cost of air transport of food was decreased; another was that a better diet was provided for our soldiers. Because workers in the fields were subject to Viet Cong attack and thus were in danger of being killed, the question was asked whether the discharged mental patients would be able to withstand the stress. Cotter replied that the stress was beneficial, pointing out that there was an appreciable drop in the number of mental breakdowns in London when it was bombed during World War II (Cotter, 1967, p. 27).

How many therapists are imitating Cotter's method is not known, but he does indicate that he has tried to pass on his newly found knowledge concerning behavior therapy to fellow psychiatrists working in Thailand, India, Lebanon, Egypt, Jordan, Turkey, Germany, Holland, and England (Cotter, 1967). In addition, his enthusiastic report on his practice was published without comment in a leading psychiatry journal, the *American Journal of Psychiatry,* and quite possibly has influenced at least some American readers of that journal. Leading behavior therapists, however, have condemned his practices (Stuart, 1973; Krasner, 1976).

The preceding cases, hypothetical and actual, illustrate at least two important points. First, it is much too simple to say that if the client consents, it is all right to use aversion therapy if it is effective. The patient may consent but not understand what he is agreeing to – the pain involved may be too great; the problem to be solved may be too small. Second, the most significant danger in the use of aversive conditioning is not that the therapy will be used subtly to manipulate the mind or behavior of people, but that it will be used to cause them unnecessary pain. In a therapeutic situation it is easy to become convinced that the infliction of pain, if it is called therapy, is in the client's interest; sometimes it is, but often it is not. It is imperative, then, that guidelines be proposed, criticized, and refined so that an individual therapist does not have to rely solely on his own intuitions about what is and is not morally permissible. With this imperative in mind, the following principles are offered as tentative guidelines, which will probably need to be revised or supplemented. Some of these principles may seem intuitively obvious, but others (particularly those discussed in the next section) require defense. Even some of the more obvious principles are worth stating explicitly because they can easily be overlooked by someone in the grip of the basic model. They conflict with the idea that the client should be "given what he wants." The letter P will precede acceptable principles and Q unacceptable ones.

One preliminary clarification is needed. Some of these principles speak of "painful therapy." How shall we define *painful?* Suppose a patient is given an oral medication with a bad taste but no side effects? Is this painful therapy? What degree of unpleasantness is required? For the purposes of this discussion, we will assume that the degree of unpleasantness is more than minimal. Taking the bad-tasting medicine, for example, does not count, but the standard sorts of aversive conditioning to be discussed shortly do. It would be nice to have an operational definition of *painful therapy,* but because any such definition must be somewhat arbitrary, we will let common sense serve as a guide to whether or not the procedure is sufficiently painful to give rise to any serious moral issue.

P_1: Painful therapy should not be used, other things being equal, if the amount of suffering it causes the client outweighs the amount of suffering it saves him.

To apply P_1 we would need to know how painful the aversion therapy is likely to be. There is now enough clinical evidence to make some rough generalizations. The kind of shock used in standard electrical aversion therapy for such problems as alcoholism, homosexuality, sexual fetishes, and cigarette smoking does not seem to be excruciatingly painful, judging by either the strength of the shock used or the patient's reaction. Most studies that identify the current have reported using 5 milliamperes or less for aversive conditioning (Tanner, 1973). In a study of the effects of electrical aversion therapy for alcoholism and for sexual problems, most clients ranked the aversion sessions as less unpleasant than visits to the dentist. The great majority of the patients were not disturbed by the electric shocks, and the reported "side effects" were few in number and mild in character (Hallam, Rachman, & Falkowski, 1972).

In the treatment of self-destructive, autistic children, the shock has had spikes as high as 1400 volts at 50,000 ohms resistance. Lovaas and Simmons (1974, p. 474) describe the shock they have used with such children as "definitely painful like a dentist drilling on an unanesthetized tooth"; the pain terminated, however, when the shock ended, which was typically after one second.

The suffering caused by chemical aversion therapy is more difficult to measure, partly because there is more variation in the way it affects different people; but some writers (e.g., Rachman & Teasdale, 1969) intimate that the typically used nausea-producing drugs are quite unpleasant compared to standard electrical aversion therapy. Other drugs that have been used in the treatment of alcoholism, such as the aforementioned scoline, are not simply very unpleasant; the experiences they produce can be terrifying.

What about the suffering caused by the client's problem? Given the great variability in the difficulties that can beset people, it would be very hard to catalogue all such problems, harder still to generalize about their effects. Even with a single sort of problem, it is often difficult to know how much suffering it will cause a particular indiviudal. For example, consider writer's cramp, which has been treated by electrical aversion therapy (Beech, 1960). Part of the suffering the problem causes may depend on what the client stands to lose if he is unable to write. Will he ever get published if he does recover? Will he earn rich rewards? It is hard to know in many cases. Suppose the patient is depressed? If he is not cured quickly, will his marriage be destroyed? Will he commit suicide? Or will the client recover fairly quickly without suffering very much? In many cases neither the client nor the therapist will have sufficient evidence to answer such questions. Still, it is possible to describe clear-cut cases where the amount of suffering a problem is likely to cause will be too minimal to justify any of the standard forms of aversion therapy. For example, a city dweller may have a snake phobia, but the problem may never cause him any anxiety or discomfort if he never sees a snake. A clear case of the opposite sort is that of certain autistic and retarded children treated by Lovaas and his associates. In some cases the children were pulling out their fingernails, biting through the flesh of their shoulders, and bloodying their heads and ears with their fists. Whether or not one has doubts about administering therapy on children without their consent, it does seem clear that their suffering was far greater than that caused by a few brief electric shocks. (In one of the worst cases, the self-destructive behavior ceased after two one-second shocks were administered [Lovaas & Simmons, 1974]). In cases in between these two extremes the therapist and client may have to act on insufficient evidence; but that is true of other sorts of cases where we try to help people. This uncertainty is not a sufficient reason to give up altogether the attempt to estimate costs and benefits.

A different sort of uncertainty arises because of the presence in P_1 of the phrase *other things being equal*. What does this mean? We can translate it as *in the absence of overriding conditions,* but it would be difficult to specify in advance all the possible conditions that can override the prohibition against causing pain to an individual that does not produce commensurate benefits for him. Nevertheless, the principle is not useless so long as we can often recognize the sorts of things that would and would not count as overriding conditions. For example, the fact that a therapist's sadistic impulses would be gratified by applying shock to the client obviously does not qualify. A more difficult issue arises when the benefits of the therapy accrue partly to society. Our city dweller may not benefit greatly from the eradication of his snake phobia, but if he is part of a well-controlled experiment others may gain from the knowledge that is acquired. A prisoner may gain slightly, all things considered, from the use of aversion therapy for his drug habit, but society may benefit substantially if he is rehabilitated. How do we weigh in these factors? In most outpatient therapy situations the therapist's primary obligation is to minimize the suffering of his client, not of others; but it seems plausible to think that in some cases other things are not equal precisely because the suffering of others would be reduced. Experimentation and the treatment of prisoners raise controversial issues that will be discussed later, but consider the case of an alcoholic who causes great suffering to his family. The elimination of their pain might tip the balance in favor of aversion therapy, even if the client's suffering did not quite exceed the pain of the therapy.

A second sort of overriding condition may occur if the client *believes* that his gain will outweigh the suffering. In our first hypothetical case, for example, the client greatly overrated his drinking problem because he had a false belief about its effects. The first move on the part of the therapist, at least in some cases, should be to dissuade the client.

Suppose, however, that a client persists in overrating his problem because of certain religious beliefs; he believes, for example, that he will suffer greatly in the afterlife because of his drinking. Even if his belief is not painful in itself – and hence its effects do not figure greatly in our calculation – at some point, a therapist should probably accede to the client's wishes even if they are misguided.

There are, then, at least two sorts of cases in which overriding conditions may be present: where changing the patient would relieve the suffering of others and where the client persists in his belief that his problem is more serious than it really is. Where these or other overriding conditions are present, not everything is equal; consequently, P_1 is not applicable. There are complexities to be faced, therefore, in invoking the principle in any given case. Sometimes, however, we can be reasonably sure that there are no overriding conditions and that the principle is being violated.

P_2: Painful therapy should not be used if less painful but equally effective techniques are readily available, other things being equal.

It seems obvious that, other things being equal, if a problem can be treated just as well by an aversive or a nonaversive procedure, then the latter should be used; and of two aversive procedures, the less painful is preferable. Complexities arise, however, when not everything is equal. For example, if treatments A and B differ with respect to cost and length of treatment, A may be preferable even if it is aversive and B is not. Or suppose that A and B are equally effective but we do not yet know that. For example, covert conditioning, which involves the use of an imagined rather than an actual stimulus, is presumably less aversive than the use of electric shock. Suppose that for a certain type of problem both procedures will be equally effective (whether or not we know this to be so), but that the evidential support for the effectiveness of covert conditioning is still minimal. In deciding which of the two treatments is preferable, the therapist may have to weigh both the likelihood and cost of failure. Making such judgments can obviously be difficult. Principles for using aversion therapy can help, but it is doubtful that they can substitute in all cases for the good sense and sensitivity of both the therapist and client.

P_3: Painful therapy should not be used, other things being equal, without obtaining the informed consent of the client if he is capable of giving his consent.

The preceding rule (and the next rule) could be amended to cover all behavior therapy, but its violation with respect to aversion therapy is generally more serious precisely because the latter is inherently painful.

What counts as *"informed* consent" is a perplexing question. Clearly, the client need not be given all the information possessed by the therapist; he need not be given Ph.D. training in psychology before proceeding with the therapy. There are some crucial items, however, that seem obviously relevant to giving one's informed consent to aversive treatment. First, and most important with respect to aversive therapy, the client should be told of the degree of pain involved. In our first hypothetical case, what is mainly objectionable is the therapist's use of scoline without describing in detail its likely effects. Second, the client should be warned of possible side effects, particularly in the use of chemical aversion therapy. Third, the goal of the therapy should be specified, preferably in behavioral terms. Fourth, the likelihood of success or failure should be made evident. Fifth, alternative, less painful procedures should be mentioned where relevant.

What of clients who are not capable of giving their consent, such as autistic or severely retarded children or mute catatonics? Because the use of aversion therapy with such people raises especially difficult problems, the question will be bypassed until the next section. P_3 neither forbids nor licenses its use on such clients. Similarly, the use of aversive conditioning on unwilling prisoners also raises special problems that will be discussed in the next section. If, as some would argue, it is permissible to use aversion therapy on prisoners who do not consent, then P_3 would have to be amended to exclude prisoners from its scope.

P_4: A therapist should not coerce a client to undergo painful therapy, other things being equal, if the client is capable of consent.

The preceding principle has a different form from the earlier ones. Why? Why not simply say that painful therapy should not be used, other things being equal, without obtaining the uncoerced consent of anyone capable of consent? The answer is that the latter principle seems too strong. Suppose a client is coerced by a court to undergo aversion therapy because he has a drug habit and has committed a crime. In some cases a therapist may have good reason to refuse to administer aversion therapy even if none of the earlier principles is violated, but that is not so merely because the client has been coerced; at least, that is not obviously true. Suppose, the client agrees that his choices – aversive conditioning or revocation of parole – are not pleasant, but argues that given these choices, he prefers, on very rational grounds, to undergo the therapy. Should a therapist refuse his request simply because he has been coerced? If one says yes, then what of the following case? An alcoholic does not want to undergo therapy, but he is pressured by his wife who threatens to leave him. The therapist knows that this is so. Should he refuse to use aversion therapy even if it is otherwise warranted?

Clearly, some degree of coercion is involved in many cases where aversive conditioning is nonetheless permissible. Social pressure often causes people to seek solutions to such problems as marital discord, sexual impotence, stuttering, alcoholism, and so on. Such people are coerced to some degree, but that in itself does not seem sufficient to deny them access to aversive conditioning, at least not in all cases. We might reply, "Well, these people are not really coerced; they still have the choice of putting up with the social pressure." That is true, at least in many such cases; but, then, if a therapist places a gun at the client's temple, the client still has the choice of being dead. Is *that* a reason for saying he was not coerced?

Perhaps what is needed is a distinction between different degrees of coercion. If the client is coerced to X degree, then do not on that account deny him the therapy; beyond that point, withhold it. This approach may be the right one, but it is exceedingly difficult to draw the distinction in a clear and precise way. Until it is drawn, we can at least require that the therapist not pressure the client to undergo aversion therapy because, for example, the therapist is interested in collecting data on its effects. What, then, of a client who is pressured simply because the therapist is an expert? The answer is not that the therapist should fail to express his judgment but that he should try to counteract the client's deference to authority and to encourage him to decide on rational grounds whether or not to undergo the therapy.

Conclusion. The preceding principles are intended to express only necessary, not sufficient, conditions for the justified use of aversion therapy. Furthermore, because they contain the vague phrase *other things being equal,* they are less informative and harder to test than other principles that might be proposed. Nevertheless, they are of some use if they help explain why aversive conditioning is objectionable in certain sorts of cases where that is not immediately obvious. They help explain, for example, what was morally objectionable in the hypothetical and actual cases cited earlier. That is, they do that *if* what they say is true. How can we tell? How, in fact, can we decide anything about the moral foundations of behavior therapy, or of anything else? This latter question is perhaps the deepest and most controversial question in philosophical ethics. It would be foolish to try to give and defend a satisfactory answer here, but the question should not be ignored altogether given the views of many behavior therapists on the rationality of ethics. For example, after explaining why Cotter's practice on his Vietnamese patients was wrong, Krasner (1976, p. 639) asks the following question: "Is my value system (or yours) better than Cotter's? By what behavioral decision does my value system (or yours) take precedence over anyone else's?" Krasner's answer seems to be that there may well be no satisfactory answer to these questions. For example, he suggests that it is bad to coerce patients to support a war effort, but refers to this suggestion as his "bias." Similarly, Stuart (1973, p. 232) concludes a sensitive and enlightening discussion of ethical issues by saying that, in many instances, ethical decisions concerning behavior therapy are "arbitrary." *The highest good,* he suggests, has many definitions. Whether or not these authors are endorsing a general moral skepticism, it is probably a widely held view among behavior therapists that science and rationality end where ethics begins; that is, there can be no rational defense of moral principles. One antidote to such skepticism would be to provide a behavioristic account of ethics (Day, 1975). For example, it has been suggested that ethical statements are really about reinforcement contingencies. Thus, *You ought to tell the truth* might be translated *If you tell the truth, you will be reinforced for doing so.* There are rational procedures for determining whether or not this second statement is true. However, a behavioristic view of this sort encounters serious problems, as has been effectively shown by Begelman (1976). One of his examples is *You ought to persecute blacks.* This statement does not mean, *If you persecute blacks, you will be reinforced for doing so.* If you live in a racist society, the latter statement may be true even if the former is not. A behaviorist is free to propose a different behavioristic translation, but we have already considered this sort of theory of meaning in Chapter 2; the problems raised there make it dubious that behavioristic translations of ethical statements will prove adequate. Our choices, however, are not limited to either moral skepticism or a behavioristic analysis. To illustrate, according to one nonbehavioristic theory, fundamental ethical principles are somewhat analogous to principles of logic (even though there are important differences as well). For example, the following principle of logic cannot be tested directly by appeal to empirical observation, but it is not arbitrary either: "If 'p' and 'if p then q' are true, then 'q' is true." Why accept this principle? First, it is intuitively plausible; second, one cannot find any credible counterexamples; third, the principle can be used to explain why certain intuitively obvious arguments are good arguments. For each of these three points, an analogous point can be made about certain ethical principles. One weakness of this position, however, is that it seems to sanction an appeal to what is intuitively obvious as having evidential value but does not explain why that is so (either for logic or ethics). One possible way around this difficulty is to bring in causal explanations of why certain simple cases and principles in ethics seem intuitively obvious to rational agents having certain characteristics. Suppose, for example, that it does seem intuitively plausible to most rational agents that we should not inflict pain on another human being for no good reason. Is it because (1) this principle is rationally credible; (2) most people uncritically accept it without adequate reflection, without trying to find counterexamples; or (3) they are being misled by some false theory; or (4) there is some other reason? If explanations 2 or 3 were correct, the appeal to the intuitions of rational agents in this case might carry little or no evidential weight; but the appeal might have some value if the first explanation were correct. Developing and defending a theory of this sort is beyond the scope of this book, but a somewhat similar account is explained in some detail in Rawls (1971); for an alternative view, see Harman (1977).

V. Behavior therapy with a captive clientele

Although issues concerning free choice and coerciveness can arise in outpatient treatment, the problems are more visible and more pervasive when the clientele is under someone's control, as in a prison or state mental institution. Some of the more serious issues arise because of an interaction between two factors: the painfulness of the treatment and the captivity of the client. For that reason we will continue to concentrate on aversive procedures; later the conclusions will be extended to other behavior therapy techniques, especially token economy programs.

Behavior therapy in prisons

Some of the public concern about behavior therapy arises from its use in prisons on nonconsenting prisoners. In 1971 the Senate Subcommittee on Constitutional Rights, chaired by Senator Sam Ervin, Jr., began an investigation into a variety of behavioral change programs. The final 651-page report, issued in 1974, raised serious constitutional and moral issues concerning some of the investigated programs, especially those used in correctional institutions. One result of the inquiry was the announcement in 1974 by the Law Enforcement Assistance Administration, U.S. Department of Justice, that it was prohibiting the use of its funds for, among other things, behavior modification research; aversion therapy in particular was cited as falling within the scope of the ban (Ervin Committee Report, 1974, p. 420). Part of the controversy that led to the ban appears to have stemmed from conceptual confusion. On one of the definitions of *behavior modification* suggested in the Ervin Committee Report (p. 1), the concept applies only to aversive procedures. On a wider definition, such techniques as lobotomies and other psychosurgery techniques were included; these are clearly not forms of behavior therapy as the term is used here. It is also true, however, that conceptual clarification will not resolve all the issues; some criticisms were made because aversion therapy *has* been used on prisoners. One such case has already been mentioned; in *Mackey* v. *Procunier* (1973), a state prisoner at Folsom State Prison in California alleged that he had been given a paralysis-inducing drug, succinylcholine, without his consent. The same drug has been used as part of an aversive treatment program at Vacaville, a psychiatric facility for criminal offenders, located in California (Ervin Committee Report, 1974, p. 14). In this second case the consent of patients was sometimes obtained; sometimes it was not. Apomorphine, a drug that induces uncontrollable vomiting, has also been used as part of an "aversive conditioning program" in the Iowa Security Medical Facility. The drug was used without the inmate's consent for such behavior as staying in bed, talking, swearing, or lying (Ervin Committee Report, 1974, p. 14).

In one of the more widely publicized cases, 90 male inmates at Atascadero, an institution populated primarily by mentally disordered criminals, received injections of succinylcholine as part of an aversion therapy program. All of those treated were forced to receive the drug; there was no signed consent (Gerber et al., 1975). Furthermore, there is some evidence that the drug was used to punish as well as treat people. For example, one inmate was selected for treatment because he was "observed in active fellatio attitude"; another was described as follows: "Uncooperative, disruptive in group. Pacing, negativistic, laughs and grins inappropriately. Muslim who stirs up race hatred" (Gerber et al., 1975).

Aversion therapy is not used in federal prisons, according to the testimony of the director of the Federal Bureau of Prisons (Ervin Committee Report, 1974, p. 230); however, the bureau does not have jurisdiction over state correctional facilities. In any event, the issue of using aversion therapy in prisons is likely to be raised again as long as the crime rate is high and more conventional rehabilitation programs are perceived as ineffective in reducing recidivism. Additional pressure is likely to be generated as the findings of Martinson and his colleagues become more widely publicized. After an exhaustive review of the literature, Martinson concluded that, on the basis of current evidence, existing treatment programs have very little effect (in most cases, no effect) on the rate of recidivism (Martinson, 1976). Some observers are likely to conclude that a plausible explanation of these findings is that the wrong kinds of programs have been used in correctional institutions; what is needed, it will be argued, is behavior therapy, and perhaps aversive conditioning in particular.

Should aversion therapy be used on unwilling prisoners if it is effective? Some would think the practice obviously wrong, but not everyone agrees. For example, McConnell (1970) argues that because a prisoner has no right to his criminal personality, it can be altered by the use of aversion therapy for the benefit of society. It does not matter whether or not the prisoner consents.

The preceding argument may seem plausible because it is not obvious that a criminal does have a right to his personality; but this may be because it is not obvious that anyone has such a right. To decide this issue, we might have to answer several puzzling questions. First, what is a personality? Is it no more than a complex set of dispositions to behave in certain sorts of ways? If that is all it is, and if the ways are criminal, then it might seem that the person has less of a claim to his personality. If someone has no right to engage in criminal activities, why should he have a right to retain his dispositions to act criminally? If, however, a personality is something more than a set of dispositions, if it is in some sense intimately related to a person's self-identity, then his claim to retain his personality might have greater strength. Second, to what extent are people generally responsible for shaping their own personalities? If an individual has the personality he has largely because of his genetic makeup and because of environmental influences outside of his control, then what has he done to give him a right to that personality? Or does one have a right to one's personality in the same way that one has a right to life; perhaps both rights are natural rights that do not depend on an individual's doing anything to earn them. Because these issues are not easily settled, given the vagueness of the idea of self-identity, it might be wise to avoid them if we can. To avoid them, let us concede that a prisoner has no right to his criminal personality. Does it follow that we have a right to use aversion therapy on him? It does not follow without the aid of some additional premise, such as the following:

Q_1: If a criminal has no right to his personality, then we have the right to use aversion therapy to alter it for the benefit of society.

The preceding principle does not seem plausible if it is not generally true that we have the right to use aversion therapy to modify for society's benefit a characteristic a person has no right to. Suppose, for example, that someone has a speech impediment, or a facial tic, or some disgusting eating habit. It seems odd, and false, to say that he has a right to such a characteristic; nevertheless, it seems wrong to inflict pain on him without his consent merely because society would benefit. If it is wrong then why is it permissible to inflict pain on the unwilling prisoner? One possibility is that it is permissible because he has not just a tic or a disgusting eating habit, but a criminal personality. Why is this a crucial difference? Presumably, because if he is released with his personality intact, he is likely to engage in criminal acts. This suggests the following principle:

Q_2: If a person's retention of his criminal personality is likely to cause him to engage in criminal behavior, then we have the right to use aversive conditioning to alter his personality.

If we rely on principle Q_2, then we will have shifted the issue. What is now crucial is not the right to keep one's personality, but society's right to inflict pain on someone to prevent some future misdeed. It is not clear that society has this right. If Q_2 were correct, it would license the infliction of pain on an innocent individual simply to benefit other people. What would be crucial would be not what he had done, but what he was likely to do. For example, consider some of the studies funded by the National Center for the Study of Crime and Delinquency that deal with the prediction of criminal behavior. Some studies have attempted to relate a disposition to behave criminally to chromosome abnormalities; some to the repetition of such behavior in families. Others appear to involve direct electrical stimulation of the brain in an effort to discover and "neutralize" neurological sources of violence (Ervin Committee Report, 1974, pp. 27–8). If any of these studies were successful in finding characteristics predictive of criminal behavior, Q_2 would license the treatment of individuals possessing these characteristics even if they were innocent of any wrongdoing. We would be permitted not only to deprive them of their freedom but to use painful procedures to "neutralize" the source of their potential criminality. Q_2, then, appears to license too much; it should not be accepted unless supported by a compelling argument.

Perhaps Q_2 can be defended. Consider the following case. A convicted murderer will complete this sentence in three months and will then be released. Suppose we know for certain that he will murder someone unless his criminal personality is altered. If the use of aversion therapy will prevent the murder, should it not be employed if its use, and only its use, can achieve that result? It seems plausible to say yes. But, then, is it really crucial that the potential murderer has already murdered? If the sole justification for the use of the therapy is to prevent the anticipated murder, then why not use it even if the subject has never broken the law? If we should, then why object to Q_2 on the grounds that it licenses the use of aversion therapy on innocent people? The answer is that we should not. If the loss of utility is sufficiently great, and we know with certitude that treatment and only treatment will prevent that loss, then it is not necessary that the subject be guilty of any wrongdoing. It is not even necessary that he be a *potential* wrongdoer. Suppose we know with certitude that unless someone is forced to undergo painful medical therapy, he will cause someone's death by inadvertently transmitting a deadly virus. We might then be justified in giving the therapy without the subject's consent (although we might not be if the treatment were sufficiently painful or were to last a long time). The defect of Q_2 is not that it licenses the coerced treatment of the innocent in some cases, but that it permits this as a matter of general policy. The principle does not require that the potential wrongdoing be as serious as murder, or that we know for certain that without the therapy the loss of utility will occur, or that we know for certain that the therapy will be effective. All that Q_2 requires is that a person's retention of his criminal personality is likely to cause him to engage in criminal behavior, whether or not he is guilty of any legal or moral wrongdoing; again, this principle licenses too much. It is not an adequate defense of the principle, then, merely to point out that forced treatment of innocent, competent adults is justified in cases where we know for certain that a tremendous loss of utility will occur in the absence of the therapy. What has to be shown is that even in cases lacking these features, coerced treatment is justified if the conditions of the principle are satisfied.

We could retain the basic idea of Q_2 but build into the principle additional requirements; for example, we might stipulate that the potential crime be very serious, that we know for certain that in the absence of therapy the crime will be committed, and that the forced therapy will be effective. The modified principle might then be acceptable, but would it be applicable to very many prisoners? There is reason to doubt that it would, at least if the revision were along the lines just indicated. It is doubtful that we have reliable criteria for predicting the commission of serious crimes, and it is doubtful that standard forms of aversion therapy will be generally effective with nonpsychotic, nonretarded prisoners who do not cooperate with the therapist. The current situation may change dramatically if new therapies and new predictors of criminal behavior are developed, but rather than specualte on what may occur, let us try a different approach. Perhaps we need a principle very different from Q_2. What might be crucial is not what the prisoner is likely to do, but what he has done: He has engaged in criminal behavior and thus has forfeited whatever rights he had, including the right to be free from aversion therapy.

This idea, that the prisoner is "legally dead" once he passes through the jailhouse entrance, has been upheld by various courts and is still reflected in current statutes. It was upheld, for example, in the case of *Ruffin* v. *Commonwealth* (1871), in which the prisoner was said to be the temporary "slave of the state." It is reflected in the New Jersey statute that prohibits prisoners from suing the state until they are released from confinement (Singer & Statsky, 1974, p. 581). In the 1960s, however, federal and state courts became more attentive to complaints of prisoners. In the 1970s the idea that the prisoner has no legal rights has been decisively rejected by the Supreme Court. For example, in writing the majority decision in *Wolff* v. *McDonnell* (1974), Justice White concluded: "But though his rights may be diminished by the needs and exigencies of the institutional environment, a prisoner is not wholly stripped of constitutional protections when he is imprisoned for crime. There is no iron curtain drawn between the Constitution and the prisons of this country" (Singer & Statsky, 1974, p. 790). If it is asserted that prisoners lose all their *moral* rights, even though they retain certain legal rights, then this claim seems even more dubious. There is no good reason to believe that it is morally permissible to do whatever we like to prisoners – to whip, starve, to torture them – merely because they have committed a crime. Assuming that prisoners do retain at least some legal and moral rights, it has to be explained why they lose in particular the right to be free from aversion therapy. So far we have not done that.

The positive reason for thinking that prisoners do have the right to be free from coerced aversive conditioning is that to subject a nonconsenting prisoner to painful therapy is tantamount to inflicting on him an extra punishment to which he has not been sentenced. It might be replied that the treatment is "therapy" and not punishment, provided that it is given to benefit the prisoner and not to exact retribution for wrongdoing. If this is the justification, then, again, it needs to be explained why nonprisoners capable of rational consent cannot be legitimately treated in the same manner. The difference cannot be simply that some people are prisoners and others are not; this difference would vanish whenever we imprisoned innocent citizens who would benefit from the treatment. In the absence of some further argument it seems reasonable to accept the following principle:

P_5: Prisoners capable of rational consent should not be forced to undergo painful therapy if their sentence does not explicitly provide for its use.

The preceding principle should be interpreted as stating a strong presumption against coerced painful treatment, but not an absolute ban on its use. As indicated earlier, there might be overriding reasons for such treatment in exceptional cases if the gain in utility were sufficiently great. The principle also does not rule out coerced painful therapy if the law is changed so that certain sentences do explicitly provide for its use. Should we change the law in this way? One possible justification is purely retributive: Those who commit certain heinous crimes, it might be said, should be made to undergo painful treatment simply because they deserve to suffer. This kind of justification may or may not be acceptable, but if we rely on it there is no point in specifying that aversion *therapy* be used. If the sole goal is to cause the criminal to suffer, then it does not matter whether the procedure has therapeutic value or not; it is sufficient that the procedure be painful.

Another possible justification is utilitarian: by making the suggested change in the law, we can maximize long-run utilities for society. It might be argued, for example, that by explicitly allowing for the use of painful treatment on nonconsenting prisoners, we can deter potential lawbreakers or perhaps reduce recidivism. There are other possibilities as well. Although I do not think it likely that an adequate utilitarian justification will be found, that possibility need not be ruled out. That such a justification can be found must be demonstrated by the advocate of legal change. Under present law, aversion therapy should not be used on nonconsenting prisoners capable of rational consent.

What of prisoners who want to undergo aversive conditioning? Should they be granted their wish? The problem in doing so is that there is likely to be some degree of coercion present even if they give their consent. Suppose we have three prisoners: A, B, and C. Prisoner A is told that unless he agrees to aversion therapy, he will be transferred to a particularly violent cellblock, where he will probably be beaten up and raped. Prisoner B is told that the cost of his not undergoing aversive therapy is that his term will not be shortened by several years, as he thought it might be. Prisoner C is not threatened in any way, but he does believe that by undergoing aversive conditioning he will win favor with the prison authorities and the parole board. The first two cases clearly seem to be cases of involuntary treatment even if the prisoner gives his consent: malevolent authorities can force consent without using a gun or lash. What about case C? Is this also a case of involuntary treatment? Some writers would probably agree that it is. For example, in one important case, *Kaimowitz ex rel. John Doe* v. *Department of Mental Health for the State of Michigan* (1973), it is argued that involuntarily confined mental patients live in an inherently coercive institutional environment and are not able to voluntarily give informed consent because of the inherent inequality in their position. Although the decision concerned not aversive conditioning but experimental psychosurgery, the preceding principle, if sound, could be extended to cover the former as well. It is true that there are important differences between the two types of procedures – psychosurgery, for example, generally produces irreversible organic changes – but this is a difference in the effects of the treatment, not a difference in degree of coerciveness. If simply being a prisoner in a mental or penal institution makes it impossible to give one's voluntary consent, then voluntary consent cannot be given under these conditions to either type of treatment. Should we say, then, that prisoner C, as well as A and B, is not voluntarily accepting the aversion therapy?

Suppose prisoner C is not in any way moved to undergo the therapy by the pressures generated by being in prison. For example, suppose that he had been undergoing aversion therapy for drug addiction before he was sent to prison and that he would continue the therapy even if he were released. He has simply decided on rational grounds that it is in his interest to solve his drug problem and that the use of aversion therapy is the best way to accomplish his goal. His decison may then be voluntary despite his being in prison; the coercive prison pressures are there, but they are not affecting *this* prisoner in this instance. More generally, it is an empirical question whether any particular prisoner is caused to seek a certain form of therapy by the coercive pressures generated by his prison situation. He may or may not be moved by these pressures. A prisoner who requests a shot of penicillin, for example, may believe that he is currying favor with the authorities, but his reason for asking for the drug may be different; it may simply be that he feels sick. We cannot, then, reasonably deny just any prisoner access to aversion therapy on the grounds that he is being coerced; he may not be coerced at all, and even if he is coerced to some extent, that may also be true of some nonprisoners in outpatient settings who, quite reasonably, are given the therapy they request. Should we, then, give prisoner C what he requests? There is a case to be made for denying him what he wants, but not on the grounds that we are protecting his interests. We may in fact know that that is not true. He really wants that aversion therapy, let us say, and would benefit from it; he may even have a *prima facie* right to it, just as he has a *prima facie* right to adequate medical care. Either right may be overridden, however, in the interests of protecting the prison population at large. It is all too easy for prison authorities to institute unlawful and immoral punishment and to christen it *therapy*. Given this great potential for mischief, it might be reasonable to deny inmates access to aversion therapy, just as it might be reasonable to ban prefrontal lobotomies in prisons even if the latter procedure were effective. The proper justification for the ban in each case would seem to be a utilitarian one. We want to protect the prison population as a whole from a great evil even if that means sacrificing the interests of a few. This suggests the following principle:

P_6: Painful therapy should not be used in prisons even on a voluntary basis unless there exist adequate safeguards against abuse.

P_6 should be quite uncontroversial even for those who recommend using aversive conditioning on nonconsenting prisoners. What might be controversial is the empirical claim that adequate safeguards do not now exist. That might not be true of some prison systems but it is probably true of most prisons in the United States. It is likely to remain true so long as it is difficult in practice to distinguish the prisoner wanting therapy for its own value and the prisoner being pressured by the promise of parole or the simple need to curry favor with those who control his life. However, there might be some way to solve this problem, perhaps by using review committees to protect the interests of the prisoner. Even without such safeguards, painful procedures of a certain type might justifiably be used if the benefits were great enough – if, for example, the treatment were required to save the prisoner's life. P_6, like all the principles stated so far, expresses a *prima facie* obligation; the obligation may be overridden in exceptional cases.

State mental institutions

What of the use of aversion therapy on those incapable of rational consent, such as some of the inmates of state mental institutions? The sort of case raising the most difficult issues is where the therapy is used "paternalistically." By this I mean that it is used primarily to improve the welfare of the patient, but without his or her consent. It might be thought that the key issues here can be resolved by pointing out that the patient has a right to adequate treatment. If he does, it might be argued, simply select an effective procedure and use it whether the patient consents or not. However, this is too simple. If it seems plausible to postulate a right to adequate treatment, it also seems plausible to attribute a right to decline treatment. Consider a cancer patient who refuses to undergo chemotherapy to prevent the recurrence of the disease. We presumably would not be justified in coercing him even if we knew that the treatment would improve his welfare. Although there may be exceptions, we generally do not have the right to hurt people without their consent even if what we do benefits them. A nonutilitarian may explain this fact partly on the basis of utilitarian considerations and partly on the grounds that people sometimes have the right to damage their own interests even if overall utility is diminished. A utilitarian can use only the first sort of explanation, but he still has a good deal of scope for pointing out the bad effects of too much intrusion by the state. The classic presentation of the utilitarian case against paternalism is contained in John Stuart Mill's *On Liberty:* "the only purpose," he writes, "for which power can be rightfully exercised over any member of a civilized community, against his will, is to prevent harm to others" (Mill, 1975). However, Mill explicitly excludes children from the scope of his antipaternalism rule, and this exception seems warranted. For example, consider again an autistic child who has the habit of ripping out his fingernails and bloodying his head by banging it sharply against the wall. Subject to certain obvious constraints, it would seem permissible to use a few one-second, relatively painful electric shocks if this would eliminate the self-destructive behavior. The obvious constraints are, for example, that the benefit of the therapy outweigh the cost, that there be no less painful but equally effective procedure available, and so on. These kinds of constraints are expressed in the principles, P_1 through P_4, cited earlier in discussing aversion therapy. I will henceforth assume that in the cases being discussed, these principles will be satisfied, where applicable, if aversion therapy is to be used. We might also insist that the child's parents and an independent review committee approve the therapy. Subject to these conditions, the paternalistic use of aversion therapy seems justified in this sort of case. Assuming that this is so, what explains this fact?

A traditional answer, endorsed by the American Psychiatric Association (Editorial, 1972), is that some people should be treated without their consent because they need treatment but are incapable of making a free and informed decision to accept or reject it. What does one need to make a "free and informed decision"? It is not enought that the patient receive all the relevant information concerning his problem and possible treatment procedures; if he is psychotic, he may be unable to process such information. He may have lost his capacity to reason. It would seem, then, that at least this much is required; the patient must have the capacity to make a rational decision. This suggests the following principle:

Q_3: A patient may be subjected to painful therapy without his consent if it would benefit him and he is incapable of making an informed, rational decision to either accept or reject the therapy.

The preceding principle appears to make a rather weak claim. It states only a sufficient condition for the paternalistic use of therapy and then only if we tacitly presuppose the satisfaction of the obvious constraints referred to earlier. Furthermore, it would not apply in a case where someone has been declared incompetent and subjected to involuntary confinement but nevertheless is able to make an informed, rational decision concerning his treatment. Someone who occasionally hallucinates, for example, may be quite lucid in thinking about some matters. Despite the narrowness of Q_3, however, it appears to cover too many cases. Consider again the cancer patient who refuses to undergo chemotherapy. His refusal might be rational: The avoidance of the treatment's side effects may be more valuable to him than, for example, the gain of an extra six months of life. However, we presumably would not be justified in forcing him to undergo the treatment even if it were needed to save his life and even if his decision were irrational. It might be thought that the situation would be radically different if the cancer patient had lost altogether his capacity for making a rational decision, but why should that make a difference? If we knew before his loss of capacity that he had made a firm and irrevocable decision not to undergo the therapy, and if we were not justified then in forcing the treatment on him, why would we be justified now? It is easy to confuse two different cases: the present case and one in which we know of no such decision. In the second case, we might try to justify our decision to compel treatment on the grounds that it is reasonable to believe that the patient would want the treatment if he were rational. We might be quite reasonable in believing this, but then our grounds for coercing the patient are not simply that he needs treatment and is incapable of rational consent; rather, it is our belief that we are giving the patient what he would want if he were rational. Anyone who held a similar belief in the first case would be wrong. Let us assume we would know that; we would know that the patient would reject the treatment even if he regained his rationality. Under these conditions it seems wrong to go against the patient's wishes, assuming that coerced treatment would have been wrong prior to his loss of capacity. If this is right, then need of treatment and loss of rational capcity are not sufficient conditions for forcing a patient to undergo painful treatment.

Perhaps we need to add another ingredient to our first principle: that the patient would approve of the treatment if he were to become rational. Suppose someone in a highly emotional state is about to commit suicide. What justifies our using force to restrain him? It seems plausible to say that we believe the person is temporarily irrational and would approve of what we did to him if he were to become rational. If we later find that in a calmer, rational state of mind, he still wants to kill himself, then our justification seems less clear (although in some cases the protection of his life may be necessary to safeguard the vital interests of others). This sort of case suggests the following principle:

Q_4: A patient may be subjected to painful therapy without his consent if (1) it would benefit him; (2) he is incapable of making an informed, rational decision to either accept or reject the therapy; and (3) he would approve of the therapy if he were to become rational.

The preceding principle is plausible, and it may prove to be correct, but there are problems.

First, it is even narrower in scope than our first principle. In particular, it does not apply where an incompetent patient still has the capacity to make an informed, rational decision about his treatment; nor does it apply where he lacks the capacity but condition 3 is not satisfied. This is not a problem if our goal is merely to explain why the paternalistic use of therapy is justified in the case of the autistic child; but it may be a problem if we want to justify many of the current paternalistic practices in mental hospitals.

Second, it will often be difficult to get empirical evidence that condition 3 of the principle is satisfied. It is not enough that we determine that an ideally rational agent would prefer the treatment. It is not even sufficient that we know that, given the goals and interests of the patient, the treatment is rationally preferable. People who retain a capacity for rational thought often make decisions that are irrational even relative to their own goals. The cancer patient who is irrationally afraid of loss of hair may thwart his most important goals by refusing chemotherapy. The seriously depressed patient who wants most to return to his family and job may, nevertheless, refuse the only treatment that will bring about that result. He may have the capacity to make a rational decision but may fail to exercise that capacity in this case. Because people often fail in this way, we cannot assume an identity between what a particular patient would approve of if he were to regain his capacity for rational thought and what is rational given his overall preference scheme.

The third problem is even more serious; it concerns the correctness of the principle. Suppose a paranoid-schizophrenic regains his capacity for rational decision making as a result of coerced treatment. It is likely that other changes will have taken place as well, including, perhaps, changes in his fundamental goals and preferences. Given his new set of goals and preferences, he may approve of what we did; but if he had not changed in this way, he might disapprove even if he were rational. Why place so much weight on his new preferences? It is tempting to bring in here a bit of metaphysics (see, for example, Shapiro, 1974, p. 289). The true self of a person, it might be said, is his rational self. If his true self is temporarily eclipsed by mental illness but wants and needs help, then provide the necessary treatment; the true self will exhibit gratitude when, and if, it regains visibility. One can accept Q_4 without accepting this metaphysical view, but making the view explicit may help explain why the principle seems attractive to some people. The metaphysics, however, is quite dubious. Many of us are incompetent, ignorant, stupid, or irrational, but when we choose to ruin our lives and to reject unwanted help, it is we who are choosing, not some phenomenal reflection of a "deeper" or "truer" self. We want to gamble or drink, to become fascists or communists, to become religious zealots or crusading atheists; it is *we* who make these choices. We might choose very differently if we were very different sorts of people; if we were to change, we might agree later that we should have been coerced to undergo treatment, but that hardly shows that we should be given what we now reject. The religious zealot who is drugged or shocked into atheism may later be grateful; that might also be true of the socialist who is brainwashed into becoming a fascist (if that were possible). But even if such people are better off and later thank us, why does that show that we were right to force therapy on them? People can always change their minds and say that we did not violate their rights, but that is hardly conclusive. They may say that now because they have changed radically, and they may simply be wrong. It may be objected that these cases are not counterexamples to Q_4, even if the people should not be coerced, unless all three conditions of the principle are satisfied. True. However, assume that a certain religious zealot and socialist are incapable of making an informed, rational decision; that a certain painful therapy would benefit them; and that they would approve of the therapy if they were to become rational. If, as seems plausible for some cases of this sort, coerced painful therapy is still unjustified, then Q_4 is false.

If neither of our two principles satisfactorily explains why it is permissible to hurt people for their benefit without their consent, then what justifies the practice in our paradigm case of self-destructive children? It might be that this kind of case is a very special one, and that its salient features are not present in many other cases. First, the recipients of the therapy are children. It is not clear how we should weigh this factor, especially because the more general issue of what rights children have is a very difficult one, but it is plausible to think that this factor might make some difference. Second, some of these children cannot at all consent or refuse the therapy; sometimes they cannot even talk, or understand what is being said to them. It is not just that they are incapable of making either an informed or rational decision; as noted earlier, that may also be true of certain religious or political fanatics. Why should inability to consent at all, as opposed to inability to give one's informed or rational consent, make a difference? One possible answer is that if lack of consent is explained by inability to consent or dissent, then, in the absence of evidence to the contrary, we are not doing to the patient what he does not want done to him. It is true that the autistic child may not want to be shocked; we can get behavioral evidence of that even if he cannot talk. It is not clear, however, that he does not want to be *shocked for the purpose of saving him from self-destruction.* He probably does not even understand what this means; he lacks the concept. In contrast, the religious and political fanatics (and many residents of state mental institutions) do possess the concept, even though, because of their irrationality, they do not fully appreciate or care about the beneficial consequences of the therapy being proposed. A third important feature of our paradigm case is that the consequences of withholding the therapy are so immediate and so awful. The child is pulling out his fingernails, bloodying his ears with his fist, and destroying crucial body tissue. It is not a question of merely altering the child's life-style (as with a political zealot) or running a risk of death (as with a cancer patient or heavy smoker), nor is it merely a matter of getting the patient out of the mental institution and returning him to his previous way of living (as with Cotter's schizophrenic patients). If we refuse to use a few brief electric shocks with some of these autistic children, we know that the consequence will be disastrous. The last feature, the certitude and gravity of the result, may well be the most important feature to be cited in explaining why we can justifiably subject some autistic and severely retarded children to painful treatment without their consent. Consider a child in a coma who will die without an operation that will subsequently cause him pain. In the absence of very special conditions the operation seems warranted. Suppose the child also had a deformity that could also be altered for his benefit by means of another pain-producing operation. The justification of the second operation seems much less weighty. It appears to diminish further if the patient is an adult, and to vanish altogether if the patient had indicated before the onset of the coma that he did not want the second operation to be performed.

Is it being claimed that the three conditions pointed to in our paradigm case are necessary, that without the patient's consent aversive treatment must be withheld unless he (1) is a child; (2) is incapable of consent or dissent; and (3) will surely suffer disastrous consequences without the treatment? No. For example, meeting conditions 2 or 3 might be enough in some cases. The point, rather, is that if it is the presence of these three conditions that explains why it seems obviously right to treat the autistic child, then we should not be confident that we can export the justification to many other sorts of cases. In many of the more standard cases of psychotic, institutionalized patients where painful treatment is often thought justifiable, none of these three conditions is present. Perhaps other conditions will suffice; we have not run through all the possibilities. What has been argued is the inadequacy of two standard justifications:

Q_3: The patient would benefit from the treatment and is incapable of making an informed, rational decision to accept or reject the therapy.

Q_4: The patient meets condition Q_3 and would approve the treatment if he were to become rational.

Where the only apparent justification is the appeal to either of these two dubious justifications, then the burden of proof is on him who wants to coerce the patient. This suggests the following principle:

P_7: Where the only justification for coerced painful treatment is that it would benefit the patient and he is not capable of informed, rational consent but would approve if he were to become rational, then the therapy should not be used.

Even if P_7 is acceptable, the loss of rational capacity might still have an important connection with the justification of paternalistic treatment. Perhaps what is needed is a specification of a certain type of incapacity for rational thought; if such an account can be worked out, then perhaps such treatment can be justified in a much wider range of cases.

One additional justification for coerced painful treatment might be that it is needed because the patient is dangerous. This justification also presents problems; it too would underwrite the treatment of innocent people living outside of mental institutions. However, we shall not discuss these problems here. If it is true, as some writers contend (Szasz, 1972; Ennis, 1972), that relatively few inmates of mental institutions present any danger to themselves or others, then this justification would be relevant only in relatively few cases.

The principles discussed so far, P_1 through P_7, are mainly applicable to aversive conditioning, but they also cover other kinds of behavior therapy techniques insofar as they are painful. For example, consider so-called operant techniques. It was suggested earlier that the use of such techniques sometimes involves giving rewards but not inflicting pain. That might be true, for example, of using candy to condition severely retarded children. In other instances it is not true. For example, in the case described by Cotter (1967), food was given as a reinforcer, but only after very painful conditions of deprivation were forced on the subjects; they were starved for three days. More generally, our principles apply to the use of any operant technique in which painful conditions of deprivation are forced on the patients in order to make certain rewards reinforcing. In particular, it applies to some of the token economy programs in use in state mental institutions. Wexler (1973) points out that some of these programs may also prove to be illegal. Although the law in this area is still unsettled, a problem is posed particularly by the decision in *Wyatt* v. *Stickney* (1972), which specifies certain minimum living conditions the patient in a state mental institution cannot be legally denied. These include a comfortable bed, a closet or locker for the patient's personal belongings, a chair, a bedside table, a television set, nutritionally adequate meals, and the rights to have visitors, exercise, wear one's own clothes, attend religious services, and so on. If this decision is accepted in other jurisdictions, then many token economy programs could be ruled illegal if they deprive patients of such items until certain specified behavior is exhibited. Many programs have done just that (Wexler, 1973). An additional problem is posed by the requirement of the "least restrictive alternative" as set forth in *Lake* v. *Cameron* (1966) and *Covington* v. *Harris* (1969). As some lawyers interpret this doctrine, the conditions of deprivation used in many token economy programs would fail to meet the requirement if less painful programs, such as that developed by Fairweather (1969), are equally effective (Wexler, 1973; Martin, 1975). This is not to say that token economy programs are inherently immoral or illegal. In at least some cases the patient's consent can be obtained and the more aversive elements can be eliminated; the patient can be rewarded without first being starved or deprived of basic comforts to which he is entitled.

VI. The treatment of social deviance

The moral problems considered so far arise because of special characteristics of the therapy (e.g., it is painful), or of the client (he is incapable of rational consent), or of the therapeutic setting (it is a prison or mental hospital). Dilemmas can also arise because of the nature of the problem to be treated. Some conditions, such as schizophrenia, *directly* cause pain or disablement to the subject, even if his problems may be enlarged because of the intolerance of others. The schizophrenic, like the cancer victim, may suffer from job discrimination, but schizophrenia and cancer would affect people adversely even if such intolerance were to vanish. That need not be true of certain other conditions. For example, many homosexuals would not be pained by their condition if it were not for the reactions of people who disapprove of homosexuality. Let us use the term *social deviance* (in a technical sense) to refer to these *conditions* (in a neutral sense) that are problematic for clients primarily because of the mediation of others, and the term *social deviants* to refer to clients having such conditions. Some conditions, such as homosexuality, may qualify as social deviance in some cases but not in others, depending on the source of the problem (if there is one).

The existence of social deviance poses an additional problem for what we earlier called the basic model. According to that model, the client makes the moral decision, if one is needed, as to whether his behavior should be changed; the therapist decides on empirical grounds how best to achieve the goal the client has selected. There are at least two reasons why the model is unsatisfactory if applied to social deviants. First, the client may say that he is freely deciding to have his behavior altered, but in fact he may be coerced by societal pressures. Second, in giving the client what he wants, a behavior therapist may be contributing to the maintenance of society's intolerance. The good that he does for the client may thus be cancelled or overridden by the evil he does to others by helping to perpetuate an unjust system or practice.

One sort of social deviance involves the holding of unpopular moral, religious, or political beliefs. For example, consider the belief of some vegetarians that it is morally wrong to eat meat. It has recently been argued that a belief in vegetarianism is a sign of mental illness (Friedman, 1975). If this argument were accepted, vegetarians might be pressured into seeking therapeutic help for their "problem"; that would pose a serious moral issue for therapists who want to give the client what he requests. The same sort of issue might arise if a behavior therapist were asked to reconvert someone who had adopted the beliefs of an unpopular religious sect, such as the Hare Krishna. A third and more serious example is the use of psychiatry in the Soviet Union to treat people with dissident political beliefs. If reports are accurate the patients are forced to undergo treatment; their main problem is their tendency to express political beliefs that are unacceptable to certain political authorities (Medvedev & Medvedev, 1972).

A second sort of case involves behavior that is not harmful to the subject, but is disapproved of by those in charge of certain institutions. For example, Winett and Winkler (1972) charge that behavior modification has been used extensively in schools to support the status quo. Children are rewarded for being docile, quiet, and orderly. In this way the behavior modifier, it is charged, has been helping school officials achieve what, in many cases, are undesirable goals. O'Leary (1972) challenges the empirical claims of Winett and Winkler about what has taken place, but agrees about the moral issue – that the behavior modifier should question the desirability of the proposed change. Another example is the use of token economy programs in mental institutions for the purpose of getting the clients to exhibit behavior acceptable to the custodial staff. Sometimes it is in the client's interest to exhibit such "acceptable" behavior, but sometimes it is not. One leading theorist of token economy programs has concluded that his work in setting up such programs was helping to maintain a social institution, the mental hospital, that in its current form is no longer desirable in our society (Krasner, 1976). Consequently, he has announced that he will no longer develop token economy programs in mental hospitals.

A third sort of case involves the treatment of sexual deviance. A client who has a sexual fetish, for example, may desire to change simply because his marriage is being affected adversely. Other sexual deviants would have no desire to change were it not for the antipathy of society. The most widely discussed such case is that of homosexuality. Because of its intrinsic interest and because it can serve as a stand-in for other sorts of social deviance, we will focus on this case.

Some writers have recently raised moral doubts about the use of behavior therapy with homosexuals (Begelman, 1975); at least one behavior therapist has proposed that all such treatment be terminated (Davison, 1976). The main reasons for the doubts are (1) it is questionable whether the consent of homosexual clients is truly voluntary; and (2) one of the effects of using behavior therapy with homosexuals is the maintenance of society's unfavorable attitude. These reasons are connected in that consent is thought to be not truly voluntary because of societal pressure, which in turn is due primarily to ignorance and prejudice, which in turn is being sustained by the practice of treating homosexuality as something pathological, something to be cured. It has been suggested, therefore, that clinicians cease trying to help homosexuals change their sexual orientation and instead concentrate on improving the quality of their interpersonal relationships (Davison, 1976).

There is doubtlessly a serious moral issue being raised here, and it cannot be disposed of simply by saying that we should give the client what he voluntarily requests; the request may not be voluntary, and catering to it may be wrong even if it is. One might disagree, however, with the solution being proposed by those who raise the problem, particularly if, as already suggested, homosexuality is only part of a larger pattern of social deviance. Consider stuttering. Some stutterers might desire fluent speech even if they were not subjected to ridicule. Many stutterers seeking treatment, however, are pressured at least indirectly by the reactions of others. The reaction need not be overt ridicule; a display of embarrassment or uneasiness in his presence may suffice. In using behavior therapy with such a client, the therapist may be helping to maintain the practice of treating stutterers unkindly. The message is conveyed, as with homosexuality, that the behavior is undesirable and needs to be eliminated. Homosexuality, then, is part of a larger and deeper problem that can develop whenever the behavior or state of a client is problematic to him primarily because of the reactions of others. It can arise not only for the homosexual, but also for the transvestite and the fetishist; not only for the stutterer, but for anyone who is shy or has anxiety over speaking in public. Indeed, it can arise for almost anyone who displays behavior thought to be socially inappropriate. To withhold behavior therapy in all such cases would be unacceptable because it would cause too much suffering; too many people would be condemned to live with a condition that at least indirectly causes them grief. It might be that some of these cases should be treated differently; homosexuality, for example, may be a special case. We need to consider that possibility, but at least we should not recommend the withholding of treatment as a general solution to the problem of social deviance.

The first reason for withholding therapy from the homosexual who asks for it is that his request may not be truly voluntary. Suppose that were the only reason; suppose that the effect of societal attitudes was negligible and that no other effect was unfavorable. How much weight should this first reason be accorded? Suppose a gay person says to a therapist: "It is true that I want to change my sexual orientation primarily because of the prejudice of others. It would be better if such prejudice did not exist, but given that it does, I will be better off if I change. My decision may be coerced to some extent, but it is nonetheless rational (it has been reached after much reflection on the relevant evidence) and it is correct (I will be helped, and no one will be harmed)." Under these conditions, to withhold the therapy merely because the decision is not wholly voluntary seems to be unjustified paternalism. It is not like the case discussed earlier of withholding aversive therapy from the prisoner; there the justification was to protect the interests of others. Here we are assuming for the moment, there is no such justification. It is hard to explain in this case, then, why a sufficient reason to deny the client's request is that his decision is the terminal result of a causal chain that began in ignorance and prejudice. Things would be different if the client unthinkingly reacted to the prejudice of society and decided to change without considering any alternatives. In that case the therapist should explain whatever options exist and perhaps help the client to try a less drastic option first. After that is done, if the client decides on rational grounds that it is in his interest to change, then it is hard to see why his request should be denied merely on the grounds that it can ultimately be traced to the prejudice of others.

The more interesting reason for withholding therapy is to protect the interests of other people. Suppose that the practice of helping homosexuals to change their sexual orientation makes an important causal contribution to reinforcing the belief that homosexuality is bad, as claimed by Begelman (1975). If that is true, and assuming that the result is evil, then this might provide a powerful reason for withholding the therapy. A puzzle might still arise if the evil were to result only from the cumulative efforts of many behavior therapists. The case might be analogous to voting in a national election: If no one votes, disaster results, but my failure to vote makes no difference. Analogously, an individual therapist might well reason that his practice makes little or no difference to the reinforcement of society's prejudice; it is only if other therapists also help change homosexuals that the bad effect occurs. It is tempting to say in such cases that the individual acts permissibly: I do no wrong by not voting if my omission makes little or no difference. This may be the correct solution, but such cases may still seem puzzling; no individual does anything wrong, and yet the cumulative effect of many such actions may be a great evil. If this *is* puzzling, we might refuse to take sides on this issue and try to answer the following question: If participating in a practice is wrong, given that its cumulative effect is a great evil, should a behavior therapist stop participating in the practice of trying to change the sexual orientation of homosexuals? Suppose we lived in a society where helping Jews to convert to Christianity or Marxism played an important role in reinforcing anti-Semitism; this might constitute a strong reason for not assisting such conversions. In this case and the homosexuality case, the evil that is avoided by withholding help would still have to be weighed against the good that is lost, but it just might be true that the balance is tipped in favor of withholding help. It might be true, but is it? The main reason for being skeptical in the homosexuality case is that it is questionable that the practice of behavior therapists makes an *important* contribution to the maintenance of society's antigay attitudes. The practice might make some difference, but clearly such attitudes existed before behavior therapy did. Would such attitudes change significantly if behavior therapists announced that they would stop the practice of trying to alter homosexual behavior? They might. But what evidence is there that the change in attitudes would be significantly greater than that brought about by some less drastic move, one that does less immediate damage to the interests of homosexuals seeking therapy? For example, behavior therapy associations might announce that in the view of their members: (1) there is no firm evidence that homosexuality is an illness; and (2) sexual change programs should be open to heterosexuals as well as homosexuals. As long as there are ways to influence those who are misinformed other than by withholding treatment, the more drastic and unfair alternative is less preferable.

Conclusion. Social deviance poses a problem for those who believe that we should simply give the client what he wants, but there is no general solution to the problem. For that reason, we shall not attempt to state any positive general principle. The relevant facts are different in different sorts of cases, and in many cases are hard to ascertain. Assuming the accuracy of reports from the Soviet Union, certain political dissidents clearly have little or no choice about being subjected to psychiatric treatment. In other cases it may be difficult to tell whether a particular client with a particular problem is being coerced by others to seek therapy. How much coercion is there? Someone with a drinking or sexual problem may be reacting to pressure from others, but in a cool hour he may nonetheless have rationally decided that it is in his interest to change. Whether or not that is so, there might still be grounds for withholding therapy to protect the interests of others. If a token economy program is used in a given society to teach fascist values to schoolchildren, there would be good reason not to participate in such a program. But most cases are not so clear-cut. Given the paucity of hard empirical data about the long-term effects of token economy programs, it is often hard to tell whether a given program will do more harm than good. Even if a program is used primarily to teach children to be docile and orderly in the classroom, what are the effects of achieving these goals – more and better education – or simply more docility? Where offering the therapy clearly makes some contribution to the perpetuation of an unjust system, there might be a variety of remedies available. One might be to withhold therapy, but another might be to try to change the system while offering the therapy. Once stated, all this seems obvious, but then it should also seem obvious that neither "give the client what he wants" nor "refuse to treat him" will do as a general solution to the problem of how to deal with social deviance. This suggests the following negative principle:

P_8: Aversion therapy should be neither banned altogether as a treatment for social deviance nor given to whomever requests it.

VII. Back to the basic model

Some behavior therapists insist that their techniques are morally neutral; or as Bandura puts it: Behavior therapy is not a system of ethics (1969, p. 87). There is a point to saying this. What are often thought of as basic principles (such as the law of effect) do not say what ought to be done, or what is good or evil; they do not contain any terms of moral evaluation. The same is true of the descriptions of the techniques. What about the techniques themselves, assuming that one can distinguish them from their descriptions? A behavior therapy technique is an abstract entity, neither good nor bad. It is just as morally neutral as a truth table technique for testing the validity of arguments. However, to *apply* a behavioral technique is to do something to someone, and that action might sensibly be characterized in moral terms. Was using *this* technique with *this* client under *these* conditions morally wrong, permissible, or perhaps obligatory? Behavior therapy, then, is morally neutral in the preceding sense, but its *application* can give rise to moral questions. The main point of the basic model is not to deny this but to indicate that in most cases the issue for the therapist is relatively clear-cut. Nothing more subtle is required than some such principle as: It is right to help suffering people when they seek help. Any remaining moral issue as to what changes are desirable is a decision for the client: "There is no justification for therapists imposing their value preferences upon clients, who must bear the consequences of whatever changes they undergo" (Bandura, 1974, p. 19). When properly understood, this view is very plausible – the main moral justification for using behavior therapy is to give the client the sort of help he wants – but the view has to be restricted to certain sorts of cases. Whether or not it is true of most cases where behavior therapy is used is an empirical question that is hard to answer; we need not answer it here. What is important is that the basic model cannot serve by itself to justify the practice of behavior therapy in general; it needs to be supplemented with additional principles.

As suggested earlier, principles are needed, first, to cover cases where the therapy is painful. Most such cases involve the use of aversion therapy, but almost any behavior technique can be painful. Covert conditioning, for example, makes use of an imagined rather than an actual painful stimulus, but the discomfort the client feels is not itself imaginary. Even in systematic desensitization, the client may find it unpleasant to run through the so-called anxiety hierarchy. Modeling might seem to be an exception; it might appear to be a wholly painless procedure. But a child, for example, may find it quite upsetting to witness someone in close contact with an object that is phobic to the client. Unlike aversion therapy, pain is not necessarily present when these other procedures are used – and where it is, it may be too minimal to give rise to any serious moral question. Consequently, the issues are not generally the same as those arising from aversion therapy. Nevertheless, moral principles applicable to aversion therapy, such as P_1 through P_8, are potentially applicable to almost any behavioral technique as applied in at least some cases.

Other areas where supplementary principles are needed include those already discussed: (1) where the client is incapable of informed, rational consent; (2) where the therapy is dispensed in an institutional setting, such as a prison or a mental hospital; and (3) where the problem is one of social deviance. Finally, there is at least one additional area where the basic model is inapplicable, that of experimentation. Here it is clearly not enough to say: "Give the client what he wants." At best, a client agrees to participate in an experiment; its purpose is usually to satisfy not any of his goals but those of the experimenter. Furthermore, he is often deceived about crucial details of the experiment. The issues in this area concern the study of therapy rather than its application (although the two are often intertwined). Many of the same issues arise for the nonclinical psychologist and for the medical researcher; they are too complex to be explored here in great detail. One issue worth mentioning, however, concerns the kinds of experimental designs commonly used in behavior therapy research. For example, consider the single subject designs favored by many of those working in an operant tradition. One of the simplest, the so-called *ABA* reversal design, normally involves: (1) a recording of baseline behavior, (2) the introduction of therapy, (3) the withdrawal of the therapy, (4) a reinstatement of the therapy. If the target behavior decreases in frequency after the introduction of the therapy and increases after its withdrawal, the therapy is assumed to have made a difference. A moral problem can arise because the experimenter deliberately tries in phase 3 to reverse the effects of the therapy; it is partly by doing this that he provides evidence of effectiveness. The problem may be minor if the client's problem is minor, but a serious moral issue can arise if the client's problem is serious. For example, if an autistic child suffers greatly from his self-destructive behavior, it would be hard to defend the deliberate reinstatement of this behavior. The problem is compounded if irreversible effects take place in phase 3. For example, if a man seeks help for sexual impotence in order to save his marriage, the reinstatement of his problem, even for a brief period, is objectionable if the result is divorce. In cases where a single-subject reversal design should not be used, we might use a group design; but this too can cause moral problems.

A group design normally involves one or more control groups that do not receive treatment. Often one group is assigned to a placebo condition and another to a "wait" condition (they will receive treatment at a later date). The key moral issue here concerns the withholding of therapy, at least for a time, that the therapist thinks to be effective. The problem is mitigated somewhat if the controls receive some other type of therapy, say short-term psychoanalysis; but there is still a problem so long as the therapist has good reason to believe that the withheld therapy is superior. Again, if the client's difficulty is minor – for example, if he is a college student with a minor snake phobia – the ethical issue may be minor; but if he is seeking help for a serious problem requiring immediate attention, the ethical dilemma may be serious. A seriously depressed patient, for example, may need immediate help if he is not to commit suicide.

One possible solution to the preceding problem is to cease doing experiments on clients seeking therapy. This solution has appealed to some psychoanalysts who object on moral grounds to the use of group designs with their patients. It is not likely to appeal to behavior therapists; nor should it. The result would probably be the continued survival of worthless therapies. That in turn would result in a great waste of resources and an increase in the suffering of clients.

A second solution would be to continue to use group designs, but to try to justify their use on moral grounds. For example, Leitenberg (1973, p. 395), although he supports single-subject designs for epistemic reasons, suggests that it is "somewhat spurious" to contend that the use of group designs is at the expense of the client not receiving treatment. The contention is spurious because we still do not know how to care for the client in the first place. If we did, the research would not, he suggests, be needed. Leitenberg's reply is relevant, but not sufficient. Even where a therapy is being initially tested there are usually antecedent reasons for thinking it better than no treatment at all. As more and more evidence becomes available, without yet obviating the need for further testing, the therapist acquires more and more reason to believe that the withheld therapy is more effective than a placebo. He may not *know* that this is so, but he does have some supporting evidence. Another sort of justification might appeal to the welfare of society: The common good is maximized by finding out which therapies work and which do not. We need not be utilitarians to make this appeal; we can add that it is also fair that certain clients be temporarily denied therapy so long as a fair criterion is used in deciding who gets assigned to the no-treatment conditions. For epistemic reasons, the assignment is usually decided on a random basis; consequently, it might be argued that the criterion is a fair one. Here epistemic considerations and considerations of justice happily merge. This justification helps, but it is not totally adequate. Suppose a doctor gives me a placebo for my ear infection instead of a treatment that probably works but is still being studied. If he used a randomizing device in assigning me to the placebo condition, that is fairer than, for example, selecting me on the basis of my skin color or political views. Nevertheless, I still have some grounds for complaint. I came with the reasonable expectation of receiving effective therapy; instead, I was deceived and received either no treatment or inadequate treatment. I could have been treated worse, but I was still treated badly. My grounds for complaint would be strengthened further if my illness were more serious, for example, if I had heart trouble or cancer.

A third approach to our aproblem would be to try to reduce the unfairness to the untreated patient. One way to do this would be to introduce compensatory elements into our research practices in order to (1) reduce the harm and (2) increase the benefits to the untreated controls. For example, Stuart (1973) suggests that we can reduce the harm by monitoring the untreated client to ensure that his condition is not seriously deteriorating. If it is, then we can offer immediate therapeutic help. One problem with this procedure, as Stuart points out, is that by deleting the most negative cases from a comparison group, one decreases the likelihood of obtaining positive experimental findings. However, some sort of trade-off of this kind between evidential and moral gains may be necessary. One way to increase the benefits to the client would be to return some or all of the fees he pays. The amount of reduction in fees might be prorated depending on the seriousness of his problem and the amount of time effective treatment is withheld.

As noted earlier, it is not the behavior therapist alone who must face the moral problems associated with controlled studies of human subjects. At present, however, behavior therapists are responsible for much of the research being done in clinical psychology. For that they deserve credit, but they also take on the responsibility of diminishing whatever unfairness exists in such experiments. The preceding suggestions are only illustrations of what might be done; clearly, additional remedies need to be developed.

Conclusion. We began with a statement of the basic model: "The practice of behavior therapy needs no moral foundation except for the following: (1) It is right (permissible or obligatory) to help people who request help." What is basically right in this model is the idea that principle 1 is fundamental; what is basically wrong is the idea that a more complex moral foundation for the practice of behavior therapy is not needed. The following list is certainly not complete and may need some revision, but it includes some of the more important supplementary principles:

P_1: Painful therapy should not be used, other things being equal, if the amount of suffering it causes the client outweighs the amount of suffering it saves him.

P_2: Painful therapy should not be used if less painful but equally effective techniques are readily available, other things being equal.

P_3: Painful theapy should not be used, other things being equal, without obtaining the informed consent of the client if he is capable of giving his consent.

P_4: A therapist should not coerce a client to undergo painful therapy, other things being equal, if the client is capable of rational consent.

P_5: Prisoners capable of rational consent should not be forced to undergo painful therapy if their sentence does not explicitly provide for its use.

P_6: Painful therapy should not be used in prisons even on a voluntary basis unless there exist adequate safeguards against abuse.

P_7: Where the only justification for coerced painful treatment is that it would benefit the patient and he is not capable of informed rational consent but would approve if he were to become rational, then the therapy should not be used.

P_8: Aversion therapy should neither be banned altogether as a treatment for social deviance nor given to whomever requests it.

References

Alanen, Y. O., Rekola, J., Stewen, A., Takala, K. & Tuovinen, M. The family in the pathogenesis of schizophrenic and neurotic disorders. Acta Psychiatry and Neurology Scandinavia, 1966, 42 (Suppl. 189).

Albee, G. Emerging concepts of mental illness and models of treatment: the psychological point of view. American Journal of Psychiatry, 1969, 125, 870–6.

The emperor's model. International Journal of Psychiatry, 1970, 9, 29–31.

Allyon, T. Intensive treatment of psychotic behavior by stimulus satiation and food reinforcement. Behaviour Research and Therapy, 1963, 1, 53–61.

Allyon, T. & Haughton, E. Control of the behavior of schizophrenic patients by food. Journal of the Experimental Analysis of Behavior, 1962, 5, 343–52.

Modification of symbolic verbal behavior of mental patients. Behaviour Research and Therapy, 1964, 2, 87–97.

Allyon, T. & Michael, J. The psychiatric nurse as a behavioral engineer. Journal of the Experimental Analysis of Behavior, 1959, 2, 324–34.

American Psychiatric Association. *Diagnostic and Statistical Manual of Mental Disorders II* (Washington, D.C.: American Psychiatric Association), 1968.

Anant, S. A note on the treatment of alcoholics by a verbal aversion technique. Canadian Psychologist, 1967, 80, 19–22.

Armstrong, D. M. *A Materialist Theory of the Mind* (New York: Humanities Press), 1968.

Atthowe, J. M. Behavioral innovation and persistence. American Psychologist, 1973, 23, 34–41.

Atthowe, J. M. & Krasner, L. Preliminary report on the application of contingent reinforcement procedures (token economy) on a "chronic" psychiatric ward. Journal of Abnormal Psychology, 1968, 73, 37–43.

Azrin, N. H. & Holz, W. C. "Punishment," in *Operant Behavior: Areas of Research and Application,* Hoenig, W. K. (ed.) (New York: Appleton-Century-Crofts), 1966.

Bachrach, A., Erwin, W. & Mohr, J. "The Control of Eating Behavior in an Anorexic by Operant Conditioning Techniques," in *Case Studies in Behavior Modification,* Ullmann, L. & Krasner, L. (eds.) (New York: Holt, Rinehart & Winston), 1965.

Bancroft, J. Aversion Therapy. DPM Dissertation, University of London, 1966.

Bandura, A. "Vicarious Processes: A Case of No-Trial Learning," in *Advances in Experimental Social Psychology,* Vol. 2, Berkowitz, L. (ed.) (New York: Academic Press), 1965.

Principles of Behavior Modification (New York: Holt, Rinehart & Winston), 1969.

"Psychotherapy Based upon Modeling Principles," in *Handbook of Psychotherapy and Behavior Change: An Empirical Analysis,* Bergin, A. & Garfield, S. (eds.) (New York: Wiley), 1971.

"The Ethics and Social Purposes of Behavior Modification," in *Annual Review of Behavior Therapy Theory and Practice,* Franks, C. & Wilson, G. T. (eds.) (New York: Brunner/Mazel), 1975.

Behavior theory and the models of man. American Psychologist, 1974, 28, 859–69.

Self-efficacy: Toward a unifying theory of behavioral change. Psychological Review, 1977, 84, 191–215.

Bandura, A. & Adams, N. E. Analysis of self-efficacy theory of behavioral change, Cognitive Theory and Research, 1977, in press.

Bandura, A., Adams, N. E. & Beyer, J. Cognitive processes mediating behavioral changes. Journal of Personality and Social Psychology, 1977, 35, 125–139.

Bandura, A., Blanchard, E. & Ritter, B. The relative efficacy of desensitization and modeling approaches for inducing behavioral, affective, and attitudinal changes. Journal of Personality and Social Psychology, 1969, 13, 173–99.

Bandura, A. Grusec, J. E. & Menlove, F. L. Vicarious extinction of avoidance behavior. Journal of Personality and Social Psychology, 1967, 5, 16–23.

Bandura, A., Jeffery, R. & Wright, C. Efficacy of participant modeling as a function of response induction aids. Journal of Abnormal Psychology, 1974, 83, 56–64.

Bandura, A. & Walters, R. *Social Learning and Personality Development* (New York: Holt, Rinehart & Winston), 1963.

Barlow, D. Increasing heterosexual responsiveness in the treatment of sexual deviation: a review of the clinical and experimental evidence. Behavior Therapy, 1973, 4, 655–71.

Barlow, D., Agras, W. S., Blanchard, E. B. & Young, L. D. Biofeedback and reinforcement to increase heterosexual arousal in homosexuals. Behaviour Research and Therapy, 1975, 13, 45–50.

Barlow, D., Reynolds, E. J. & Agras, W. S. Gender identity change in a transsexual. Archives of General Psychiatry, 1973, 28, 569–76.

Beck, A. Cognitive therapy: nature and relation to behavior therapy. Behavior Therapy, 1970, 1, 184–200.

Beech, H. R. "The Symptomatic Treatment of Writer's Cramp," in *Behavior Therapy and Neuroses,* Eysenck, H. J. (ed.) (London: Pergamon Press), 1960.

Begelman, D. A. "Ethical and Legal Issues of Behavior Modification," in *Progress in Behavior Modification,* Hersen, R. M., Eisler, R. M. & Miller, P. M. (eds.) (New York: Academic Press), 1975.

Discussion of contributions to a symposium on a behavioristic analysis of ethics. Presented at the 84th Annual Convention of the American Psychological Association, Washington, D.C., 1976.

Benda, C. E. Neurosis of conscience. Journal of Existentialism, 1967, 7, 425–42.

Bergin, A. Cognitive therapy and behavior therapy: foci for a multidimensional approach to treatment. Behavior Therapy, 1970, 1, 205–12.

"The Evaluation of Therapeutic Outcome," in *Handbook of Psychotherapy and Behavior Change: An Empirical Analysis,* Bergin, A. & Garfield, S. (eds.) (New York: Wiley), 1971.

Bergin, A. & Suinn, R. Individual psychotherapy and behavior therapy. Annual Review of Psychology, 1975, 27, 509–56.

Bergmann, G. The contribution of John B. Watson. Psychology Review, 1956, 63, 265–76.

Biglan, A. & Krass, D. The empirical nature of behavior therapies. Behaviorism, 1977, 5, 1–15.

Birk, L., Huddleston, W., Miller, E. & Cohler, B. Avoidance conditioning for homosexuality. Archives of General Psychiatry, 1971, 25, 314–323.

Birky, H. J., Chambliss, J. E. & Wasden, R. A comparison of residents discharged from a token economy and two traditional psychiatric programs. Behavior Therapy, 1971, 2, 46–51.

Blakemore, C. B., et al. Application of faradic aversion conditioning to a case of transvestism. Behaviour Research and Therapy, 1963, 3, 78–85.

Boorse, C. On the distinction between disease and illness. Philosophy and Public Affairs, 1975, 5, 49–68.

Boring, E. G. A History of Experimental Psychology (New York: Appleton), 1950.

Borkovec, T. D. Effects of expectancy on the outcome of systematic desensitization and implosive treatments for analogue anxiety. Behavior Therapy, 1972, 3, 29–40.

Borkovec, T. D. & Nau, S. D. Credibility of analogue therapy rationales. Journal of Behavior Therapy and Experimental Psychiatry, 1972, 3, 257–60.

Bower, G. Imagery as a rational organizer in associative learning. Journal of Verbal Learning and Verbal Behavior, 1970, 9, 529–33.

Breger, L. & McGaugh, J. L. A critique and reformulation of "learning theory" approaches to psychotherapy and neurosis. Psychological Bulletin, 1965, 63, 335–58.

Brewer, W. "There is No Convincing Evidence for Operant or Classical Conditioning in Adult Humans," in Cognition and the Symbolic Processes, Weimer, W. & Palermo, D. (eds.) (Hillsdale, N.J.: Lawrence Erlbaum Associates), 1974.

Bridgman, P. W. Reflections of a Physicist (New York: Philosophical Library), 1955.

Bromberg, W. & Simon, F. The "protest" psychosis: a special type of reactive psychosis. Archives of General Psychiatry, 1968, 19, 155–60.

Brown, H. A. Role of expectancy manipulation in systematic desensitization. Journal of Consulting and Clinical Psychology, 1973, 41, 405–11.

Brown, R. & Herrnstein, R. Psychology (Boston: Little, Brown), 1975.

Bucher, B. & Lovaas, I. "Use of Aversive Stimulation in Behavior Modification," in Miami Symposium on the Prediction of Behavior, M. R. Jones (ed.) (Coral Gables: University of Miami Press), 1968.

Buchwald, A. M. Effects of immediate and delayed outcomes in associative learning. Journal of Verbal Learning and Verbal Behavior, 1967, 6, 317–20.

    Effects of "right" and "wrong" on subsequent behavior: a new interpretation. Psychological Review, 1969, 76, 132–43.

Cahoon, D. D. Symptom substitution and the behavior therapies: a reappraisal. Psychological Bulletin, 1968, 69, 149–56.

Carlin, A. S. & Armstrong, H. E. Aversive conditioning: Learning or dissonance reduction? Journal of Consulting and Clinical Psychology, 1968, 32, 674–78.

Carlson, C. G., Hersen, M. & Eisler, R. M. Token economy programs in the treatment of hospitalized adult psychiatric patients: current status and recent trends. Journal of Nervous and Mental Diseases, 1972, 155, 192–204.

Carnap, R. "Testability and Meaning," in Readings in the Philosophy of Science, Feigl, H. & Brodbeck, M. (eds.) (New York: Appleton-Century-Crofts), 1953.

Carrol, J. "Reinforcement: Is It a Basic Principle, and Will It Serve in the Analysis of Behavior," in The Nature of Reinforcement, Glaser, R. (ed.) (New York: Academic Press), 1971.

Cautela, J. R. Covert sensitization. Psychological Record, 1967, 20, 459–68.
The treatment of overeating by covert conditioning. Psychotherapy: Theory, Research and Practice, 1972, 9, 211–16.
Covert processes and behavior modification. Journal of Nervous and Mental Disease, 1973, 157, 27–36.
Chomsky, N. Review of verbal behavior. Language, 1959, 35, 26–58.
Aspects of the Theory of Syntax (Cambridge, Mass.: MIT Press), 1965.
"The Case Against B. F. Skinner," in For Reasons of State (New York: Random House), 1971.
"Problems and Mysteries in Language Study," in Language in Focus: Foundations, Methods and Systems, Kasher, A. (ed.) (Dordrecht, Holland: D. Reidel), 1976.
Coles, R. The limits of psychiatry. The Progressive, 1967, 31, 32–4.
Colgan, D. Effects of instructions upon the skin resistance response. Journal of Experimental Psychology, 1970, 86, 108–112.
Cooper, L. & Shepard, R. "Chronometric Studies of the Rotation of Mental Images," in Visual Information Processing, Chase, W. G. (ed.) (New York: Academic Press), 1973.
Cotter, L. H. Operant conditioning in a Vietnamese mental hospital. American Journal of Psychiatry, 1967, 124, 23–8.
Covington v. Harris, 1969, 419 F. 2d 617, D.C.
Davison, G. Systematic desensitization as a counter-conditioning process. Journal of Abnormal Psychology, 1968, 73, 91–9.
"Counter-Control in Behavior Modification," in Behavior Change: Methodology, Concepts and Practice, Hamerlynck, L., Handy, L. & Mash, E. (eds.) (Champaign, Ill.: Research Press), 1973.
Homosexuality: The ethical challenge. Journal of Consulting and Clinical Psychology, 1976, 44, 157–62.
Davison, G. & Neale, J. Abnormal Psychology: An Experimental Clinical Approach (New York: Wiley), 1974.
Davison, G. & Stuart, R. B. Behavior therapy and civil liberties. American Psychologist, 1975, 30, 755–63.
Davison, G. & Valins, S. Maintenance of self-attributed behavior change. Journal of Personality and Social Psychology, 1969, 11, 25–33.
Davison, G. & Wilson, G. T. Critique of "desensitization: Social and cognitive factors underlying the effectiveness of Wolpe's procedure." Psychological Bulletin, 1972, 78, 28–31.
Processes of fear-reduction in systematic desensitization: cognitive and social reinforcement factors in humans. Behavior Therapy, 1973, 4, 1–21.
Dawson, M. E. Cognition and conditioning: effects of masking the CS-UCS contingency on human GSR classical conditioning. Journal of Experimental Psychology, 1970, 85, 389–96.
Dawson, M. E. & Furedy, J. J. The role of relational awareness in human autonomic discrimination classical conditioning. Unpublished manuscript, University of Toronto, 1974.
Dawson, M. & Grings, W. Comparison of classical conditioning and relational learning. Journal of Experimental Psychology, 1968, 76, 227–31.
Day, W. F. Ethical philosophy and the thought of B. F. Skinner. West Virginia Conference on Behavioral Analysis and Ethics, Morgantown, West Virginia, 1975.

Delahunt, J. & Curran, J. Effectiveness of negative practive and self-control techniques in the reduction of smoking behavior. Journal of Consulting and Clinical Psychology, 1976, 44, 1002–7.

Denney, D. & Sullivan, B. Desensitization and modeling treatments of spider fear using two types of scenes. Journal of Consulting and Clinical Psychology, 1976, 44, 573–9.

De Nike, L. D. The temporal relationship between awareness and performance in verbal conditioning. Journal of Experimental Psychology, 1964, 68, 521–9.

Diament, C. & Wilson, G. T. An experimental investigation of the effects of covert sensitization in an analogue eating situation. Behavior Therapy, 1975, 6, 499–509.

Dinsmoor, J. "Operant Conditioning," in Handbook of General Psychology, Wolman, B. (ed.) (Englewood Cliffs, N.J.: Prentice-Hall), 1973.

Dulaney, D. Hypothesis and habits in verbal "operant conditioning." Journal of Abnormal and Social Psychology, 1961, 63, 251–63.

"On the Support of Cognitive Theory in Opposition to Behavior Theory: A Methodological Problem," in Cognition and the Symbolic Processes, Weimer, W. & Palermo, D. (eds.) (Hillsdale, N.J.: Lawrence Erlbaum Associates), 1974.

D'Zurilla, T., Wilson, G. T. & Nelson, R. A. A preliminary study of the effectiveness of graduated prolonged exposure to the treatment of irrational fears. Behavior Therapy, 1973, 4, 672–85.

Elliot, C. & Denney, D. Weight control through covert desensitization and false feedback. Journal of Consulting and Clinical Psychology, 1975, 43, 842–50.

Ellis, A. Reason and Emotion in Psychotherapy (New York: Lyle Stuart), 1962.

Should some people be labelled mentally ill? Journal of Consulting Psychology, 1967, 31, 435–46.

"A Twenty-Three-Year-Old Girl Guilty About Not Following Her Parents' Rules," in Growth Through Reason, Ellis, A. (ed.) (Palo Alto, Calif.: Science and Basic Books), 1971.

Emmelkamp, P. Self-observation versus flooding in the treatment of agoraphobia. Behavior Research and Therapy, 1974, 12, 229–37.

Emmelkamp, P. & Walta, C. Effects of therapy set on electrical aversion therapy and covert sensitization. Behavior Therapy, 1978, 9, 185–88.

Ennis, B. Prisoners of Psychiatry (New York: Harcourt Brace Jovanovich), 1972.

Ervin Committee Report. Individual Rights and the Federal Role in Behavior Modification (Washington: Government Printing Office), 1974.

Erwin, E. The Concept of Meaninglessness (Baltimore: Johns Hopkins Press), 1970.

"The Confirmation Machine," in Boston Studies in the Philosophy of Science, Buck, R. & Cohen, R. (Dordrecht, Holland: D. Reidel), 1971.

Are the notions "a priori truth" and "necessary truth" extensionally equivalent? Canadian Journal of Philosophy, 1973, 3, 591–602.

Estes, W. K. "Reinforcement in Human Learning," in Reinforcement and Behavior, Tapp, J. (ed.) (New York: Academic Press), 1969.

"Reward in Human Learning: Theoretical Issues and Strategic Choice Points," in The Nature of Reinforcement, Glaser, R. (ed.) (New York: Academic Press), 1971.

Everaerd, W., Rijken, H. & Emmelkamp, P. A comparison of "flooding" and successive approximation in the treatment of agoraphobia. Behaviour Research and Therapy, 1973, 11, 105–17.

Eysenck, H. J. The effects of psychotherapy: an evaluation. Journal of Consulting Psychology, 1952, 16, 319–24.

Behavior Therapy and the Neuroses (London: Pergamon Press), 1960.

(ed.). *Experiments in Behavior Therapy* (New York: Pergamon Press), 1964.

The Effects of Psychotherapy (New York: International Science Press), 1966.

Behavior therapy is behavioristic. Behavior Therapy, 1972, 3, 609–13.

Psychological theories and behavior therapy. Psychological Medicine, 1975, 5, 219–21.

"Behavior Therapy – Dogma or Applied Science?" in *Theoretical and Experimental Bases of the Behavior Therapies,* Broadhurst, A. & Feldman, M. P. (eds.) (New York: Wiley), 1976.

Eysenck, H. J. & Beech, R. "Counterconditioning and Related Methods," in *Handbook of Psychotherapy and Behavior Change: An Empirical Analysis,* Bergin, A. & Garfield, S. (eds.) (New York: Wiley), 1971.

Fairweather, G. W., Sanders, D. H., Cressler, D. L. & Maynard, H. *Community Life for the Mentally Ill* (Chicago: Aldine), 1969.

Feldman, M. & MacCulloch, M. *Homosexual Behavior: Therapy and Assessment* (Oxford: Pergamon Press), 1971.

Ferster, C. B. & Skinner, B. F. *Schedules of Reinforcement* (New York: Appleton), 1957.

Fodor, J. *The Language of Thought.* (New York: Crowell), 1975.

Fodor, J. & Katz, J. *The Structure of Language: Readings in the Philosophy of Language* (Englewood Cliffs, N.J.: Prentice-Hall), 1964.

Fordyce, W., Fowler, R., Lehmann, J., DeLateur, B., Sand, P. & Trieschmann, R. Operant conditioning in the treatment of chronic pain. Archives of Physical Medicine and Rehabilitation, 1973, 54, 399–408.

Foreyt, J. P. & Hagen, R. L. Covert sensitization: conditioning and suggestion? Journal of Abnormal Psychology, 1973, 82, 17–23.

Franks, C. M. "Behavior Therapy and Its Pavlovian Origins," in *Behavior Therapy: Appraisal and Status,* Franks, C. M. (ed.) (New York: McGraw-Hill), 1969.

Franks, C. M. & Wilson, G. T. (eds.). *Annual Review of Behavior Therapy Theory and Practice* (New York: Brunner/Mazel), 1973.

Annual Review of Behavior Therapy Theory and Practice (New York: Brunner/Mazel), 1975.

Franks, G. *Psychiatric Diagnosis: A Review of Research* (Oxford: Pergamon Press), 1975.

Friedman, S. On vegetarianism. Journal of the American Psychoanalytic Association, 1975, 23, 396–406.

Fromm, E. *The Crisis of Psychoanalysis* (Greenwich, Conn.: Fawcett), 1970.

Fuhrer, M. & Baer, P. Cognitive processes in differential GSR conditioning: effects of a masking task. American Journal of Psychology, 1969, 82, 168–80.

Gaupp, L. A., Stern, R. M. & Galbraith, G. C. False heartrate feedback and reciprocal inhibition by aversion relief in the treatment of snake avoidance behavior. Behavior Therapy, 1972, 3, 7–20.

Gelder, M., Bancroft, J., Gath, D., Johnston, D., Mathews, A. & Shaw, P. Specific and non-specific factors in behavior therapy. British Journal of Psychiatry, 1973, 123, 445–62.

Gelder, M. & Marks, I. Severe agoraphobia: a controlled prospective therapeutic trial. British Journal of Psychiatry, 1966, 112, 309–19.

Gerber, M., Hiller, C., Keith C. & Taylor, J. Behavior modification in maximum security settings: one hospital's experience. The American Criminal Law Review, 1975, 13, 85–99.

Gerwirtz, J. L. "The roles of Overt Responding and Extrinsic Reinforcement in 'Self' and 'Vicarious Reinforcement,' Phenomena and in 'Observational Learning' and Imitation," in *the Nature of Reinforcement,* Glaser, R. (ed.) (New York: Academic Press), 1971.

Gittleman, M. Behavior rehearsal as a technique in child treatment. Journal of Child Psychology and Psychiatry, 1965, 6, 251–5.

Glover, J. *Responsibility* (Atlantic Highlands, N.J.: Humanities Press), 1970.

Goldfried, M. R., Decenteceo, E. T. & Weinberg, L. Systematic rational restructuring as a self-control technique. Behavior Therapy, 1974, 5, 247–54.

Goldfried, M. R. & Goldfried, A. P. "Cognitive Change Methods," in *Helping People Change,* Kanfer, F. H. & Goldstein, A. P. (eds.) (New York: Pergamon Press), 1975.

Goldfried, M. & Kent, R. Traditional vs. behavioral assessment: a comparison of methodological and theoretical assumptions. Psychological Bulletin, 1972, 77, 409–20.

Goldfried, M. R. & Merbaum, M. (eds.). *Behavior Change Through Self-Control* (New York: Holt, Rinehart & Winston), 1973.

Goldfried, M. R. & Sobicinski, D. The effects of irrational beliefs on emotional arousal. Journal of Consulting and Clinical Psychology, 1975, 43, 504–10.

Goldfried, M. & Sprafkin, J. *Behavioral Personality Assessment* (Morristown, N.J.: General Learning Press), 1974.

Greenson, R. R. "The Classic Psychoanalytic Approach," in *American Handbook of Psychiatry,* Arieti, S. (ed.) (New York: Basic Books), 1959.

Greenspoon, J. "Verbal Conditioning and Clinical Psychology," in *Experimental Foundations of Clinical Psychology,* Bachrach, A. J. (ed.) (New York: Basic Books), 1962.

Grings, W. "The Role of Consciousness and Cognition in Autonomic Behavior Change," in *The Psychophysiology of Thinking.* McGuigan, F. J. & Schoonover, R. A. (eds.) (New York: Academic Press), 1973.

Grings, W., Schell, A., & Carey, C. Verbal control of an autonomic response in a cue reversal situation. Journal of Experimental Psychology, 1973, 99, 215–221.

Grings, W. & Sukoneck, H. Prediction probability as a determiner of anticipatory and preparatory behavior. Journal of Experimental Psychology, 1971, 90, 136–40.

Grunbaum, A. "Causality and the Science of Human Behavior," reprinted in *Readings in the Philosophy of Science,* Feigl, H. & Brodbeck, M. (eds.) (New York: Appleton-Century-Crofts), 1953.

Haber, R. N . & Haber, R. B. Eidetic imagery: 1. frequency. Perceptual and Motor Skills, 1964, 19, 131–8.

Hall, E. M. Self-control and therapist control in the behavioral treatment of overweight women. Behaviour Research and Therapy, 1972, 10, 59–68.

Hallam, R., Rachman, S. & Falkowski, W. Subjective, attitudinal and physiological effects of electrical aversion therapy. Behaviour Research and Therapy, 1972, 10, 1–13.

Hand, I., Lamontagne, Y. & Marks, I. Group exposure (flooding) in vivo for agoraphobics. British Journal of Psychiatry, 1974, 124, 588–602.

Hare, R. D. *Psychopathy: Theory and Research* (New York: Wiley), 1970.

Harman, G. *The Nature of Morality: An Introduction to Ethics* (New York: Oxford University Press), 1977.

Heap, R. F., Boblitt, W. E., Moore, C. H. & Hord, J. E. Behavior-milieu therapy with chronic neuropsychiatric patients. Journal of Abnormal Psychology, 1970, 76, 349–54.

Hedberg, A. & Campbell, L. A comparison of four behavioral treatments of alcoholism. Journal of Behavior Therapy and Experimental Psychiatry, 1974, 5, 251–6.

Hempel, C. "A Logical Appraisal of Operationism," in *The Validation of Scientific Theories*, Frank, P. (ed.) (Boston: Beacon Press), 1956.

Aspects of Explanation (New York: Free Press), 1965.

Hempel, C. & Oppenheim, P. Studies in the logic of explanation. Philosophy of Science, 1948, 15, 135–75.

Hersen, M., Eisler, R. & Miller, P. "Historical Perspectives in Behavior Modification: Introductory Comments," in *Progress in Behavior Modification*, Vol. 1, Hersen, M., Eisler, R. & Miller, P. (eds.) (New York: Academic Press), 1975.

Heston, L. L. Psychiatric disorders in foster home reared children of schizophrenic mothers. British Journal of Psychiatry, 1966, 112, 819–25.

Hilgard, E. R. & Bower, G. *Theories of Learning* (Englewood Cliffs, N.J.: Prentice-Hall), 1966, 1975.

Hilgard, E. & Marquis, D. *Conditioning and Learning* (New York: Appleton-Century-Crofts), 1961.

Hollingsworth, R. & Foreyt, J. Community adjustment of released token economy patients. Journal of Behavior Therapy and Experimental Psychiatry, 1975, 6, 271–4.

Homme, L. E. Control of coverants, the operants of the mind. Psychological Record, 1965, 15, 501–11.

Horne, A. & Matson, J. A comparison of modeling, desensitization, flooding, study skills, and control groups for reducing test anxiety. Behavior Therapy, 1977, 8, 1–8.

Hull, C. L. Thorndike's fundamentals of learning. Psychological Bulletin, 1935, 32, 807–23.

Humphreys, M. S., Allen, G. & Estes, W. K. Learning of two-choice, differential reward problems with informational constraints on payoff combinations. Journal of Mathematical Psychology, 1968, 5, 260–80.

Hunt, W. A. & Matarazzo, J. D. Three years later: Recent developments in the experimental modification of smoking. Journal of Abnormal Psychology, 1973, 81, 107–14.

Hyman, E. & Gale, E. The galvanic skin response and reported anxiety during systematic desensitization. Journal of Consulting and Clinical Psychology, 1973, 40, 108–14.

Jacobsen, E. *Progressive Relaxation* (Chicago: University of Chicago Press), 1938.

James, W. & Rotter, J. B. Partial and 100% reinforcement under chance and skill conditions. Journal of Experimental Psychology, 1958, 55, 397–403.

Jones, M. C. The elimination of children's fears. Journal of Experimental Psychology, 1924, 7, 383–90.

A laboratory study of fear: the case of Peter. Journal of Genetic Psychology, 1924, 31, 308–15.

A 1924 pioneer looks at behavior therapy. Journal of Behavior Therapy and Experimental Psychiatry, 1975, 6, 181–7.

Jones, R. T. & Kazdin, A. E. Programming response maintenance after withdrawing token reinforcement. Behavior Therapy, 1975, 6, 153–64.

Kaij, L. *Alcoholism in Twins: Studies on the Etiology and Sequels of Abuse of Alcohol* (Stockholm: Almquist and Wiksell), 1960.

Kaimowitz ex rel. John Doe v. *Department of Health for the State of Michigan,* 42 U.S.L. Week 2063 (Mich. Cir. Ct., Wayne Cty.), 1973.

Kanfer, F. "Self-Regulation: Research, Issues and Speculation," in *Behavior Modification in Clinical Psychology,* Neuringer, C. & Michael, J. L. (eds.) (New York: Appleton-Century-Crofts), 1970.

Kanfer, F. & Karoly, P. Self-control: A behavioristic excursion into the lion's den. Behavior Therapy, 1972, 3, 398–416.

Kanfer, F. & Phillips, J. *Learning Foundations of Behavior Therapy* (New York: Wiley), 1970.

Kanfer, F. H. & Saslow, G. "Behavioral Diagnosis," in *Behavior Therapy: Appraisal and Status,* Franks, C. M. (ed.) (New York: McGraw-Hill), 1969.

Kantor, J. R. *The Scientific Evolution of Psychology* (Chicago: Principia), 1969.

Katahn, M. & Koplin, J. Paradigm clash: comment on some recent criticisms of behaviorism and learning theory with special reference to Breger and McGaugh and to Chomsky. Psychological Bulletin, 1968, 69, 147–8.

Kazdin, A. E. Covert modeling, model similarity, and reduction of avoidance behavior. Behavior Therapy, 1974a, 5, 325–40.

Effects of covert modeling and reinforcement on assertive behavior. Journal of Abnormal Psychology, 1974b, 83, 240–52.

Covert modeling, imagery, assessment, and assertive behavior. Journal of Consulting and Clinical Psychology, 1975, 43, 716–24.

Kazdin, A. E. & Bootzin, R. R. The token economy: an evaluative review. Journal of Applied Behavior Analysis, 1972, 5, 343–72.

Kazdin, A. E. & Wilcoxon, L. Systematic desensitization and nonspecific treatment effects: a methodological evaluation. Psychological Bulletin, 1976, 83, 729–58.

Keller, L., Cole, M., Burke, C., & Estes, W. K. Reward and information values of trial outcomes in paired-associate learning. Psychological Monographs, 1965, 79 (Whole No. 605).

Kendler, H. & Spence, J. "Tenets of Neobehaviorism," in *Essays in Neobehaviorism: A Memorial Volume to Kenneth W. Spence,* Kendler, H. & Spence, J. (eds.) (New York: Appleton-Century-Crofts), 1971.

Kety, S. S., Rosenthal, D., Wender, P. H., & Schulsinger, F. "The Types and Prevalence of Mental Illness in the Biological and Adoptive Families of Adopted Schizophrenics," in *The Transmission of Schizophrenia,* Rosenthal, D. & Kety, S. S. (eds.) (London: Pergamon Press), 1968.

Kety, S., Rosenthal, D., Wender, P., Schulsinger, F. & Jacobsen, F. "Mental Illness in the Biological and Adoptive Families of Adopted Individuals Who Have Become Schizophrenic: A Preliminary Report Based on Psychiatric Interviews," in *Genetic Research in Psychiatry,* Fieve, R., Rosenthal, D. & Brill, H. (eds.) (Baltimore: Johns Hopkins University Press), 1975.

Kim, J. On the psycho-physical identity theory. American Philosophical Quarterly, 1966, 3, 227–35.

Kline, P. *Fact and Fantasy in Freudian Theory* (London: Methuen), 1972.

Koch, S. "Psychology and Emerging Conceptions of Knowledge as Unitary," in *Behaviorism and Phenomenology*, Wann, T. W. (ed.) (Chicago: University of Chicago Press), 1964.

Kolodny, R. C., Masters, W. H., Hendryx, J. & Toro, G. Plasma testosterone and the semen analysis in male homosexuals. New England Journal of Medicine, 1971, 285, 1170–4.

Kosslyn, S. M. "Scanning Visual Images: Some Structural Implications," in *Perception and Psychophysics*, 1973, 14, 90–4.

Kosslyn, S. M. & Alper, S. N. On the pictorial properties of visual images: effects of image size on memory for words. Canadian Journal of Psychology, 1977, 31, 32–40.

Kosslyn, S. M. & Pomerantz, J. R. Imagery, propositions, and the form of internal representations. Cognitive Psychology, 1977, 9, 52–76.

Kraepelin, E. "Clinical Psychiatry," in *Theories of Psychopathology and Personality*, Millon, T. (ed.) (Philadelphia: Saunders), 1973.

Krasner, L. Studies of the conditioning of verbal behavior. Psychological Bulletin, 1958, 55, 148–70.

"Assessment of Token Economy Programs in Psychiatric Hospitals," in *The Role of Learning in Psychotherapy*, R. Porter (ed.) (London: Churchill), 1968.

Behavior therapy. Annual Review of Psychology, 1971a, 22, 483–532.

"The Operant Approach in Behavior Therapy," in *Handbook of Psychotherapy and Behavior Change: An Empirical Analysis*, Bergin, A. & Garfield, S. (eds.) (New York: Wiley), 1971b.

"Behavior Modification: Ethical Issues and Future Trends," in *Handbook of Behavior Modification and Behavior Therapy*, Leitenberg, H. (ed.) (Englewood Cliffs, N.J.: Prentice-Hall), 1976.

Kripke, S. "Naming and Necessity," in *Semantics of Natural Language*, Davidson, D. & Harman, G. (eds.) (Dordrecht: Reidel), 1972.

Kuhn, T. *The Structure of Scientific Revolutions* (Chicago: University of Chicago Press), 1962.

Kushner, M. "The Reduction of a Long-Standing Fetish by Means of Aversive Conditioning," in *Case Studies in Behavior Modification*, Ullmann, L. & Krasner, L. (eds.) (New York: Holt, Rinehart & Winston), 1965.

Kushner, M. & Sandler, L. Aversion therapy and the concept of punishment. Behaviour Research and Therapy, 1966, 4, 179–86.

Laing, R. D. *The Politics of Experience* (London: Penguin Books), 1971.

Lake v. *Cameron*, 364 F. 2d. 657, D.C., 1966.

Lang, P. J. "Experimental Studies of Desensitization Psychotherapy," in *The Conditioning Therapies*, Wolpe, J., Salter, A., & Reyna, L. (eds.) (New York: Holt, Rinehart & Winston), 1964.

Lang, P. J. & Lazovik, A. The experimental desensitization of a phobia. Journal of Abnormal and Social Psychology, 1963, 66, 519–25.

Lazarus, A. New methods in psychotherapy: A case study. South African Medical Journal, 1958, 33, 660–4.

Behavior Therapy and Beyond (New York: McGraw-Hill), 1971.

Lefcourt, H. Internal versus external control of reinforcement: a review. Psychological Bulletin, 1966, 65, 206–20.

Leifer, R. The medical model as ideology. International Journal of Psychiatry, 1970, 9, 13–21.

Leitenberg, H. The use of single-case methodology in psychotherapy research. Journal of Abnormal Psychology, 1973, 82, 87–101.

Levine, B. Treatment of trichotillomania by covert sensitization. Journal of Behaviour Therapy & Experimental Psychiatry, 1976, 7, 75–6.

Levis, D. "Behavioral Therapy: The Fourth Therapeutic Revolution?" in *Learning Approaches to Therapeutic Behavior Change,* Levis, D. (ed.) (Chicago: Aldine), 1970.

Levitz, L. & Stunkard, A. A therapeutic coalition for obesity: behavior modification and patient self-help. American Journal of Psychiatry, 1974, 131, 423–7.

Lewis, D. An argument for the identity theory. Journal of Philosophy, 1966, 63, 17–25.

Lick, J. R. Expectancy, false galvanic skin response feedback and systematic desensitization in the modification of phobic behavior. Journal of Consulting and Clinical Psychology, 1975, 43, 557–67.

Lick, J. R. & Bootzin, R. R. Expectancy, demand characteristics and contact desensitization in behavior change. Behavior Therapy, 1970, 1, 176–83.

Expectancy factors in the treatment of fear: methodological and theoretical issues. Psychological Bulletin, 1975, 82, 917–31.

Lindsay, R. B. A critique of operationalism in physics. Philosophy of Science, 1937, 4, 456–70.

Lindsley, O. R., Skinner, B. F. & Solomon, H. C. *Studies in Behavior Therapy: Status Report 1* (Waltham, Mass.: Metropolitan State Hospital), 1953.

Lloyd, R. W. & Salzberg, H. C. Controlled social drinking: an alternative to abstinence as a treatment goal for some alcoholics, Psychological Bulletin, 1975, 82, 815–42.

Locke, E. Is behavior therapy behavioristic? Psychological Bulletin, 1971, 76, 318–27.

London, P. The end of ideology in behavior modification. American Psychologist, 1972, 27, 913–20.

Loraine, J. A., Adamopoulos, D. A., Kirkham, E. E., Ismail, A. A. & Dove, G. A. Patterns of hormone excretion in male and female homosexuals. Nature, 1971, 234, 552–5.

Lovaas, I., Berberich, J., Kassorla, I., Klynn, G. & Meisel, J. Establishment of a texting and labeling vocabulary in schizophrenic children. Unpublished manuscript, University of California at Los Angeles, 1966.

Lovaas, I., Dumont, D., Klynn, G. & Meisel, J. Program for the establishment of appropriate speech and intellectual skills in schizophrenic children. Unpublished manuscript, University of California at Los Angeles, 1966.

Lovaas, I. & Simmons, J. "Building social behavior in autistic children by use of electric shock," in *Perspectives in Behavior Modification with Deviant Children* Lovaas, O. & Bucher, B. (eds.) (Englewood Cliffs, N.J.: Prentice-Hall), 1974.

Lovibond, S. H. *Conditioning and Enuresis* (New York: Macmillan), 1964.

Lycan, W. G. Noninductive evidence: recent work on Wittgenstein's "criteria." American Philosophical Quarterly, 1971, 8, 109–25.

MacCorquodale, K. Chomsky's review of verbal behavior. Journal of the Experimental Analysis of Behavior, 1970, 13, 83–99.

Mackey v. *Procunier,* 477, F. 2d. 877, 9th Cir., 1973.

Mahoney, M. *Cognitive Behavior Modification* (Cambridge: Ballinger), 1974.

Mahoney, M., Kazdin, A. & Lesswing, N. "Behavior Modification: Delusion or Deliverance?" in *Annual Review of Behavior Therapy: Theory and Practice,* Franks, C. & Wilson, G. T. (eds.) (New York: Brunner/Mazel), 1974.

Mahoney, M., Monra, N. & Wade, T. Relative efficacy of self-reward, self-punishment, and self-monitoring techniques for weight loss. Journal of Consulting and Clinical Psychology, 1973, 40, 404–7.

Mahoney, M. & Thoreson, C. (eds.). *Self-Control: Power to the Person* (Monterey, Calif.: Brooks/Cole), 1974.

Malcolm, N. "Behaviorism as a Philosophy of Psychology," in *Behaviorism and Phenomenology,* Wann, T. W. (ed.) (Chicago: University of Chicago Press), 1964.

Marks, I. M. The current status of behavioral psychotherapy: theory and practice. American Journal of Psychiatry, 1976, 133, 253–61.

Marks, I. M. & Gelder, M. G. Transvestism and fetishism: clinical and psychological changes during faradic aversion. British Journal of Psychiatry, 1967, 119, 711–30.

Marlatt, G. A. Loss of control drinking in alcoholics: an experimental analogue. Journal of Abnormal Psychology, 1973, 81, 233–41.

Martin, R. *Legal Challenges to Behavior Modification* (Champaign, Ill.: Research Press), 1975.

Martinson, R. California research at the crossroads. Crime and Delinquency, 1976, 22, 180–91.

Matson, F. (ed.). *Without-Within: Behaviorism and Humanism* (Monterey, Calif.: Brooks-Cole), 1973.

McConnell, J. V. Stimulus/response. Criminals can be brainwashed—now. Psychology Today, 1970, 3:11, 14–18.

McFall, R. & Lillesand, D. Behavior rehearsal with modeling and coaching in assertion training. Journal of Experimental Psychology, 1971, 80, 364–8.

McFall, R. & Twentyman, C. Four experiments on the relative contributions of rehearsal modeling, and coaching to assertion training. Journal of Abnormal Psychology, 1973, 81, 199–218.

McNeil, E. *The Quiet Furies* (Englewood Cliffs, N.J.: Prentice-Hall), 1967.

McReynolds, W. T., Barnes, A. R., Brook, S. & Rehagen, N. J. The role of attention-placebo influences in the efficacy of systematic desensitization. Journal of Consulting and Clinical Psychology, 1973, 41, 86–92.

Medvedev, Z. & Medvedev, R. *A Question of Madness* (New York: Random House), 1972.

Meehl, P. On the circularity of the law of effect. Psychological Bulletin, 1950, 47, 52–75.

Meichenbaum, D. H. Cognitive factors in behavior modification. Research Report No. 25, Dept. of Psychology, University of Waterloo, 1971a.

"Cognitive Factors in Behavior Modification: Modifying What Clients Say to Themselves," in *Annual Review of Behavior Therapy: Theory and Practice,* Franks, C. M. & Wilson, G. T. (eds.) (New York: Brunner/Mazel), 1971b.

Meichenbaum, D. H. & Cameron, R. "The Clinical Potential of Modifying What Clients Say to Themselves," in *Self-Control—Power to the Person,* Mahoney, M. & Thoresen, M. (eds.) (Monterey, Calif.: Brooks/Cole), 1974.

Melnick, J. A comparison of replication techniques in the modification of minimal dating behavior. Journal of Abnormal Psychology, 1973, 81, 51–9.

Meyer, V. Comments on A. J. Yates' "Misconceptions about behavior therapy: A point of view." Behavior Therapy, 1970, 1, 108–12.

Mill, J. S. *On Liberty* (New York: W. W. Norton & Co.) 1975.

Miller, S. B. The contribution of therapeutic instructions to systematic desensitization. Behaviour Research and Therapy, 1972, 10, 159–70.

Moleski, R. & Tosi, D. Comparative psychotherapy: rational-emotive therapy versus systematic desensitization in the treatment of stuttering. Journal of Consulting and Clinical Psychology, 1976, 44, 309–11.

Moore, N. Behavior therapy in bronchial asthma: a controlled study. Journal of Psychosomatic Research, 1965, 9, 257–76.

Morganstern, K. Implosive therapy and flooding procedures: a critical review. Psychological Bulletin, 1973, 79, 318–34.

Murray, E. & Jacobson, L. "The Nature of Learning in Traditional and Behavioral Psychotherapy," in *Handbook of Psychotherapy and Behavior Change: An Empirical Analysis,* Bergin, A. & Garfield, S. (eds.) (New York: Wiley), 1971.

Nathan, P. E. "Alcoholism," in *Handbook of Behavior Modification and Behavior Therapy,* Leitenberg, H. (ed.) (Englewood Cliffs, N.J.: Prentice-Hall), 1976.

Nau, S. D., Caputo, J. A. & Borkovec, T. D. The relationship between therapy credibility and simulated therapy response. Journal of Behavior Therapy and Experimental Psychiatry, 1974, 5, 129–33.

Nawas, M., Fishman, S. T. & Pucel, J. A standardized desensitization program applicable to group and individual treatments. Behaviour Research and Therapy, 1970, 8, 49–56.

Neale, J. M. & Liebert, R. M. *Science and Behavior: An Introduction to Methods of Research* (Englewood Cliffs, N.J.: Prentice-Hall), 1973.

Nedelman, D. & Salzbacher, S. "Dickey at 13 Years of Age: A Long Term Success Following Early Application of Operant Conditioning Procedures," in *Behavior Analysis and Education,* Semb, G. (ed.) (Lawrence, Ka.: University of Kansas), 1972.

Neisser, U. *Cognitive Psychology* (New York: Appleton), 1967.

Nisbett, R. & Schachter, S. The cognitive manipulation of pain. Journal of Experimental Social Psychology, 1966, 2, 227–36.

Nisbett, R. & Valins, S. *Perceiving the Cause of One's Own Behavior* (Morristown, N.J.: General Learning Process), 1971.

O'Connor, R. D. Modification of social withdrawal through social modeling. Journal of Applied Behavior Analysis, 1969, 2, 15–22.

Relative efficacy of modeling, shaping, and the combined procedures for modification of social withdrawal, Journal of Abnormal Psychology, 1972, 79, 327–34.

O'Leary, K. D. Behavior modification in the classroom: a rejoinder to Winett and Winkler. Journal of Applied Behavior Analysis, 1972, 5, 505–11.

O'Leary, K. D. & Drabman, R. Token reinforcement programs in the classroom: a review. Psychological Bulletin, 1971, 75, 379–98.

O'Leary, K. D., Poulos, R. & Devine, V. Tangible reinforcers: bonuses or bribes? Journal of Consulting and Clinical Psychology, 1972, 38, 1–8.

O'Leary, K. D. & Wilson, G. T. *Behavior Therapy: Application and Outcome* (Englewood Cliffs, N.J.: Prentice-Hall), 1975.

Pap, A. *An Introduction to the Philosophy of Science* (New York: Free Press), 1962.

Paivio, A. *Imagery and Verbal Processes* (New York: Holt, Rinehart & Winston), 1971.

"Psychophysiological Correlates of Imagery," in *The Psychophysiology of Thinking,* McGuigan, F. & Schoonover, R. (eds.) (New York: Academic Press), 1973.

"Images, Propositions and Knowledge," in *Images, Perception and Knowledge,* Nicholas, J. M. (ed.) (Dordrecht: Reidel), 1976.

Penick, S., Filion, R., Fox, S. & Stunkard, A. Behavior modification in the treatment of obesity. Psychosomatic Medicine, 1971, 33, 49–55.

Paul, G. L. *Insight vs. Desensitization in Psychotherapy* (Stanford, Calif.: Stanford University Press), 1966.

Insight vs. desensitization in psychotherapy two years after termination. Journal of Consulting Psychology, 1967, 31, 333–48.

"Outcome of Systematic Desensitization. II: Controlled Investigations of Individual Treatment, Technique Variations and Current Status," in *Behavior Therapy: Appraisal and Status,* Franks, C. M. (ed.) (New York: McGraw-Hill), 1969.

Paul, G. L. & Bernstein, D. A. *Anxiety and Clinical Problems: Systematic Desensitization and Related Techniques* (Morristown, N.J.: General Learning Press), 1973.

Phillips, L. & Draguns, J. Classification of the behavior disorders. Annual Review of Psychology, 1971, 22, 447–81.

Place, W. T. Is consciousness a brain process? British Journal of Psychology, 1956, 47, 44–50.

Pomerleau, O., Pertschuk, M. & Stinnett, J. A critical examination of some current assumptions in the treatment of alcoholism. Journal of Studies on Alcohol, 1976, 37, 849–67.

Posner, M. *Cognition: An Introduction* (Glenview, Ill.: Scott, Foresman), 1973.

Powell, J. & Azrin, N. H. The effects of shock as a punisher for cigarette smoking. Journal of Applied Behavior Analysis, 1968, 1, 63–71.

Premack, D. Toward empirical behavior laws: I. Positive reinforcement. Psychological Review, 1959, 66, 219–33.

"Reinforcement Theory," in *Nebraska Symposium on Motivation,* Levine, D. (ed.) (Lincoln: University of Nebraska Press), 1965.

"Catching Up with Common Sense or Two Sides of a Generalization: Reinforcement and Punishment," in *The Nature of Reinforcement,* Glaser, R. (ed.) (New York: Academic Press), 1971.

Putnam, H. "Brains and Behavior," in *Analytical Philosophy,* Second Series, Butler, R. J. (ed.) (Oxford: Blackwell), 1965.

Quine, W. V. "Linguistics and Philosophy," in *Language and Philosophy,* Sidney Hook (ed.) (New York: New York University Press), 1969.

Rachlin, H. On the tautology of the matching law. Journal of the Experimental Analysis of Behavior, 1971, 15 249–51.

Rachlin, H. & Green, L. Commitment choice and self-control. Journal of the Experimental Analysis of Behavior, 1972, 17, 15–22.

Rachlin, H. & Lacey, H. Behavior, cognition and theories of choice. Unpublished manuscript, 1978. State University of New York at Stony Brook.

Rachman, S. Studies in desensitization —II: Flooding. Behaviour Research and Therapy, 1966, 4, 1–6.

The Effects of Psychotherapy (London: Pergamon Press), 1971.

Rachman, S. & Eysenck, H. J. Reply to a critique and reformulation of behavior therapy. Psychological Bulletin, 1966, 65, 165–9.

Rachman, S., Hodgson, R. & Marks, I. The treatment of chronic obsessive-compulsive neurosis. Behaviour Research and Therapy, 1971, 9, 237–47.

Rachman, S. & Teasdale, J. *Aversion Therapy and Behavior Disorders: An Analysis* (Coral Gables, Fl.: University of Miami Press), 1969.

Rawls, J. *A Theory of Justice* (Cambridge, Mass.: Harvard University Press), 1971.

Raymond, M. A case of fetishism treated by aversion therapy. British Medical Journal, 1956, 2, 854–6.

Rhoads, J. M. & Feather, B. Application of psychodynamics to behavior therapy. American Journal of Psychiatry, 1974, 131, 17–20.

Rimm, D. & Litvak, S. Self-verbalization and emotional arousal. Journal of Abnormal Psychology, 1969, 74, 181–7.

Rimm, D. C. & Masters, J. C. *Behavior Therapy: Techniques and Empirical Findings* (New York: Academic Press), 1974.

Risely, T. The effects and side effects of punishing the autistic behavior of a deviant child. Journal of Applied Behavior Analysis, 1968, 1, 21–34.

Risely, T. & Wolf, M. Establishing functional speech in echolalic children. Behaviour Research and Therapy, 1967, 5, 73–88.

Ritter, B. Treatment of a dissection phobia. Unpublished manuscript, Queens College, 1965.

The group treatment of children's snake phobias, using vicarious and contact desensitization procedures. Behaviour Research and Therapy, 1968, 6, 1–6.

"Eliminating Excessive Fears of the Environment Through Contact Desensitization," in *Behavioral Counseling: Cases and Techniques* J. B. Krumboltz and C. E. Thorenson (eds.) (New York: Holt, Rinehart & Winston), 1969a.

Treatment of acrophobia with contact desensitization. Behaviour Research and Therapy, 1969b, 7, 41–5.

Roe, A., Burks, B., & Mittleman, B. "Adult Adjustment of Foster Home Children of Alcoholic and Psychotic Parentage and the Influence of the Foster Home," in *Memoirs of the Section on Alcohol,* Yale University, 1945.

Rogers, C. & Skinner, B. F. Some issues concerning the control of human behavior: a symposium. Science, 1956, 124, 1057–65.

Romanczyk, R. G. & Goren, E. R. Severe self-injurious behavior: the problem of clinical control. Journal of Consulting and Clinical Psychology, 1975, 43, 730–9.

Rosen, G. M. Therapy set: its effect on subjects' involvement in systematic desensitization and treatment outcome. Journal of Abnormal Psychology, 1974, 83, 291–300.

Rosen, G. M., Glasgow, R. E. & Barrera, M. A controlled study to assess the clinical efficacy of totally self-administered systematic desensitization. Journal of Consulting and Clinical Psychology, 1976, 44, 208–17.

Rosen, G. M., Rosen, E. & Reid, J. B. Cognitive desensitization and avoidance behavior: a reevaluation. Journal of Abnormal Psychology, 1972, 80, 176–82.

Rosenthal, D. *Genetics of Psychopathology* (New York: McGraw-Hill), 1971.

Ruffin v. *Commonwealth,* 62 Va. 790, 796, 1871.

Ryan, V. & Gizynski, M. Behavior therapy in retrospect: patients' feelings about their behavior therapists. Journal of Consulting and Clinical Psychology, 1971, 37, 1–9.

Ryle, G. *The Concept of Mind* (New York: Barnes & Noble), 1949.

Salzinger, K. & Feldman, R. (eds.). *Studies in Verbal Behavior: An Empirical Approach* (New York: Pergamon Press), 1973.

Sandifer, M. G., Pettus, C. & Quade, D. A. A study of psychiatric diagnosis. Journal of Nervous and Mental Disease, 1964, 139, 350–6.

Sarbin, T. R. On the futility of the proposition that some people be labeled "mentally ill." Journal of Consulting Psychology, 1967, 5, 445–53.

Scheff, T. The role of the mentally ill and the dynamics of mental disorder. Sociometry, 1963, 26, 436–53.

Schmahl, D., Lichtenstein, E. & Harris, D. Successful treatment of habitual smokers with warm, smoky air and rapid smoking. Journal of Consulting and Clinical Psychology, 1972, 38, 105–11.

Schmauk, F. J. Punishment, arousal, and avoidance learning in sociopaths. Journal of Abnormal Psychology, 1970, 76, 443–53.

Schultz, D. *A History of Modern Psychology* (New York: Academic Press), 1969, 1975.

Scriven, M. "Explanations, Predictions, and Laws," in *Minnesota Studies in the Philosophy of Science,* Vol. III, Feigl, H. & Maxwell, G. (eds.) (Minneapolis: University of Minnesota Press), 1962.

Shapiro, M. Legislating the control of behavior control: autonomy and the coercive use of organic therapies. Southern California Law Review, 1974, 47, 237–336.

Shepard, R. The mental image. American Psychologist, 1978, 33, 125–37.

Shepard, R. & Metzler, J. Mental rotation of three-dimensional objects. Science, 1971, 171, 701–3.

Sherman, J. Use of reinforcement and imitation to reinstate verbal behavior in mute psychotics. Journal of Abnormal Psychology, 1965, 70, 155–64.

Singer, R. & Statsky, W. *Rights of the Imprisoned* (Indianapolis: Bobbs-Merrill), 1974.

Skinner, B. F. *The Behavior of Organisms: An Experimental Analysis* (New York: Appleton), 1938.

The operational analysis of psychological terms. Psychological Review, 1945, 52, 270–7, 291–4.

Are theories of learning necessary? Psychological Review, 1950, 57, 193–216.

Science and Human Behavior (New York: Macmillan), 1953.

A critique of psychoanalytic concepts and theories. The Scientific Monthly, 1954, 79, 300–305.

Verbal Behavior (New York: Appleton-Century-Crofts), 1957.

Behaviorism at fifty. Science, 1963, 140, 951–8.

Beyond Freedom and Dignity (New York: Bantam Books), 1971a.

Personal communciation, 1971b.

About Behaviorism (New York: Knopf), 1974.

Sloane, H., Johnston, M. K. & Harris, F. R. "Remedial Procedures for Teaching Verbal Behavior to Speech Deficient or Defective Young Children," in *Operant Procedures in Remedial Speech and Language Training,* H. N. Sloane & B. A. Mac Aulay (eds.) (Boston: Houghton Mifflin), 1968.

Sloane, R. B., Staples, F. R., Cristol, A. H., Yorkston, N. J. & Whipple, K. *Psychotherapy Versus Behavior Therapy* (Cambridge, Mass.: Harvard University Press), 1975a.

Short-term analytically oriented psychotherapy versus behavior therapy. American Journal of Psychiatry, 1975b, 132:4, 373–84.

Smart, J. J. C. Sensations and brain processes. Philosophical Review, 1959, 68, 141–56.

Sobell, M. & Sobell, L. Individualized behavior therapy for alcoholics. Behavior Therapy, 1973, 4, 49–72.

Solomon, R. L. Punishment. American Psychologist, 1964, 19, 239–53.

Spector, M. *Methodological Foundations of Relativistic Mechanics* (South Bend, Ind.: University of Notre Dame Press), 1973.

Spielberger, C. D. & DeNike, L. D. Descriptive behaviorism versus cognitive theory in verbal operant conditioning. Psychological Review, 1966, 73, 306–26.

Staats, A. "A Case in and a Strategy for the Extension of Learning Principles to Problems of Human Behavior," in *Research in Behavior Modification,* Krasner, L. & Ullmann, L. (eds.) (New York: Holt, Rinehart & Winston), 1965.

Stahl, J. R. & Leitenberg, H. "Behavioral Treatment of the Chronic Mental Hospital Patient," in *Handbook of Behavior Modification and Behavior Therapy,* Leitenberg, H. (ed.) (Englewood Cliffs, N.J.: Prentice-Hall), 1976.

Stampfl, T. G. & Levis, D. J. The essentials of implosive therapy: a learning-theory-based psychodynamic behavioral therapy. Journal of Abnormal Psychology, 1967, 72, 496–503.

Steffy, R., Meichenbaum, D. & Best, A. Aversive and cognitive factors in the modification of smoking behavior. Behaviour Research and Therapy, 1970, 8, 115–26.

Steinmark, S. W. & Borkovec, T. D. Active and placebo treatment effects on moderate insomnia under counterdemand and positive demand instructions. Journal of Abnormal Psychology, 1974, 83, 157–63.

Sternback, R. *Pain: A Psychophysiological Analysis* (New York: Academic Press), 1968.

Stillings, N. A., Allen, G. A. & Estes, W. K. Reaction time as a function of noncontingent reward magnitude. Psychonomic Science, 1968, 10, 337–8.

Stolz, S., Wienckowski, L. & Brown, B. Behavior modification: a perspective on critical issues. American Psychologist, 1975, 30, 1027–48.

Strupp, H. *An Introduction to Freud and Modern Psychoanalysis* (Woodbury, N.Y.: Barron's), 1967.

Stuart, R. B. A three-dimensional program for the treatment of obesity. Behaviour Research and Therapy, 1971, 9, 177–86.

"Notes on the Ethics of Behavior Research and Intervention," in *Behavior Change: Methodology, Concepts, and Practice,* Hamerlynck, L., Handy, L. & Mash, E. (eds.) (Champaign, Ill.: Research Press), 1973.

Stunkard, A. & Mahoney, M. "Behavioral Treatment of the Eating Disorders," in *Handbook of Behavior Modification,* Leitenberg, H. (ed.) (Englewood Cliffs, N.J.: Prentice-Hall), 1976.

Szasz, T. *The Myth of Mental Illness* (New York: Hoeber-Harper), 1961.

"Introduction," in *Prisoners of Psychiatry,* Ennis, B. (New York: Harcourt Brace Jovanovich), 1972.

The myth of mental illness: three addenda. Humanistic Psychology, 1974, 14, 11–19.

Tanner, B. Shock intensity and fear of shock in the modification of homosexual behavior in males by avoidance learning. Behaviour Research and Therapy, 1973, 11, 213–18.

Task Report 5, *Behavior Therapy in Psychiatry* (Washington, D.C.: American Psychiatric Association), 1973.

Tate, B. G. & Baroff, G. S. Aversive control of self injurious behavior in a psychotic boy. Behaviour Research and Therapy, 1966, 4, 281–7.

Thistlethwaite, D. A critical review of latent learning and related experiments. Psychological Bulletin, 1951, 48, 97–129.

Thomas, G. V. & Blackman, D. E. "Operant Conditioning and Clinical Psychology," in *Theoretical and Experimental Bases of the Behavior Therapies,* M. P. Feldman & Broadhurst, A. (eds.) (New York: Wiley), 1976.

Thorndike, E. L. *Animal Intelligence* (New York: Macmillan), 1911.

Tori, C. & Worrel, L. Reduction of human avoidant behavior: a comparison of counterconditioning, expectancy, and cognitive informative approaches. Journal of Consulting and Clinical Psychology, 1973, 41, 269–78.

Ullmann, L. On cognitions and behavior therapy. Behavior Therapy, 1970, 1, 201–4.

Ullmann, L. & Krasner, L. *Case Studies in Behavior Modification* (New York: Holt, Rinehart & Winston), 1965.

Psychological Approach to Abnormal Behavior (Englewood Cliffs, N.J.: Prentice-Hall), 1969, 1975.

United States v. *Brawner,* 471 F. 2d 969, D.C. Cir., 1972.

Wachtel, P. *Action and Insight* (New York: Basic Books), 1977.

Waters, W. F., McDonald, D. G. & Koresko, R. L. Psychophysiological responses during analogue desensitization and nonrelaxation control procedures. Behaviour Research and Therapy, 1972, 10, 381–93.

Watson, J. B. Psychology as a behaviorist views it. Psychological Review, 1913, 20, 158–77.

Psychology from the Standpoint of a Behaviorist (Philadelphia: Lippincott), 1919.

Behaviorism (New York: Norton), 1924.

Watson, J. B. & Raynor, R. Conditioned emotional reactions. Journal of Experimental Psychology, 1920, 3, 1–14.

Watson, L. S. *Child Behavior Modification: A Manual for Teachers, Nurses and Parents* (Oxford: Pergamon Press), 1973.

Waters, W. F. & McCallum, R. N. The basis of behavior therapy, mentalistic or behavioristic? A reply to E. A. Locke. Behaviour Research and Therapy, 1973, 11, 157–63.

Weitzman, B. Behavior therapy and psychotherapy. Psychological Review, 1967, 74, 300–17.

Wender, P. H., Rosenthal, D. & Kety, S. S. "A Psychiatric Assessment of the Adoptive Parents of Schizophrenics," in *The Transmission of Schizophrenia,* Rosenthal, D. & Kety, S. S. (eds.) (London: Pergamon Press), 1968.

Werry, J. S. Psychotherapy – a medical procedure? Canadian Psychiatric Association Journal, 1965, 10, 278–82.

Wexler, D. Token and taboo: behavior modification, token economies and the law. California Law Review, 1973, 61, 81–109.

Wiest, W. Some recent criticisms of behaviorism and learning theory with special reference to Breger and McGaugh and to Chomsky. Psychological Bulletin, 1967, 67, 214–25.

Wilcoxon, H. "Historical Introduction to the Problem of Reinforcement," in *Reinforcement and Behavior,* Tapp, J. (ed.) (New York: Academic Press), 1969.

Wilde, G. J. Correspondence. Behaviour Research and Therapy, 1965, 2, 313.

Wilson, G. T. Effects of false feedback on avoidance behavior: "cognitive" desensitization revisited. Journal of Personality and Social Psychology, 1973, 28, 115–22.

Wilson, G. T. & Davison, G. Behavior therapy and homosexuality: a critical perspective. Behavior Therapy, 1974, 5, 16–28.

Wilson, G. T., Leaf, R. C. & Nathan, P. E. The aversion control of excessive alcohol consumption by chronic alcoholics in the laboratory setting. Journal of Applied Behavior Analysis, 1975, 8, 13–26.

Wilson, G. T. & Thomas, M. Self- versus drug-produced relaxation and the effects of instructional set in standardized systematic desensitization. Behaviour Research and Therapy, 1973, 11, 279–88.

Wilson, G. T. & Tracey, D. An experimental analysis of aversive imagery versus electrical aversive conditioning in the treatment of chronic alcoholics. Behaviour Research and Therapy, 1976, 14, 41–51.

Wilson, F. & Walters, R. H. Modification of speech output of near-mute schizophrenics through social-learning procedures. Behaviour Research and Therapy, 1966, 4, 59–67.

Winnett, R. & Winkler, R. Current behavior modification in the classroom: be still, be quiet, be docile. Journal of Applied Behavior Analysis, 1972, 5, 499–504.

Wisdom, J. *Philosophy and Psychoanalysis* (London: Methuen), 1952.

Wisocki, P. A. The successful treatment of a heroin addict by covert conditioning techniques. Journal of Behavior Therapy and Experimental Psychiatry, 1973, 4, 55–61.

Wittgenstein, L. *Philosophical Investigations* (Oxford: Blackwell), 1953.

Wolff v. *McDonnell* (June 26, 1974), U.S.

Wolpe, J. *Psychotherapy by Reciprocal Inhibition* (Stanford: Stanford University Press), 1958.

The Practice of Behavior Therapy (New York: Pergamon Press), 1973.

Behavior therapy and its malcontents. 1. Denial of its bases and psychodynamic fusionism. Journal of Behavior Therapy and Experimental Psychiatry, 1976, 7, 1–5.

Inadequate behavior analysis: the Achilles heel of outcome research in behavior therapy. Journal of Behavior Therapy and Experimental Psychiatry, 1977, 8, 1–3.

Wyatt v. *Stickney,* 344 F. Suppl. 373, 344 F. Supp. 387 (M.D. Ala. 1972) aff'd *sub nom. Wyatt* v. *Aderholt,* 503 F. 2d. 1305 (5th Cir. 1974), 1974.

Young, E. R., Rimm, D. E. & Kennedy, T. D. An experimental investigation of modeling and verbal reinforcement in the modification of assertive behavior. Behaviour Research and Therapy, 1973, 11, 317–19.

Young, G. C. & Turner, R. K. CNS stimulant drugs and conditioning treatment of nocturnal enuresis. Behaviour Research and Therapy, 1965, 3, 93–101.

Yates, A. J. *Behavior Therapy* (New York: Wiley), 1970.

Name index

Subject index

1